Positioning Pensions for the Twenty-First Century

Pension Research Council Publications

A complete listing of PRC publications appears at the back of this volume.

Positioning Pensions for the Twenty-First Century

Edited by Michael S. Gordon,
Olivia S. Mitchell, and Marc M. Twinney

Published by

The Pension Research Council
The Wharton School of the University of Pennsylvania

and

University of Pennsylvania Press
Philadelphia

Copyright © 1997 The Pension Research Council of the Wharton School
of the University of Pennsylvania
Printed in the United States of America on acid-free paper

10 9 8 7 6 5 4 3 2

Published by
University of Pennsylvania Press
Philadelphia, Pennsylvania 19104-6097

Library of Congress Cataloging-in-Publication Data

Positioning pensions for the twenty-first century / edited by Michael S. Gordon, Olivia S.
    Mitchell and Marc M. Twinney.
        p.   cm.
    Includes bibliographical references and index.
    ISBN 0-8122-3391-3 (acid-free paper)
    1. Pensions—United States.   I. Gordon, Michael S.   II. Mitchell, Olivia S.
III. Twinney, Marc M.
    HD7125.P67   1997
    331.25'2'0973–dc21   96-53837
                                                                                              CIP

Contents

Preface

An ever-growing fraction of the United States population is beginning to contemplate with alarm its future in retirement. How can pensions, both public and private, help protect against the likelihood of poverty in old age? In this volume we take a critical look at how effective pensions will be in ensuring retirement security, noting where they have succeeded and failed over the last several decades and pointing to emerging and positive new developments in the pension arena.

The most important contribution of this book is that it develops new perspectives on the challenges facing the United States pension system, both public and private. Contributors include economists and financial experts, actuaries, lawyers, corporate benefits managers, and policymakers, rendering the volume an invaluable compendium for those concerned with pensions in the decades to come.

Topics of critical interest to pension plan participants, designers, and policymakers include new plan options such as hybrid and cash-balance plans. Other topics of current concern to defined benefit pension experts include pension funding rules and recent regulations affecting pension insurance premiums. On the defined contribution front, the volume offers a unique collection of three in-depth studies of participant-directed investments, focusing on thousands of individual workers allocating their pension savings in 401(k) and related plans. We also explore emerging public pension plan developments, including pension plan administrative costs and pension obligation bonds. Finally, of urgent importance to all those interested in retirement, we discuss how employer pensions can be configured against an increasingly delicately financed social insurance system. Policy specialists reporting on possible regulatory change include members of the Social Security Advisory Council, the National Academy of Science, and the United States Congress.

Sponsorship for the research described in this volume was generously provided by The Wharton School, the American Council on Life Insurance, the Ford Motor Company, and the United States Department of Labor. We also gratefully acknowledge support from the Institutional Members of the Pension Research Council. As is true with all Council-sponsored work, the authors retain responsibility for any opinions contained herein.

On behalf of the Pension Research Council at The Wharton School, I thank the many participants contributing to this volume, as well as our reviewers, who included Vincent Amoroso, Betsy Bailey, Marshall Blume, Zvi Bodie, Martin Holmer, and Michael Useem. Thanks too are due my hardworking co-editors, Michael Gordon and Marc Twinney, to readers Anna Rappaport and Vince Amoroso, and to Elizabeth Woods, Kirk Hitesman, and Juan Tang for help in the production phase of this work.

OLIVIA S. MITCHELL
Executive Director
Pension Research Council

Chapter 1
Introduction: Assessing the Challenges to the Pension System

Olivia S. Mitchell, Michael S. Gordon, and
Marc M. Twinney

A growing fraction of the U.S. population is beginning to contemplate
its future in retirement with alarm. In this volume we take a critical look
at how effectively private and public pensions will contribute to the future of retirement well-being, make careful note of where they have
succeeded and failed over the last several decades, and highlight emerging and promising pension innovations. In addition, we examine public
policy developments affecting pensions and point to issues in the pension policy arena likely to be of growing concern over the next decade.

Several issues frame the discussion. In the United States, lack of productivity growth combined with resistance to higher taxes is forcing recognition of the Social Security system's pending insolvency (along with
that of other government-provided retirement benefits). In turn, this is
focusing renewed attention on company pensions, with experts asking
how to position these employment-based benefit plans more effectively
to meet the challenges of the next several decades. Critical reforms must
soon be enacted with respect to how pensions are offered, managed, and
regulated in the United States in order to build on their strengths and
rectify their weaknesses.

In recent years there has also been a tremendous change in the pension environment, with new pensions being created primarily of the defined contribution or 401(k) type. Defined benefit plans, seen in the past
as the right plan for the majority of the workforce, are losing ground and
losing popularity. Whether this shift is desirable is a matter of great debate; some participants as well as plan sponsors express concern that defined contribution plans will undermine retirement income security. By
contrast, other analysts see defined contribution plans as ideally suited

to the complex investment and personal financial concerns driving the modern labor market. From this perspective, defined contribution plans offer the appeal of individually determined retirement savings levels, individually directed investment allocations, and, at retirement, individually tailored benefit payouts. What to expect from each plan type in the future is a theme running through this volume.

In this introductory chapter, we first offer a discussion of why some employers offer pensions and why pensions appeal to some employees, and focus on the important distinctions between defined benefit and defined contribution plans. Second, we review recent pension developments in the United States, a perspective which is essential in assessing some of the emerging economic, regulatory, and social issues confronting those seeking to enhance retirement saving in this country. The discussion emphasizes ways in which the pension system has greatly contributed to the increased retirement security of the elderly, along with an assessment of where upcoming challenges lie. Finally, we offer an interpretive discussion of the book's remaining sections, in which we outline strengths and weaknesses of the pension system to meet the challenges of the twenty-first century.

An Overview of the United States Pension System [1]

In the United States, employer-sponsored pensions are best understood as long-term compensation arrangements. Each year the employee is with a company offering a pension, he or she accrues an additional right to an eventual retirement income benefit, typically a function of lifetime pay, age, and/or years of service. The precise form of the pension benefit depends on the type of plan offered by the firm. Experts usually distinguish between two plan types, the defined benefit (DB) and the defined contribution (DC) pension. In a DB plan, the sponsoring employer specifies a formula for retirement income based on the worker's pay and service, as well as the age at retirement. In a DC plan, the company and often the employee make contributions to the plan, often a fraction of pay. Benefits at retirement then depend on the total contribution the worker has accumulated into the plan by retirement age.

There has been a substantial change in the mix of defined contribution and defined benefit plans over time in the United States. Table 1 reveals that the number of defined contribution plans has grown from 66 percent to 85 percent of all plans since the mid-1970s. Defined benefit plans now represent a mere 15 percent of the plan universe, down from 33 percent in 1975. Since DB plans tend to be larger than DC plans, the total number of DB plan participants has dropped more modestly, but the decline in relative share is still startling. Over the period 1975–

TABLE 1 Recent Trends in Private Pension Plans

	Year			
	1975	*1985*	*1990*	*1991*
No. of plans:				
Total (100%)	311,094	632,135	712,308	699,294
DB	33%	27%	16%	15%
DC	66%	73%	84%	85%
No. of participants (thousands):				
Total (100%)	44,511	74,665	76,924	77,662
DB	75%	49%	51%	50%
DC	25%	51%	49%	50%
US$ assets (millions):				
Total (100%)	259,963	1,252,739	1,674,139	1,936,271
DB	72%	66%	57%	57%
DC	28%	33%	43%	43%

Source: U.S. DOL (1995), pp. 60, 64, 70.

1991 in the United States, the fraction of pension participants covered by DC plans doubled—to half the covered population—with participants with DB plans accounting for only half the covered group, down from three-quarters in the sixteen-year period. Perhaps the most striking pattern in Table 1 is the massive change in plan assets over this fairly short time horizon. Defined contribution plans in 1975 held only about one-quarter of the total pension asset pool, and now hold more than 40 percent.

Why have pension patterns changed so substantially over time? Why do some employers offer, and some employees participate in, company pensions, while others do not? One reason some employers offer a pension is that they feel they assist in labor recruitment and retention. For example, a company having a pension plan might attract employees willing to invest in their jobs as well as in themselves. Providing matches to workers' pension contributions, available only after a vesting period, would appeal to (and help retain) employees interested in remaining with the company for a relatively long term. A pension can also help induce employees to exert greater effort, take fewer days away from work, and in general be more motivated. At the end of the work life, pensions help ease the retirement process, providing incentives for older employees to retire after a particular age or number of years of service. On the whole, then, pensions can be a key element in a carefully thought out human resource policy, an element used by companies needing a long-term stable workforce. Such employers will be more likely to offer pensions and will also tailor their plan features to meet compensation policy goals. Conversely, firms pursuing a low-wage employment strategy would be unlikely to offer a pension at all, and, if they did, it would tend to be a less expensive plan that did not necessarily reward long-term firm attachment.

While this explanation for pensions emphasizes how employers gain from offering a pension, there are clearly several reasons some employees desire company-sponsored pensions as well. Perhaps the most obvious rationale is that company pensions hold tax-favored status if they meet certain nondiscrimination requirements, rules that require pension savings to be spread across a wide cross section of a company's workforce. The tax protection afforded contributions makes it appealing for middle and upper tax bracket employees to save for retirement in a tax-qualified plan. As many have pointed out, however, it has become increasingly costly and difficult to meet these legal nondiscrimination requirements in recent years, making the tax deferral motive for pensions somewhat less valuable than years ago.

Other factors making pensions appealing to employees include the fact that company pensions offer relatively low cost access to investment markets because of scale economies and can provide access to group risk pools, thus avoiding costly individually purchased annuities. In addition, analysts emphasizing the psychological aspects of pensions note a strong element of self-control in company pensions, whereby the automatic deferral of pay (either via salary reduction or employer contributions) makes it easier for workers to save for retirement. In general, workers who desire pensions are more likely to be relatively highly paid and expect to be long-lived; conversely, those unlikely to want a pension, and who would probably not participate in a pension plan if it were offered, are likely to be lower paid employees not planning on long-term attachment to that company, as well as those who do not value saving for retirement, particularly in a group format. Moreover, if an employer's finances permit subsidization of employee medical benefits but not both medical and pension benefits, workers (particularly younger ones) are less likely to favor pensions.

Having pointed out that pensions are seen as retirement insurance and more, the question arises as to whether defined benefit or defined contribution plans meet these needs more effectively. This is not an easy question to answer, since participants and plan sponsors assume different types of risk in each plan. For instance, DC plan participants increasingly can decide, as individual workers, how much money will be deposited into the plan and how these pension contributions will be invested. In addition, many 401(k) plans allow loans and lump-sum cash-outs, making the money more accessible than under other plan types. These features imply that the task of forecasting retirement income needs and investment risks as well as returns increasingly falls on individual employees rather than on the employer. In other words, a typical DC plan imposes on participants the uncertainty about eventual benefits due to inability to forecast lifetime earnings and capital market risk. Offsetting these risks is the fact that participants seem to like the opportunity to handle their own pension investments. Finally, DC plans often impose longevity risk on the plan member, since a majority of DC plans allow retirees to take their accumulations in the form of a lump sum. In this event, the retiree confronts the possibility of outliving his or her pension assets, a risk that would be handled quite differently had the funds been converted to a group annuity.

Many but not all of these risks are handled differently in a defined benefit plan. In conventional DB pensions, the employee accrues a right to an annuity payable at retirement based on age, service, and lifetime earnings. Often these pension plans provide a minimum benefit for all workers attaining a minimum length of service, so plan participants are somewhat protected against sharp drops in earnings (particularly at the low end of the pay scale). Also, DB plans tend to provide greater protection against inflation since their benefit formulas are usually related to salary increases over the course of the worker's career with the firm.

Many DB plans also have a degree of disability protection, paying workers with health problems income continuation if they cannot work. And as already mentioned, DB plans tend to require that pension payments take the form of an annuity, providing risk pooling within the employment group against longevity. Finally, the company sponsoring a DB plan is responsible for funding the promised level of retirement benefits. If the plan is underfunded (i.e., the pension plan's liabilities exceed pension assets), the sponsoring firm is obligated to pay pension benefits just as it must repay other long-term debt. As a result, workers in a DB plan bear less general capital market risk, having shifted some of it to the pension fund and implicitly to the sponsoring company. In turn, they are instead exposed to the risk of possible company bankruptcy when the plan is underfunded. In the United States and many other nations, the government-run pension guarantee system further spreads this type of underfunding risk across all DB sponsors.

In sum, there are several root explanations for the rapid changes experienced in the pension environment over the last several years. The fact that DC plans doubled during the 1980s and multiplied again during the 1990s can partially be explained by the fact that many covered workers now have both plan types. In fact, about half of all pension participants now have a secondary DC plan on top of a DB pension. Others are starting DC plans afresh, producing more than 10,000 new plans reported to the IRS per year.

Successes and Failures of the United States Pension System [2]

Many observers would judge the United States retirement system to be one of great achievement, with employer-sponsored pensions playing a key role. Of course Social Security benefits have also contributed to the elderly's rising economic status, but today an increasing fraction of the over-65 receive a pension, comprising a substantial portion of retirement income. In addition, most employer-sponsored pension plans are well funded, and the benefits earned are usually deemed secure, in part because of good funding and government insurance through the Pension Benefit Guaranty Corporation. In addition, large pension plans have been able to adopt sophisticated asset management techniques, relying on modern portfolio theory in the development and implementation of investment programs. Consequently, pension plan investment results have been excellent in many defined benefit plans over the last decades, in private as well as public sector plans (Bodie, Mitchell, and Turner 1996).

In other areas, success has been more mixed and there are worrisome signs on the horizon. Small employers have been particularly hard hit by competitive labor and product markets, and the complexity of pension regulation has driven many smaller companies out of the defined benefit pension market. There have also been problems with multi-employer plans, or defined benefit plans covering employer and union groups in certain sectors such as trucking and construction. In the past, employers joining such plans anticipated that their pension commitment would be met in full by paying assessed contribution amounts, but the Multi-Employer Amendments Act recently imposed "withdrawal liabilities," levying on participating firms a share of the plan's unfunded liabilities if they withdraw. This change in contractual pension obligations has decreased firms' interest in entering new multi-employer arrangements in the near term. Additionally, though private plans are well funded in general, some are underfunded and becoming increasingly so. This situation arises in part because negotiated pensions are regularly amended as benefit increases are bargained but the pension can often fall behind in funding since these increases may not be paid for until adopted.

Furthermore, on a broader level, the failure of pension coverage to rise in the workforce as a whole is of concern to those looking ahead to the baby boomers' retirement. Research shows that this coverage drop resulted from changes in the employer mix, decreases in firm size as well as unionization, and the national trend toward falling real wages, particularly for low-skilled employees.

Developments in the arena of defined contribution plans also indicate mixed success, depending on plan type and structure. Many employees are now offered the opportunity to invest their 401(k) funds in a wide range of assets, including company stock as one of the options. This pattern has both opportunities and pitfalls, since company stock has performed well in some cases but poorly in others, reminding participants too late of the need for diversification. Whether participants are able to make sensible asset allocation decisions is a matter requiring further study, and important new research is presented in this volume on this point.

Public sector pension plans are another area of research and some policy concern. In contrast to private pensions, subject to the Employee Retirement Income Security Act (ERISA) since 1974, there are no public sector rules requiring national accounting, funding, and reporting standards. While most public plans appear to be managed rather well and are close to fully funded, others are clearly not, the most notorious probably being the virtually insolvent Washington, DC plan. Indeed, the 1996 report of the Social Security Advisory Council proposed extending many ERISA regulatory requirements to the public sector to strengthen the pension plans covering one of five workers in the land.

Finally, there are problems with the United States retirement system at the national level, problems stemming from the fact that the overall saving rate is troublingly low and has been for some time. This is in part a result of the fact that there is neither a national retirement policy nor any coherent legislative or economic framework shaping pension legislation and regulation. As a result, pension laws are changed frequently—on average once a year between 1985 and 1995—and these changes have been driven more by revenue needs than by logic. The many law changes have also been combined with delays in the issuance of interpretive regulations helping plan sponsors implement the laws, making the environment for pension design one of substantial uncertainty.

Research Developments in the Pension Arena

In examining the challenges faced by the pension system entering the new millennium, this volume begins with a focus on specific pension plan issues and then discusses broader environmental and policy issues. Examining first defined benefit plans, Marc Twinney asks whether larger employers are reevaluating, and perhaps considering dropping, their long-standing commitment to defined benefit plans as the pension of choice. Twinney surveys twenty benefits managers at large United States manufacturing companies and, based on his analysis, concludes that there has been relatively little change in their benefit and pension perspective. He also identifies several corporate policies toward provision of retirement income, noting that recent policy developments have begun to worry the corporate sector. In particular, he places great weight on recent and proposed changes in Social Security, insofar as they will affect company pensions. For example, defined benefit plans are required to treat age 65 as the normal retirement age, though for Social Security purposes this age is being raised to 67 over the next several years. Twinney's conclusion, that there needs to be a coherent national retirement policy, is one that many will applaud.

A discussion by Anna Rappaport, Michael Young, Christopher Levell, and Brad Blalock is of keen interest to those focusing on new developments in the defined benefit pension arena. They write with great expertise about the cash balance pension, a new institutional form that maintains some of the advantages of the defined benefit pension while including an accumulation aspect employees will see as akin to the defined contribution pension. Since these plans are rather new, the authors offer a unique description of the novel format and compare this plan type with other alternatives.

Turning next to developments in the defined contribution plan arena, we have collected three unique and fascinating studies of these popular plans, each of which asks and answers questions about participants' asset allocation strategies. Using data on a large United States manufacturing firm, Jack L. Vanderhei and Vickie Bajtelsmit study asset allocation of pension participants using a variety of empirical and multivariate models. Their contribution is to develop and analyze a unique new data set on managerial employees in a large firm to ask how people allocate their pension assets when they have some choice in a self-directed DC/401(k) plan. In particular, the chapter assesses how account allocations vary with socioeconomic factors, including age, sex, pay level, and tenure. The authors also offer expert judgment regarding the wisdom with which plan participants appear to be investing their self-directed accounts. After concluding that few older workers hold very much of their retirement account in equities, they examine various explanations about what this implies for retirement well-being. The authors also supply new evidence on the extent to which plan participants take out loans, withdraw cash from their plans, and buy employer stock, exploiting the uniqueness of this company-level data set.

Expanding on the question of how defined contribution participants allocate their investments, Sylvester J. Schieber and Gordon Goodfellow explore a rich cross-company data file on about 36,000 participants in 24 nationwide DC plans. Examining how participants hold their retirement money, the authors find that the older the participant, the higher the pension balance; most DC assets are held in GICs (guaranteed investment contracts), and the fraction of assets held in GICs is low among the young but rises rapidly with age. A third analysis of defined contribution participants' behavior takes up a very different question. Richard Hinz, David McCarthy, and John Turner ask whether women appear to be more conservative investors than men, and find some evidence in this direction. Taken together, these studies using employer-side pension data offer some of the first microeconomic insights into rapidly growing self-directed pension accounts, about which very little is known to date in research and practical circles.

Turning to emerging pension policy issues, the focus expands to cover a wider range of topics. Mark Warshawsky investigates how defined benefit pensions are drawing on a pair of publicly available data sets as well as a new Internal Revenue Service study on the same issue. The author reviews the evolution of legal regulations on funding, beginning with ERISA and ending with the 1994 Retirement Protection Act, and summarizes accounting standards regarding funding, which often conflict with Internal Revenue Service regulations. He concludes that defined benefit pension plan funding worsened in the last several years, despite the apparent goal of policy to increase funding.

Moving to a different and also controversial pension topic, Robert Monks describes some changes that have recently rocked pension trustee boards under the rubric of corporate governance. His thesis is that, in both the public and the private sectors, pension trustees now hold such a substantial portion of publicly traded company equity that the trustees tend to become involved in managing these firms—willingly at times, but unwillingly at others. Monks reviews changes pension managers have begun to demand (and receive), including relaxation of rules for shareholder communications, report cards, proxy voting, confidential board elections, and related matters.

Aspects of pension decisionmaking in the public sector are taken up in turn in separate chapters by Robert Lang and by Ping-Lung Hsin with Olivia Mitchell. Lang first describes the financial risks confronted by participants and sponsors of state and local pension funds. He then goes on to describe pension obligation bonds, a unique method of financing recently undertaken by some state and local governments to meet these risks. Taking a different tack, Hsin and Mitchell focus on pension plan managerial efficiency, and challenges to it, in the public sector. Reducing the high costs of public pensions without cutting the quality of retirement services provided by these plans is an important issue of public concern everywhere. Analysis of a large number of United States state and local pension plans reveals that, on average, administrative expenditures per participant are high but not apparently higher than in private pension plans. Evidently public pension plans could benefit from scale economies by merging and coalescing into larger pension pools. Additionally, the study shows that pension administrative costs could be substantially reduced if the systems were operated more efficiently. Factors associated with greater efficiency are identified, and include requirements that administrative budgets be authorized by a group other than the pension board.

The final segment of this volume turns to the future, where several different specialists look ahead to directions for the pension system. Constance Citro and Eric Hanushek summarize the work of a National Academy of Sciences panel conducting an overview of retirement income modeling efforts and call for the development of more open, and more policy-relevant, pension models which are integrated with other economic and policy concerns. Social Security policy also has a potent effect on retirement income and on the role that employer pensions must fill in ensuring retirement security. The final set of chapters in the volume therefore includes two pieces on Social Security, one by economist Edward Gramlich and the other by U.S. Representative John Porter (R-Ill.). In the process of guiding debate on the Social Security Advisory Council, Gramlich has explored many of the policy options available to resolve the system's forecasted insolvency. In his chapter, he outlines the choices, thereby making all the more clear the role of employment-based pensions in response to system changes. Porter's work takes a different tack, that of converting a portion of the Social Security payroll tax to individual pension accounts. How this would alter the role of public versus private sectors in providing retirement income is a subject that commands much attention in this chapter, and will certainly generate debate in years ahead.

Notes

1. This discussion draws on Bodie and Mitchell (1996), Gustman and Mitchell (1992), and Gustman, Mitchell, and Steinmeier (1995).

2. This discussion benefited from the input and advice of Anna Rappaport, to whom we are most grateful.

References

Bodie, Zvi and Olivia S. Mitchell. "Pension Security in an Aging World." In Zvi Bodie, Olivia S. Mitchell, and John A. Turner, eds., *Securing Employer-Based Pensions: An International Perspective*. Philadelphia: Pension Research Council and University of Pennsylvania Press, 1996.

Bodie, Zvi, Olivia S. Mitchell, and John A. Turner, eds. *Securing Employer-Based Pensions: An International Perspective*. Philadelphia: Pension Research Council and University of Pennsylvania Press, 1996.

Gustman, Alan and Olivia S. Mitchell. "Pensions and Labor Market Activity: Behavior and Data Requirements." In Zvi Bodie and Alicia H. Munnell, eds. *Pensions and the Economy: Sources, Uses, and Limitations of Data*. Philadelphia: Pension Research Council and University of Pennsylvania Press, 1992.

Gustman, Alan, Olivia S. Mitchell, and Thomas Steinmeier. "Retirement Research Using the Health and Retirement Survey." *Journal of Human Resources* 30 (supp.) (1995): 557–83.

United States Department of Labor (USDOL), Pension and Welfare Benefits Administration. Abstract of 1991 Form 5500 Annual Reports. Private Pension Plan Bulletin No. 4, Winter 1995. Washington, DC: USGPO, 1995.

Part I
Defined Benefit and Defined Contribution Plans

Chapter 2
A Fresh Look at Defined Benefit Plans: An Employer Perspective

Marc M. Twinney

This chapter compares the characteristics of defined benefit, defined contribution, and hybrid plans, and reviews recent trends, particularly among large plan sponsors. Benefit policies of a set of large employers are surveyed, followed by a discussion of remedies to some of the practical problems faced by defined benefit plans.

My views and observations regarding defined benefit plans are drawn from a lifetime as a practitioner in providing and delivering benefits in the private sector. These views are not abstract theories, nor do they represent ardent advocacy. While they have evolved from an employer's perspective and priorities, they also strive to seek a balance among competing viewpoints of employees, plan sponsors, and the public. They recognize the priority of meeting employees' retirement needs in a world of complex law and custom, where age discrimination in employment is elaborately proscribed and employers cannot mandate an aging employee's retirement.

Pension Plan Types and Goals

Three major types of pension plans provide retirement income: defined benefit (DB), defined contribution (DC), and hybrid plans. The key factor differentiating the basic types is whether the plan defines a lifetime benefit or the annual contribution. In a hybrid plan, features of both basic types are combined, blurring the differences. One such hybrid is the cash balance plan, wherein each plan participant has an individual account for contributions, but because the plan guarantees a specified interest rate on the account as well as conversion rates for commutation to a lifetime benefit, the plan assumes the characteristics of a defined benefit plan.

There are several important differences between plan types (see also Rappaport et al., this volume). In DB and some hybrid plans, the retiree benefit must be stated in the form of an annuity (one that often may be converted to a lump sum). In DC plans as well as some hybrid plans, the benefit is stated in the form of a lump sum (that also may be converted to an annuity). DB benefits are normally based on pay and/or service. In contrast, DC and hybrid account balances normally grow based on annual employer contributions or credits equal to a percentage of the employee's pay, plus earnings on the assets in the account. Hybrid plans guarantee the interest rate on accounts and/or the annuity rates for conversion to lifetime benefits.

The funding status of DB and hybrid plans is determined actuarially. In other words, contributions are determined based on actuarial assumptions and are designed to provide the promised benefit at retirement. Moreover, all the DB plan's assets stand behind all the benefits. In a DC plan, by contrast, contributions are made to individual accounts and determined by the plan formula; the assets in each separate account determine the benefit. In a hybrid plan, a "phantom" account is maintained for each employee, but the total value of such accounts at any given point in time may differ from the trust fund value (i.e., the plan may be underfunded or overfunded). For this reason, some funding flexibility exists in DB and hybrid plans, whereas the DC plan affords no flexibility in funding without changing the benefit.

The funding differences translate into differential patterns of risk borne by stakeholders in the plans. Thus the employer bears the pension plan investment risk and reward in a DB plan, whereas in a DC plan the employee bears the investment risk and reward. In the hybrid plan case, the sponsoring employer bears plan investment risk because the employee receives a guaranteed interest rate on his or her account. Of course, employers can manage and control this risk by establishing reasonable interest rate guarantees. A related reason DC plans are growing in favor is that the sponsoring employer's costs tend to be more predictable and less volatile that in a DB pension. This difference arises because, in the DB plan, the employer assumes more investment and inflation risk, as well as more of the turnover, disability, and mortality risk, than in a DC pension.

Additional important differences between plan types refer to the employee's rights over the pension prior to retirement. An employee terminating employment prior to retirement eligibility is entitled to a deferred vested benefit that generally does not change after termination in the DB case (in nominal terms). In contrast, in the DC and hybrid case, a terminating employee typically may withdraw the account balance and roll it over into an Individual Retirement Account (IRA). Alternatively the funds may be reinvested elsewhere. In this sense, DC and hybrid plans offer greater portability than their counterparts. On the other hand, DB pensions (and, to a lesser extent, hybrid plans) facilitate disability, survivor, and early retirement benefits because they often specify supplementary benefits payable at early ages or on the occasion of death or invalidity.

One factor increasingly noted by large employers is that, for equivalent cost levels, DB plans tend to benefit older, highly paid employees. Conversely, DC and hybrid pensions tend to be more age-neutral and often provide higher benefits to short-term employees and people who change employers. In addition, some companies have found that employees appreciate DC and hybrid plans because their account balances are quantifiable; the concern is that this appreciation may sometimes stem from a poor understanding of the size of the accumulation amount necessary to provide retirement income. Analysts have found in practice that a DB plan will often have lower costs than DC and hybrid plans, even assuming equal investment results on pension assets, because the value of deferred vested benefits in a defined benefit pension is less than the value of account balances accumulated in DC or hybrid plans for those who terminate employment prior to retirement.

Defined Benefit Plan Goals

Academics and practitioners have many theories regarding why employers sponsor defined benefit pension plans (Schmitt 1993). For the present discussion, my perspective is that large industrial firms prefer the defined benefit form as the primary plan to meet their retirement objectives. They do so less because of cost efficiency than the effectiveness of this type of pension in achieving desired objectives. Specifically, the DB plan is the most effective human resource mechanism available to remove older, less efficient employees from the workforce in a humane and socially responsible way. In other words, pensions at these large firms are not designed primarily to recruit employees or to tie core employees to the workforce so as to avoid training costs. The fact that these additional results might occur to a greater extent under a DB pension plan than with a DC plan is incidental to the primary goal. These secondary effects result from efforts to control the costs of providing retirement income, and are acceptable to the firm and to employees.

In seeking to design sensible compensation offerings, employers normally start by measuring the cost/benefit ratios of alternative packages, seeking to achieve their ultimate goal. The costs usually considered naturally include retirement benefits and the salary/wages saved at the point of contemplated retirement, but in my experience typically do not include an assessment of recruiting and training costs for replacement employees. For many firms, replacements are either assumed not to be required (as in a case where the firm is reducing in size) or are seen as part of the normal attrition and growth process.

Some firms attempt to reduce plan cost levels and benefit levels by substituting a DC plan in place of their old DB offering. This has been done in instances where the newly framed individual account appears more valuable to younger workers than did the old DB plan's benefits, which were only available at a future retirement age. However, the problem that can arise is that lower retirement benefits delivered by the DC plan may cause older workers to delay retirement. As a consequence, the effort to reduce costs may fail, and the firm may ultimately pay because it is compensating less efficient workers toward the end of their careers.

A related issue is that a DB plan can deliver a particular retirement benefit or income replacement ratio with precision, whereas the benefit to be generated by a DC account is much less certain and ultimately depends on market share values or other random factors; that is, an employer can focus a defined benefit plan's replacement ratio on selected retirement ages or have it maximized after a specific period of service. This enables the sponsoring firm to ensure orderly retirement planning, a factor employers find important given legal restrictions over the employer's right to terminate employment selectively. It is likely that orderly scheduling of retirements over reasonable time horizons makes the firm more efficient and the organization more energetic.

These defined benefit advantages are demonstrated by comparing outcomes under DC and DB plan types for a given date, such as the year of normal retirement, which is when an employer intends retirement to occur and the pension benefit is paid without reduction. Under a defined benefit pension, if retirement is postponed a year, no benefit is paid. The plan saves by retaining that benefit as well as the plan's investment income for the year, but subsequently another year's service and pay increase may be charged. In my experience, these benefit savings tend to balance out in large-employer DB plans.

By contrast, in a defined contribution plan the employer sees no savings when an employee postpones retirement one year because the employee retains both the benefit nonpayment and the investment return. As a result, the defined contribution plan creates no incentive to retire at any specific point of time. If the employer has evidence to believe that after a certain age employee productivity does not improve (or is in fact declining), the defined benefit cost pattern is more efficient. This view assumes productivity as a factor in the provision of benefits in a competitive pay package.

A Brief Review of Trends

The trends in coverage and benefits have been surveyed and well reported during the last five years (Schieber 1995, Oliver and Patterson 1993–95). My perspective on these findings is that private pension plan coverage is not very high (only about 50 percent or so), given the 20 years since ERISA. One must be careful with this point as there are sizable differences in coverage reported by different sources. There is good evidence, for instance, that audited tax returns provide more accurate tallies of pension participation than does the Current Population Survey (CPS) based on interviews of individuals. This difference in reporting is huge, on the order of one out of three or 33 percent in some series. No doubt individuals' recollection of their coverage is not very accurate, perhaps because people are unaware or forgetful of being covered or are confused between pension coverage, pension eligibility, and pension vesting.

Despite these caveats, the number of defined benefit plans (and DB participants) has declined in the United States in recent years, whereas the number of defined contribution plans (and plan participants) has increased. Use of the DB pension has dropped less among large employers, but even among these large employers employment has declined as they "right-sized" and sought to improve productivity. In some industries these transitions have been substantial; for example, at Ford Motor Company, it took twenty-five years for the workforce to double between the mid-1950s to the end of the 1970s, but less than five years for employment to be cut in half during the recession of 1979–1982.

To assess very recent trends among large employers, I undertook a limited survey of the pension outlook at twenty companies in 1995. While this is admittedly a small sample, these are very large firms, among the largest in their lines of business. Though specific company names cannot be revealed for confidentiality reasons, the companies are principally in manufacturing; no more than two firms come from the same industry. The industries represented are automotive, chemical, communications, drug, electrical/electronics, metals, oil, retailing, tire, and energy.

To summarize my findings, there was little evidence of recent massive change in the pension offerings of these twenty companies. This was in part true because most of the respondents had both DC and DB plans; only one company relied exclusively on a DC to provide retirement income.[1] Of the group, three quarters, or fifteen of the twenty, had reviewed their pension policy between 1990 and 1994; of these fifteen, seven made changes during that time, six made no change, and two are still considering their options.

Three companies increased the DC contribution while one decreased its DC contribution during this period. One company increased the DB benefit (to remove a competitive deficiency) and two companies decreased the DB benefit for future service but not for prior service (neither of these eliminated the DB plan, however). Only one firm (included in the counts above) both increased its DC and decreased its DB plan. Two other companies continue to explore a possible shift of emphasis to the DC from the DB plan.

These counts overlook changes in benefits for negotiated groups as well as special early retirement windows. At least half the companies increased their negotiated benefits at least once during the five-year period. If these 10 DB increases are netted against the one DB decrease, the result is a net positive of nine increases.

Several possible causes for switching from DB to DC plans have been offered at the national level, prominent among them regulation and its unpredictability (Clark and McDermed 1990). In many employers' view, this regulatory complexity and instability has been increased by the enactment of the 1994 Retirement Protection Act, whose goal is to reduce private DB pension plan underfunding by making more volatile the premiums payable to the Pension Benefit Guaranty Corporation, as compared to prior law. It is my considered opinion that these increased premiums will do less to improve funding than will increased employer contributions along with the continued shift away from the DB pensions. The future does not bode well for those concerned with the broad goals of coverage and participation in pension plans guaranteeing income for life after retirement.

Employers' Retirement Income Policies

If the changing array of plans and coverages has been less evident among larger employers, it is nevertheless worthwhile to determine what policies they have followed. This section investigates the policies these large employers have followed with respect to providing cash retirement income and how they have thought about the differences between defined benefit plans and the alternatives.

The survey of twenty large plan sponsors suggests five different approaches to providing pension income, approaches followed by more than one company. These policies appear in Table 1, and may be classified as follows. First, we identified a focus on "employee security,"

TABLE 1 Survey of Large Private Sector Employers' Retirement Income Policies

Employee Security

Company A recently reviewed its employment security policy. After doing so, it reaffirmed that a long-term relationship between the firm and its core employees based on concern for the employees' security needs was in the company's best interest, and that the benefit plans should support that objective. Thus Company A did not shift from a defined benefit to a defined contribution plan simply to make it easier for employees to leave, or to enable Company A to terminate relationships more simply. Here the approach was not one of "where should retirement income come from" but rather one of "are current benefit plans consistent with company employment security objectives."

Competition

Company B has a "market-related" policy of providing benefit levels and types based on competitive surveys for Company B. The market of comparators is made up of leading United States companies in different industries (other companies use the firms in their industry). For retirement income and other post-retirement benefits of non-represented employees, Company B's objective is to provide approximately 100 percent of a benefit value index for each type of benefit and by benefit sector. Other companies using the index can select the comparators and the percentages. When benefit changes are made, the goal is to move closer to the percentage objective where possible, by increases and decreases in benefits. (When adjustments are made for the downward effect on the index of reflecting changes to conform to the 1986 Tax Reform Act, there has been almost no change in the value of the defined benefit or the defined contribution plan indices during the last five years.)

Internal Equity

Company C has evolved a policy of providing benefits that are "employment neutral" across demographic factors such as age, service, gender, and dependents. The firm's objective is for benefits to vary by merit and performance per unit of work in a way comparable with compensation. It does not wish to see the benefit plans dominate an employee's decision to stay or leave at any particular point. To the extent possible, it does not want demographics to allocate employer dollars. It expects the benefit plans to influence neither employee loyalty nor the obligation of the firm to the employee.

Desired Behavior

Company D seeks to align employee behavior with company goals of generating wealth. This is accomplished by placing primary emphasis on stockholder value and the employee in the position of a stockholder. The theme dominates the determination of contributions to benefit plans, the allocation of contributions among employees, and the form of the benefit, especially in retirement income security, which is viewed as just another aspect of compensation.

Employee Choice

Company E recently developed a policy to allow more choice by each employee in designing his/her own benefit package. Some minimum coverages are required and the first choices derive from changes to the preexisting program. The retirement plans (cash or health) or savings plan were not included in the first series of choices, but are expected to be involved in the next series. This change will lead to more emphasis of the defined contribution approach.

the traditional concern of the employer to meet the employee's security needs. Second, we found much discussion of "competition," that is, a drive to make benefits competitive with other companies as measured by a market survey or a benefit value index (much as employers match competitive salary levels). A third theme was "internal equity," where companies used benefit forms and value scales to allocate benefit accruals in relation to units of pay. Fourth, we found that some firms emphasized "desired behavior" in that they designed their pensions to encourage specific types of employee behavior. Last, some companies emphasized "employee choice," wanting to allow employee participation in the allocation of their own individual benefit packages.

In each case, the employer's concern about retiree benefits clearly extends more broadly than just decisions between DB and DC plans. Strategic benefits decisionmaking for the next decade will therefore inevitably involve more complex problems than previously. Specifically, the pension choice must be made against the backdrop of an evolving division of responsibility among the employer, the worker, and the government; the need for lifetime income versus access to accumulated wealth; retirement replacement ratios; provisions for surviving spouses; whether pensions are offered for early leavers; how disability is treated; and various macroeconomic factors including inflation and productivity growth.

Suggested Remedies

There are several specific policies that could begin to remedy some of the problems confronting defined benefit pension plans in the United States. I begin from the perspective that, for many employers and firms, combined DB/DC plans would be preferable to one dominated by DC plans alone. My list of proposed changes is not exhaustive and, given the need to avoid further destabilizing the qualified plan system, avoids drastic medicine.

Refining Pension Regulation

One regulatory change that would be most beneficial would be to revisit the rules allowing the amount of lump sums to be paid upon retirement from qualified plans. Currently many workers and retirees can take all of their accumulated amounts on termination (or retirement) in the form of a lump sum. Perhaps a better system would permit only half, or perhaps one-quarter, of the pension assets to be taken as a lump sum. A life income payment would protect better against the risk of longevity and would help assure that payments would continue during the life of the retired employee, as well as covering the surviving spouse. With growth in life expectancies, this is a vital concern. Similarly, pension withdrawals and loans should be greatly curtailed.

If we are further to restrict lump sums in DB plans, there is a parallel question of whether a DC account should be required to be taken as an annuity (or over the full lifetime with expectancy installments). It seems illogical to consider the individual account an adequate substitute for the DB plan without requiring that a portion of it be paid for life. A more complex, but in my view more just, requirement would be that an employer should designate a pension plan that is to be termed the base or life income plan, and then would require that base plan to meet the 50 percent or 75 percent life income value requirement (including Social Security benefits, most probably). Likewise, a base plan should not be allowed to provide withdrawals or loans prior to retirement and the commencement of the lifetime payments (with or without hardship). In a world of diverse plans that the government has so willingly combined for benefit limitation and tax purposes, some notion of a minimum lifetime pension could apply.

Another proposal would be to harmonize the age and service rules between defined benefit and defined contribution plans. Because service rules are much more elaborate for DB plans (particularly for breaks in service), employers have found that it is virtually impossible to run both plan types for the same group of employees with one set of service rules. For example, in a DB pension, all the employee's service except for breaks in service must be taken into account for determining the worker's nonforfeitable benefit percentage. However, rules describing a break in service vary depending on whether there was at least one year's service prior to the break. Current regulatory practice states that service before a break is not required to be counted for vesting. In my view, this form of regulatory micro-management should be eliminated.

A further change would be to allow a one-time change in pension plan normal retirement ages to bring them into alignment with Social Security rules, as amended. In 1983, Social Security's "normal" benefit age was raised, and further age changes are being discussed (see Gramlich, this volume). The regulation has vastly different effects on the two different types of plans. Initially, DB plans were required by ERISA to treat age 65 as the normal age at which unreduced benefits must be paid. Recent legislation allowed a higher age for DB, but did not change the age for existing accruals and further required the higher age for stepped-up benefits on compensation over the Social Security tax base. This distorted pension plan early retirement reductions as well as the pension system's definition of the "normal" retirement age. The rule should be changed to permit, but not require, alterations in the plan's normal and early retirement ages as well as reduction factors for accrued benefits.

Otherwise, a private plan is locked into a normal age 65 or a second plan must be created, one that pays part of the benefits at age 65 and further benefits at the Social Security age. Similarly, a remedy should be found for DB plans' past accruals that would allow some flexibility for the plan sponsor to adjust the normal retirement age and share the benefit/cost effects with the participants. This would avoid penalizing one type of plan (the DB) in favor of the other.

In order to achieve system solvency there may be further changes in Social Security's normal and early retirement ages. These proposals would therefore affect private plans that supplement Social Security. Here it is critical to give employers sufficient advance notice, and a clear explanation of what is to be done, to ensure long-term stability of retirement planning. It would be in the interest of national policy as well as of employers and employees to allow age changes in private plans. This would encourage more employees who are able to continue to work to the full Social Security age to do so.

Other changes many large employers might support would be to increase the annual benefit limit for DB plans to 100 percent of the covered compensation limit (currently US $150,000). This would make the defined benefit limit five times, not four times, the limit on annual DC contributions. This is essential to restore the relationship initially established under ERISA and would begin to reflect the underlying relation between costs/contribution and benefits values under the two types of plans. As an alternative suggestion, it might be possible to allow DB benefits to be provided under a nondiscriminatory plan, funded in a separate trust without tax deduction to the employer until benefits were paid, but with tax exemption on trust earnings, FICA taxation on the contributions when made, but deferral of other taxation to the employee until benefits were paid. This restructuring might make employers willing to deliver more via tax-qualified plan benefits, without the up-front tax loss.

Adjusting the Restrictions on Funding

Under the rubric of funding and contribution requirements/limits, a suggestion on employee contributions seems eminently sensible. Specifically, the idea would be to allow tax-exempt employee contributions to DB plans in amounts up to the same limits for 401(k) contributions. A trend has been fostered in the private sector away from contributory pensions because, at present, employee contributions to pension plans are always deposited after having paid income tax. There is no logical policy reason to discriminate in this way against the DB plan, an issue that gains in importance because of the need for employee cost sharing and employee choice in the future. (The limitation could apply to each plan individually and to the total addition to both types of plans.) This proposal would make cash balance pension plans with their automatic life income provision more competitive with other DC plans.

The 1994 Retirement Protection Act made drastic changes in minimum funding for DB plans. It increased the funding target for the plans by mandating interest and mortality standards not based on experience but based on selected standards. The 1993 Tax Act cut back the funding allowed for private plans. Neither act helped plan sponsors to fund their plans by a regular and orderly schedule of contributions. One suggestion that might help deal with these consequences would be to increase the annual limit on the employer's maximum funding that was deductible, which could be done by allowing defined benefit plans to project future inflation in the compensation considered in the benefits in the current year's maximum funding (at a minimum). Beginning in 1994, the maximum amount of pay that may be considered in determining a defined benefit for funding in the plan year was cut from US $235,840 to US $150,000. While the new limit sounds large, it is inadequate when inflation and pay growth are considered. Indexing the limit in future years does not help this year's actuarial calculation. Thus employees who earn as little as US $50,000 today and receive pay increases only slightly greater than inflation will not be able to have their benefit funded prior to retirement.

Another idea would be to increase the maximum funding limit for non-pay-related benefits from 100 percent of the current liability by permitting projection of historic benefit increases, but not in excess of 125 percent of the current liability. Consequently sponsors of flat-rate benefit plans would be permitted to continue to contribute to those plans, even when the funding ratio approached or exceeded 100 percent, and to build a reasonable cushion for periods of adverse experience.

Many pension experts have called for increasing the alternative funding maximum for pay-related benefits from 150 percent to 175 percent, which would allow sponsors of final-pay formulas with young, short-service workforces and few retirees to contribute on a more level basis with respect to payroll. This would be helpful to new businesses, including employees hired by new plants started by United States or foreign companies. Likewise, it would be useful to increase or eliminate the 25 percent payroll limitation for aggregate contributions to DB and DC plans of the same sponsor, when the contributions meet individual plan limits. The 25 percent limit is an old rule created to avoid evasion of excess profit taxes during World War II and makes little sense in the current context of high minimum requirements, variable pay, and volatile markets. Removal of the rule would help sponsors with mature workforces whose minimum requirements for DB plans can be quite large in a given year. The size of the contribution will be even more unpredictable because the 1994 law requires contributions of 90 percent of the increase in the underfunded current liability (to avoid harsher requirements) or 30 percent of the aggregate unfunded current liability, including increased underfunding from drops in interest rates and declines in security markets.

Finally, actuaries tend to agree that a reasonable mortality forecast is required for DB plans, one that is more reflective of their own experience than as the one required under current rules. Large firms have a more open, more diverse, and larger pool of lives than those used for the group annuity business. We need to avoid including the selling and profit margins, as well as the mortality selection, in establishing an accurate basis appropriate for these larger employee groups. We also need to understand the unnecessary margins that can be built into projected mortality which helps commercial annuities state a higher interest rate in the annuity basis.

Conclusion

It would be ideal if a new private retirement system could be designed from scratch. I suspect that parts of an ideal system would look quite different from what we have today even if we did not choose new goals. If we did select new goals, we would probably want rather more emphasis on adequacy and singleness of purpose for DC plans and less cumbersome and complex rules for DB plans. The layers of DB regulation were designed with the best of intentions, but their result has been self-defeating and must be seriously questioned. Because the costs and liabilities are so high, employers' motivation to provide for adequate replacement income is more fragile than many policymakers assume.

Initially, the regulatory system's goals were to foster DB coverage, to accrue benefits more proportionally with service, to vest benefits earlier, to require higher funding, and to guarantee benefits against all risks, including plan termination. The outcome of these mandates seeking perfection for the tax-qualified plan system has been perverse overall, because it has discouraged DB coverage and led to smaller DB benefits as well as more non-qualified DB benefits. The latter outcome is the most ironic because in non-qualified plans, vesting, funding, and benefit guarantees (the goals of all the reforms) are nonexistent. This is not solely an issue relevant to the highly paid worker; rather, thousands of employees are being affected today at both large and small companies.

Meanwhile, in other parts of the developed world, there is a widespread perception that funding or plan termination is not a serious problem. Germany's private plans are more than 50 percent unfunded, yet no alarm ensues (see Bodie, Mitchell, and Turner 1996); in contrast, in the United States, a unfunding of less than 5 percent brought on the worst kind of crisis predictions in Washington. In Britain, plan sponsors can contribute on an orderly, long-term basis without short-term interruptions imposed because funds hit legal full funding limits. Why is the United States government alone among western democracies in having become so distrustful of private plans and their sponsors? The rules and tax advantages were designed to foster private plans, at least initially. Why is it now a bad outcome that employers provide benefits according to their objectives and policies? Why should savings and its private investment have such a low public priority?

On both sides, there is a greater need to appeal to the people responsible for setting and applying public policy. The government must begin to realign its policy goals, to become more supportive of private plan sponsors, and to help the private sector provide reasonable financial protection for old age. Unless we develop an environment conducive to private pension plans, the nation's retirement system will remain in sorry shape. Social Security is not solvent in the medium and long run, and benefits are more likely to be cut gradually than are taxes to be increased. All this implies, in my view, that it is time for experts and policymakers jointly to seek national solutions to a problem we have little time to solve.

The views reported herein reflect the author's opinion and not the views of his former employer.

Note

1. These results cover each firm's largest employee group and may exclude or include negotiated benefits for a part of the group.

References

Bodie, Zvi, Olivia S. Mitchell, and John A. Turner, eds. *Securing Employer-Based Pensions: An International Perspective*. Philadelphia: Pension Research Council and University of Pennsylvania Press, 1996.

Clark, Robert L. and Ann A. McDermed. *The Choice of Pension Plans in a Changing Regulatory Environment*. Washington, DC: AEI Press, 1990.

Oliver, L. L. and M. Patterson. *Retirement Benefits in the 1990s*. KPMG Peat Marwick, 1993–95.

Mitchell, Olivia S. and Anna M. Rappaport. "Innovations and Trends in Pension Plan Coverage." In Ray Schmitt, ed., *The Future of Pensions in the United States*. Philadelphia: Pension Research Council and University of Pennsylvania Press, 1993.

Salisbury, Dallas L. "Pensions in a Changing Economy." Paper presented at 1995 Employee Benefits Research Institute symposium, Washington DC, January 1995.

Schieber, Sylvester J. "Retirement Income Adequacy at Risk: Baby Boomers' Prospects in the New Millennium." Watson Wyatt Worldwide working paper. Washington, DC: The Wyatt Company, 1995.

———. "Why Are Pension Benefits So Small?" *Benefits Quarterly* (Fall 1995).

Schmitt, Ray, ed. *The Future of Pensions in the United States*. Philadelphia: Pension Research Council and University of Pennsylvania Press, 1993.

Chapter 3
Cash Balance Pension Plans

Anna M. Rappaport, Michael L. Young,
Christopher A. Levell, and Brad A. Blalock

Over the last fifty years, analysts have repeatedly claimed that defined benefit plans are dead. Some of the rationales given include the views that they are old fashioned and too complex, younger employees don't appreciate them, and they are too risky for the plan sponsors.

In spite of these contentions, larger employers who have analyzed their options have often decided to continue with their defined benefit plans. One reason for this is that, for employees who stay to retirement, DBs have delivered the most return per dollar the employer contributed, a goal of many employers in designing retirement plans. Additionally, employers who have managed their assets well have been well-rewarded for taking the risks associated with offering a defined benefit pension.

The Environment of the 1990s

Many employers today are again reexamining their retirement strategies in response to major shifts in the business environment. Some of the new factors include a greater concern about employee appreciation and a focus on an evolving and different social contract.

In the past, larger employers offered what was seen as an implied promise of the availability of lifetime employment. An employee who performed could count on his or her job being there as long as the employee wanted the job. There was the option to stay to retirement. A retirement plan, which offered those who stayed to retirement the greatest share of the benefits, was generally offered by these employers. These plans offered substantial incentives to retire before "normal retirement age," usually 65, so that many employees retired between 55 and 62.

More recently, however, an oversupply of trained people resulting from the baby boom and from restructuring has changed the employment bargain. Employers often do not have to compete for good people or worry about retaining them. As a result, many organizations have implemented reengineering and downswing programs. Downsizing measures undermine the expectation of lifetime employment, and many large employers no longer offer any "promise" of lifetime employment. Employees now believe that performing well offers no guarantees since companies and jobs are often restructured. Furthermore, many companies have experienced changes in ownership of the entire organization or of parts of the organization. Individual operations are often sold to other organizations so that employees may find that they have a new employer, one with a different culture.

The transition to different cultures is difficult, both for employees and for employers. For employees over age 45 with long service, this is particularly true since many built their lives based on expectations which grew out of the old culture. In looking at the accrual pattern under a traditional defined benefit plan, one human resources officer summarized the needs of the new environment, stating, "We need to offer a plan such that if an employee leaves at any point in time we are square and treat the employee fairly. We need to protect our employees in the event we are acquired. In our industry, 25 percent to 33 percent of the employees will usually lose their jobs after an acquisition." The traditional defined benefit pension plan with its steep accrual pattern was not perceived as meeting these needs.

Plan Choices in the Present

In addition to traditional defined benefit and defined contribution plans, there are a number of hybrid plan types available. Hybrid plans offer a combination of the features of both traditional defined benefit and defined contribution plans. Two examples of hybrid plans illustrate that a range of combinations of features is possible:

1. *Cash balance plan.* A defined benefit plan where the benefit is defined as an individual account within the plan. The plan specifies the rates of contribution and investment return (independent of plan asset performance) to be credited to the participant's account. This plan looks to the participant like a defined contribution plan for benefit accrual purposes.
2. *Target benefit plan.* A defined contribution plan where the account is calculated to reproduce the benefits in a defined benefit formula by individual. The benefit accrual pattern in this type of plan is more like a defined benefit plan than a defined contribution plan

with a non-age-related contribution. This plan looks to the participant like a defined benefit plan, but it is subject to defined contribution legal requirements.

This article focuses primarily on cash balance plans, because they offer a good response to a changing employment contract, and on the pros and cons of using these plans relative to more traditional defined benefit and defined contribution plans. Table 1 compares the characteristics of cash balance, traditional final average pay defined benefit plans, and traditional defined contribution plans.

Choosing a Plan

The traditional choice between defined benefit and defined contribution plans is based on setting objectives and considering plan characteristics. However, new ways of thinking about this choice are helpful. The key differences in the *traditional* plan designs include the following:

Benefit accrual. Defined benefit (final average earnings) plans provide for larger benefit accruals later in the employee's career. In contrast, in defined contribution plans, account additions pay for greater benefit accruals earlier, if translated to income. From the individual's perspective, retirement assets grow slowly early in the employee's career in a traditional defined benefit plan, and much more rapidly in a defined contribution plan.

Method of payout. Defined benefit plans usually offer payout as monthly income, and defined contribution plans usually offer payout as lump sums. Either can offer the other form as an option.

What the employee sees. For defined benefit plans, the employee sees a monthly income at age 65, but for defined contribution plans the employee sees an account balance.

Hybrid plan designs combine the features of both defined benefit plans and defined contribution plans so that the employer can offer a plan called a cash balance defined benefit plan. Several distinctive features of this plan design stand out. First, benefits accrue as under a traditional defined contribution plan (or in a pattern selected by the employer). Second, lump-sum distributions are the usual form of benefit payout. As a defined benefit, a life income minimum is guaranteed and is the "normal form" as required by law. Third, benefit values are communicated as an "account balance." Fourth, the interest earned on the "account balance" is based on a credited rate defined by the plan. The rate may

TABLE 1

	Traditional DB	Cash Balance	Traditional DC
Allocation of dollar cost	Heavily to later years of service/older age	Heavier to early years of service/younger age (can modify with formula)	Heavily to early years of service
Investment risk is borne by	Employer; benefits do not vary based on investment results	Employer; benefits do not vary based on investment results	Employee; benefits vary substantially based on investment results (see Table 2)
Ability to grandfather prior defined benefit formula inside plan	Yes	Yes	No
Ability to offer early retirement windows inside plan	Yes	Yes	No
Investment choices available to employees	No	No	Yes
Ability to vary accruals by age/length of service	Formula does automatically	Yes, subject to passing nondiscrimination tests	Yes, subject to passing nondiscrimination tests
Can base benefits on profits	No	No	Yes
Inflation risk			
Prior to retirement	Employer	Employer	Employee
After retirement	Employee	Employee (but offset by opportunity to keep investment return)	Employee (but offset by opportunity to keep investment return)
Mortality risk after retirement	Employer	Employee; if lump sum chosen	Employee

be based on an external index (such as a T-bill rate) or it may be a fixed rate (such as 5 percent). For the plan to be a defined benefit plan, the benefit must be "definitely determinable" and the plan sponsor cannot be allowed discretion in defining the crediting rate each period. The crediting rate is not tied to the actual investment results of the plan.

Cash balance plans are like defined benefit plans along several dimensions. Most critically, assets are pooled in a single fund; there are no individual investment accounts. This reduces recordkeeping requirements. The same principles are used to manage assets as in any defined benefit plan, although, because the expected cash flow pattern can be quite different, actual asset mix may differ. Additionally, the sponsoring employer retains investment risk on plan funds. Depending on objectives, this can be seen as an advantage or disadvantage, but, overall, funds where employers have made the investment decisions generally have earned higher returns than employee-directed investments. Cash balance plans also are covered by Pension Benefit Guaranty Corporation (PBGC) insurance on the benefits side, and PBGC premiums are required. Depending on one's point of view, this might be perceived as an advantage or a disadvantage. Employers would tend to view the premium cost as a disadvantage, but the insurance is a benefit to participants. In the calculation of costs, the employer can recognize expected terminations of employment in advance. Initial costs are lower than under defined contribution plans because future non-vested terminations are recognized through actuarial assumptions rather than after they occur. In contrast, under a defined contribution plan, the impact of non-vested terminations occurs through forfeitures after the termination. Depending on the defined contribution plan type and provision, forfeitures either reduce contributions or are distributed to remaining participants.

Other ways in which a cash balance plan resembles a defined benefit pension include the facts that increases in benefits for past periods can be granted and that early retirement window benefits can be offered inside the plan (accomplished with a benefit enhancement beyond the normal account addition). Finally, a change to a cash balance formula from a traditional defined benefit plan requires a plan amendment, not a termination. If the plan is overfunded at the change, the surplus is used to reduce future contributions (as it would with the traditional plan). If the plan is underfunded, the unfunded liability is amortized as it would be in any defined benefit plan.

Method of Benefit Payout

Both defined benefit and defined contribution plans can pay out benefits as lump sums or as annual incomes. Traditional defined benefit plans usually pay benefits as monthly income, except for small accumulations. Some plans offer lump sums for all benefit levels. Traditional defined contribution plans generally offer lump sums that can be rolled over into an IRA or taken as cash, though some plans offer annuity options. Cash balance plans generally offer both lump-sum options and communicate the benefit as a lump sum, although the normal form is income.

There are risk implications from the participant's perspective of the form of benefit payout. With a lump sum, the participant assumes both the investment and mortality risk after the time of payout. With an annuity, the plan sponsor, or organization offering the annuity if insured, assumes the post-retirement mortality and investment risk. Benefit payout can be a significant issue because many employees are not in a good position to evaluate the risk of outliving their retirement funds and may not focus on the issue of mortality risk.

Annuity options are also available to pay benefits over joint lifetimes, and ERISA requires a normal form of annuity payout for married participants of a 50 percent joint and survivor annuity. The average future period of widowhood for women in their forties today has been predicted as fifteen years. On average, elderly single persons are much less well off than couples, and women are less well off after widowhood. Issues related to choice of payment option are quite important and should be considered in helping individuals plan for retirement.

Time of Access to Plan Funds

Many defined contribution plans, particularly 401(k) plans, offer the option to the employee to access funds prior to retirement through the use of loans and/or hardship withdrawals. No options for access to funds prior to termination of employment or retirement are available in cash balance plans. All defined benefit plans are likely to make available small lump sums at termination of employment. These can be rolled over and saved for retirement, but often are not. There is an important issue in retirement security: the value of plans in providing for retirement security is tied to whether the funds will still be available for retirement.

Transition to Cash Balance Plans

Several methods of transition from another defined benefit formula are possible. Under the most common method, the benefits already earned under the prior defined benefit formula are calculated as lump sums and used as opening "account balances." If the prior plan provided a final average pay formula and subsidized early retirements, there are transition issues of whether to protect the future earnings increase applied to prior service and whether to offer a benefit to compensate for the value of the prior subsidized early retirement benefit. Legally, the benefit payable if the employee terminated employment on the day before transition is protected, but many employers will want to offer a greater benefit to longer-service employees.

Several transition methods are available. One approach is to pay the greater of the benefit that would have been paid under the old plan and the benefit due under the new formula for a subset of the employees for a limited time period. Another is to extend that period until termination or retirement for the subset of employees. A third technique is to provide extra account balances at transition to make up for the greater benefit which would have been available at early retirement. This makes sense where there was heavily subsidized early retirement in the old plan. Alternatively, the employer may provide extra account additions to make up for the fact that final average earnings will not be directly used in the formula. Finally, an employer may provide a supplemental additional benefit.

The second method, known as the traditional grandfathering approach, has the drawback of being complex, taking a longer period until the new plan is accepted, and having a potentially large difference in benefits for people on the two sides of the grandfathering line. On the other hand, the main advantages of this method is that it ensures that longer-service employees will not receive less than under the prior plan.

The new cash balance formula can have credits which vary by age or length of service. When this is utilized, extra benefits during transition are usually reduced since the benefit is closest to that provided under the prior plan. Transition based only on conversion to account balances generally favors junior employees. Added benefits to longer-service employees balance the transition, so that depending on the amount of added benefits and who receives them, either a more junior or a more senior group might be favored.

Cost and Financial Implications of the Choice

We have modeled the cost from a financial statement perspective of a defined contribution plan versus a cash balance plan, both with an annual contribution level of 6 percent of pay. The annual expense for an average employee (age 40 with ten years of service and an annual salary of about US $50,000) is as follows:

Expense for defined contribution plan	US $2,932
Expense for cash balance plan	US $1,845
Ratio of cash balance to defined contribution	.63

The assumptions used in the calculation are shown in Table 2. The expense for the cash balance plan is lower because we anticipate that plan assets will earn more than the crediting rate and because forfeitures at

TABLE 2 Assumptions Used in Expense Calculation and
Modeling (US $)

Deterministic Forecasts	
Starting Salary	$30,000
Hired at age 30	Valued at age 40 with
	10 years of service
Annual Credit	6.00%*
Diversified Return	8.00%
GIC Return	6.00%
Unlucky Return	−3.00%
Cash Balance Crediting Rate	7.00%*
Discount Rate	8.00%*
Return on DB Assets	10.00%*
Salary Increases	5.00%*
% of GIC Employees	70.00%
Stochastic Forecasts	
Starting Salary	$30,000
Years in Payout	30
Inflation Expected Return	5.00%
Inflation Standard Deviation	3.00%
Contribution Level	6.00%
Portfolio Expected Return	8.00%
Portfolio Standard Deviation	14.00%

*Assumptions used in expense calculation.
Note: Salary increases were tied to the stochastic inflation system.

the time of non-vested terminations are recognized in advance. The plan sponsor is rewarded for assuming the investment risk. The expense for the defined contribution plan will ultimately drop somewhat as terminations occur and as forfeitures are recognized.

The expected benefit at age 65 from the defined contribution plan depends on the actual investment choices and returns. If the employee chooses fixed-income investments which provide an average return of 6 percent to age 65, while the cash balance plan credits participants' accounts with 7 percent, then the cash balance benefit at age 65 will be 120 percent of the defined contribution benefit. The higher balance will be a direct result of the higher investment return credit. The cost/value ratio of the defined contribution plan with a choice of fixed income investments versus the cash balance benefit can be viewed as 53 percent for the cash balance plan in this case because the cost is 63 percent and the benefit is 20 percent higher (63% divided by 120% = 53%). The differences in benefits delivered and the impact of investment returns are explored further below.

Table 3

Attribute	Cash Balance	Defined Contribution
Overall ongoing benefit cost (excluding administrative cost)	Account addition as a percentage of pay offset by value of anticipated non-vested terminations and investment earnings in excess of crediting rate	Account addition offset by prior period forfeiture amounts not added to participant accounts
Ability to consider any unfunded liability at transition in calculating costs	Can be considered; if there is surplus, it is in effect amortized and reduces ongoing cost as described above	Cannot be considered; prior plan must in effect be considered separately if continued, or terminated
Ability to consider any unfunded liability at transition in calculating costs	Can be considered; additional payment would be required to amortize	Is not considered in defined contribution cost, but this amount would be paid separately either to fund and terminate prior plan or maintain it on an ongoing basis
Ability to optimize investments for best return	Very good	Limited, since fluctuations have direct impact on individual benefits

Overall, financial implications of the choice can be summarized as shown in Table 3:

Implications of Offering Investment Choice and Shifting Investment Risk

A key difference between cash balance plans and traditional defined contribution plans is that investment risk remains with the employer in cash balance plans. In defined contribution plans, it is also common to give employees investment choices.

A key question is the significance of investment risk bearing for employees. Several issues arise, including the fact that in a defined contribution plan returns on investment directly impact each individual employee; if returns are lower, that means a lower account balance. Also, if investment choices are offered, there will be a wide variation in the actual choice made by individuals, and poor choices can have a major impact on an individual's benefits. As noted elsewhere in this volume, where employees have investment choices, they often choose conservatively, and choose fixed-income investments. Long-term investment results indicate that, by choosing fixed-income investments they give up some of the potential investment return. Finally, fluctuations in actual returns have a very different impact in defined benefit and defined contribution plans, both from year to year and at the point of retirement.

The effects of fluctuations are very important and generally are not a focus in the defined contribution setting. However, since they affect benefits rather than cost, employers have not focused on this issue in budgeting and financial planning. In contrast, in the defined benefit setting, investment return fluctuations affect the employers' costs and have been modeled extensively. They have an impact on employer contributions which can be smoothed by the use of asset valuation techniques as well as through the actuarial liability valuation method. Unless a plan is close to the full funding limit, considerable spreading of fluctuations in asset values is possible. Many plan sponsors can tolerate considerable asset fluctuation because the amount of fluctuation is modest when viewed in the context of the firm's financial structure.

Of course, in the defined contribution setting, each account is one person's benefits. Fluctuations at different points in time have a very different impact on the individual. During the time prior to withdrawal of the funds, fluctuations are tolerable, except that the individual may make decisions based on such fluctuations which are adverse to achieving a better return long term. However, at the point when the lump sum is withdrawn, the value is fixed. It can be argued that if the market is down, the lump sum can be reinvested in equities so that the fluctuation is still smoothed out, but for many participants that is not a reasonable scenario. These participants will want a more certain strategy after retirement.

To illustrate the effects of defined contribution plan fluctuations for the average employee, we have modeled plan outcomes under different investment scenarios. The investment scenarios are as follows:

A. Employee chooses a diversified portfolio and averages 8 percent.
B. Employee chooses fixed-income investments and averages 6 percent.
C. Employee makes poor choices, is unlucky, switches between asset classes at wrong time, and averages −3 percent.
D. Cash balance with crediting rate equivalent to 7 percent.

Figure 1 shows the lump-sum balances under these four scenarios at the end of ten years and at age 65 for a single employee.

Since employees will make different choices in the defined contribu-

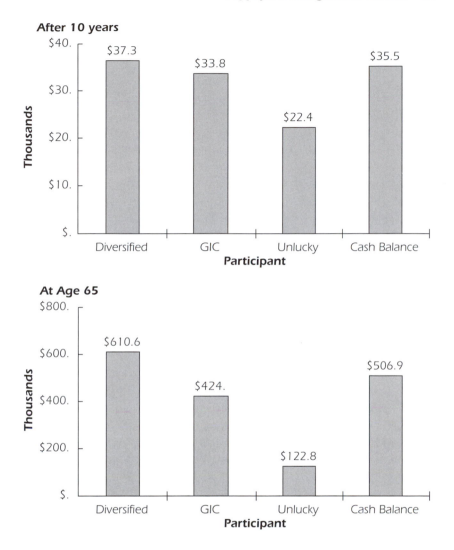

Figure 1. Individual account balances in DC plans under investment scenarios alternative.

tion plan, an average outcome will be a composite of the individuals' choices. Table 4 shows the average composite results for several different election patterns, again illustrated as lump sums at age 65, and also as age 65 replacement ratios (i.e., equivalent annual benefit as a percentage of final pay).

TABLE 4 Impact of Election Pattern on Average DC Balances versus Cash
       Balance Account at Age 65 (US $)

Defined Contribution	Sample Election Patterns			Average Balance	Income Replacement
	Diversified	GIC	Unlucky		
Sample 1	20%	80%	0%	$461,299	31%
Sample 2	30%	60%	10%	449,841	30%
Sample 3	50%	40%	10%	487,162	33%
Sample 4	70%	20%	10%	524,483	35%
Sample 5	90%	10%	0%	591,921	40%
Cash Balance	– no election permitted –			$506,891	34%

TABLE 5 Diversified Employee Percentile Ending Balances at Age 65
       (US $)

	Percentile	Balance ($US)
Defined Contribution	10	255,938
	25	364,062
	50	553,393
	75	816,248
	90	1,130,877
Cash Balance		506,891

Impact on Individual Employees

An additional concern is the impact of variation in investment returns
on individual employees. This table shows the impact of variability on an
individual employee's lump sum amount at age 65. Variability will have a
direct impact in each situation, but it is greatest in investment Scenarios
A and C. Table 5 shows results based on a simulation for the diversified
portfolio. Assumptions have been made for each asset class as to both
expected return and standard deviation. Based on this modeling, the
lump sums at age 65 are shown at different probability levels. The lowest
number is the 10th percentile; it is expected that the lump sum will exceed this number 90 percent of the time or more if investments are
chosen according to the assumptions for the diversified portfolio. The
second amount is the 25th percentile; 75 percent of the time the lump
sum will be this amount or greater. The next value is the median; half
the time the results will be equal to or greater than this amount. The
75th and 90th percentiles are also shown.

Variability of individual account balances is a major issue in defined
contribution plans. For each individual, it is only their results that count;

averaging with the rest of the group does not matter. Variability can have a major impact of the personal security of each individual.

Case Studies

In our line of business we consult with many different clients, some of whom have recently examined cash balance plans. One was a not-for-profit organization that sponsored a traditional final average earnings defined benefit plan. When this firm analyzed its culture, work patterns, and workforce it found that few employees stayed as long as ten years, and there were different job groups with different characteristics at hire, including younger professionals who joined the firm in order to get initial experience which would help them in building a career; senior professionals who came as an "end of career" or "second career" job which depended on their credibility and experience; and clerical and administrative staff who were essentially like these groups at any organization. Furthermore the existing pension plan was not valued or appreciated, and employees were not being encouraged to save although there was a savings program, but without a match.

Focus groups were conducted with both rank-and-file employees and managers. The manager group was used to test and provide input into alternative plan design concepts. The organization then implemented a cash balance plan and added a match to the savings program that worked to encourage employee savings. Longer-term employees at the time of change were given the greater of the benefit under the old plan or the cash balance plan. Benefit statements were produced which combined balances under the matched savings program and the cash balance plan, and focused employees on the total retirement program. After 10 years of operation, the organization continues to be pleased with the results.

A second case was that of a multi-location, integrated health care organization that sponsored a mix of plans. A traditional final average earnings defined benefit plan was in place at its hospitals and some of its other locations, but at other locations a defined contribution plan was in place. This organization was making acquisitions to respond to the changing market and had new services such as home health, physician offices, and nursing homes along with its traditional hospital business. In evaluating their situation, they found that the diverse approach to benefits was a barrier to transfers and to meeting federal requirements. Also, with the new businesses, the requirements for professionals were increasingly diverse. The firm's culture which had supported paternalism in the past was changing and needed to move from that attitude. Simultaneously, the existing plan was not valued or appreciated, particularly by younger employees. Employees were not being encouraged to save although there was a savings program, but without a match.

A task force of human resource and financial managers representing diverse business units studied retirement strategy and developed a policy for retirement benefits. Focus groups were conducted with rank-and-file employees. Subsequently, the organization decided to move all employees into a new cash balance approach, which permitted effective integration of groups from both prior plans. Existing employees who participated in the defined benefit plan were given the better of the two plans—their old plan or the new plan with the calculation done at termination. The existing defined benefit plan had a surplus which was used to help fund the benefits under the amended plan.

A Comparison of Cash Balance Versus Defined Contribution Plans

Cash balance plans have several pros and cons versus traditional defined contribution plans. Among the advantages are that the plan sponsor may be able to invest funds more effectively than the participant over the long term. As a result, the cost to the plan sponsor per dollar of benefit delivered should be lower in the long term due to more favorable investment returns. Additionally, employers have some flexibility in contribution timing in many situations.

Another advantage of cash balance plans is that plan termination is not required in the transition process. Surplus can be used to help fund additions to accounts, and there is time to make up any deficits. Also, retrospective benefit improvements can be offered by providing additional benefits as income or added account balances. For an organization involved in multiple acquisitions, these plans offer a reasonable transition from either defined benefit or defined contribution plans. The plan sponsor need not be concerned about the impact of fluctuations in investment returns on employees.

Of course there are also some disadvantages of cash balance plans, as compared to defined contribution pensions. First, risk is retained by the employer, and costs can fluctuate. Second, administrative and management requirements of defined benefit plans such as actuarial valuations still apply. Third, these plans are somewhat more difficult to explain than traditional defined contribution plans. Another key difference relates to payment of PBGC premiums. They are required for cash balance plans, and these plans are insured. Whether this is seen as an advantage or disadvantage depends on one's point of view.

A Comparison of Cash Balance Versus Traditional Defined Benefit Plans

Cash balance plans are increasingly perceived as more modern and are more appreciated by younger employees. They have benefit accrual patterns similar to defined contribution plans, and allocate more money to those with less service and at younger ages as well as to those who leave early. The accrual pattern can be modified by setting step accrual rates, that is, varying accruals by length of service. For example, a plan might offer 5 percent of pay as an annual credit, or it could offer 3 percent for five years, 4 percent the next five years, 5 percent for the next five years, and so on.

Cash balance plans may not be well suited to employers who find that traditional final average pay plans meet their needs, but for those who want an accrual pattern more slanted to early years of employment, this hybrid plan offers an excellent combination of features. Employers considering a transition to defined contribution plans should look at cash balance as an option.

Other Approaches to Meet the Changing Employment Environment

The cash balance approach discussed here assumes that the focus of employer-financed benefits will be a plan sponsored and managed by the employer, and we have argued that the cash balance approach is an excellent alternative for employers favoring such an approach. There are other plan options which meet some of the same goals, including a multiemployer pension scheme. One such program is TIAA-CREF (Teachers Insurance Annuity Association and College Retirement Fund), a national nonprofit pension company offering a defined contribution program to college and university faculty. Individual annuity contracts are provided to each covered person, and the employer contributions are deposited in these contracts, which are fully owned by the individuals. Plan participants are fully mobile across the academic community.

There are several reasons why this program probably would not be acceptable for business in general. One is that persons accepting teaching positions often stay within the occupation for life, although they may change institutions. This is not the case in other fields, as we have seen recently. Second, TIAA-CREF has a unique situation as compared to commercial insurance companies in that it is authorized by special legislation which makes it tax exempt. Third, TIAA-CREF has very strong acceptance and status within the academic community, but it is unlikely that an insurance company would achieve such stature with business. The program identity is with TIAA-CREF and not the employer, but this is widely accepted within the profession. Private businesses generally want more identity for their benefits and more credit for them. Contributions are often considerably higher than most private businesses are willing to devote to benefits. (This is part of the reason why TIAA-CREF accumulations tend to be considerable at the point of retirement.) At the (lower) level of contributions commonly made to defined benefit plans, results would be much less satisfactory.

Another possible model is that of the multi-employer defined benefit plan. Such plans have been common for negotiated groups and are the only way to provide effective retirement benefits for certain groups tied to a union but working for many employers. Examples are longshoremen, construction workers, and milk truck drivers. While this model is appealing in theory, it has not worked well in practice in many cases. Corporations eligible to participate in these plans for selected groups of workers are reluctant to do so. Problems with these plans have arisen when an industry declines. In this case multi-employer plans have been left with many retirees and not enough money. The surviving participating companies were often left with liabilities related to those who withdrew. This has been partly solved by requiring employers who leave the plan to pay a withdrawal liability. Nevertheless, participating employers have limited control over the plan and factors that influence their costs. In addition, these plans address the needs of the changing work environment only so long as people move within covered employment. Otherwise, they do not work well.

Conclusion

As the workforce and employment contract are changing, pension plans will also need to be revisited. For many employers, there are weaknesses in both traditional defined benefit and traditional defined contribution plans. Because cash balance plans offer an alternative well suited to many situations, they will be used increasingly in the future.

Chapter 4
Risk Aversion and Pension Investment Choices

Vickie L. Bajtelsmit and Jack L. VanDerhei

If current trends in mortality and labor force participation continue, retirees in the twenty-first century can expect to live longer and healthier lives than their twentieth-century counterparts.[1] This implies that, for those baby boomers who survive to age 65, wealth and income in retirement will need to be sufficient to support more than twenty years of retirement.[2] Since Social Security benefits replace only a small portion of average pre-retirement earnings, they cannot necessarily be viewed as an adequate safety net for individuals with insufficient savings, particularly given the future tax increases that will be necessary to support promised benefits beyond the early part of the next century.[3] It is therefore essential that today's workers be encouraged to make savings choices during their working years that will enable them to achieve their retirement income goals.

As a backdrop for exploring the future of pension policy, this chapter focuses on the emergence of defined contribution plans as primary pension vehicles and the implications of this trend for plan participants and their retirement income security. Recent theoretical and empirical evidence concerning individual investment decisionmaking suggests that individuals are more risk averse and have more diverse reasons for saving than do their employers. They are therefore expected to allocate their plan assets more conservatively, resulting in lower accumulated assets to fund retirement. Furthermore, the diversity of individual characteristics and needs implies that the allocations of individual participant accounts can be expected to exhibit a great deal of variation. If risk aversion is higher for certain groups, such as women, minorities, or low-income households, greater conservatism in retirement investment will result in lower income replacement for these groups.

Due to the lack of available data, most studies of defined contribution asset allocation have used aggregated data, and there have been relatively few studies examining individual decisionmaking. The data set used in this chapter includes information on a sample of 20,000 active management participants for a single, large United States employer, as well as valuable demographic information for each participant. We examine asset allocation decisions as a function of demographic characteristics that have been suggested in the literature to be associated with risk aversion. The empirical evidence indicates that demographic characteristics of workers are important determinants of their allocation decisions. Generally more conservative patterns of investment by women are also found to exist. We conclude with a discussion of policy implications and areas for further consideration.

The Emerging Importance of Defined Contribution Plans

Predominance of New Plans

In the last decade, there have been significant changes in pension provision. Although Yakoboski and Silverman (1994) report that the much publicized downward trend in pension sponsorship and participation rates during the 1980s has apparently reversed direction, there are still many employers that do not offer pension plans and, even when offered, not all employees choose to participate. Based on tabulations by the Employment Benefit Research Institute (EBRI) of the April Current Population Survey, 62.1 percent of all civilian nonagricultural wage and salary workers age 16 and over work for an employer where a plan is sponsored. When a plan is available, 75.9 percent of these workers choose to participate. More than half of all workers in this category are not participating in a plan.

Most new plans are of the defined contribution type, and these plans are an increasing percentage of total plans. Eighty-four percent of all plans offered are now defined contribution and, for 16 million participants, this plan is their primary plan. The total number of private-sector qualified plans increased in number by 80,000 between 1985 and 1990. However, during that period, the number of defined benefit plans declined by 57,000 and that of defined contribution plans increased by 137,000.

Key Features of Defined Contribution Plans

The increasing proportion of defined contribution plans is related to characteristics that distinguish them from defined benefit plans. The key differences are related to risk bearing and investment decisionmaking.

Risk Bearing

In defined contribution plans, ultimate retirement income is dependent on the level of contributions made to the plan and the investment performance of the participant's account. In comparison, defined benefit plans typically provide retirement benefits based on years of service and level of pay at retirement. Thus, defined contribution plan participants face much greater uncertainty regarding the expected level of retirement benefits and increasing short-term investment risk as they approach retirement. By comparison, the benefit promise to defined benefit participants becomes more certain as they approach retirement. It has been argued that the shifting of risk to employees is a trend that is detrimental to retirement income security. However, when the trends are examined carefully, it is apparent that most new plans are for small employers (two to nine employees) who did not previously provide a retirement plan at all. Since small employers are not substantially better than their employees at bearing investment or inflation risk, the trend is probably a net gain in that more individuals have access to tax-preferred savings vehicles than previously.

From the standpoint of risk bearing, an advantage of defined contribution plans over final average defined benefit plans is that they can provide lump sum "cash-outs" for workers who leave the firm. If workers change jobs several times over their working careers, participation in a different defined benefit plan at each employer will result in lower total retirement income as compared to participation in a single plan for their lifetime. This is due to the loss of inflation adjustment when benefits are determined based on the last salary earned at a previous employer. In a defined contribution plan, a participant who leaves his or her current employer can roll over plan assets into a different retirement savings vehicle, thus avoiding the penalty for mobility that is inherent in the defined benefit plan.

Investment Decisionmaking

The second important characteristic of defined contribution plans is that participants are often allowed to contribute additional funds to the plans and are required to direct the allocation of their accounts into different investment alternatives. Calculation of the current contribution levels necessary to support future retirement is an extremely complex actuarial and financial problem that requires estimates of investment returns, future inflation, life expectancy, wage growth, and many other factors. Most individuals simply do not have the mathematical skills necessary to do more than ballpark the answer. As an aid to participant de-

TABLE 1 Asset Allocations of Private Pension Plans with More Than 100 Participants, 1991

Asset Class	Percent of DC Assets	Percent of DB Assets
Cash Equivalents	13.0	6.6
Government Securities	10.0	28.7
Corporate Debt	7.8	15.5
Stock	26.6	42.9
Employer Securities	38.5	0.9
Other	4.1	5.4

Source: U.S. Department of Labor tabulations of the 1991 Form 5500s.

cisionmaking, it is increasingly common for employers or plan providers to provide participants with projections of expected retirement income. For example, TIAA-CREF routinely provides tables of replacement ratios resulting from specific investment choices for hypothetical entry and retirement age scenarios (TIAA-CREF 1994).

The contribution decision is closely tied to the allocation decision, since conservative investments will require greater current contribution levels to achieve desired retirement goals. Evidence of allocations for different types of plans indicates that defined contribution plans have had lower allocations to equities than have defined benefit plans. Based on the United States Department of Labor summary of the 1991 Form 5500 Annual Reports, Table 1 provides the percentage allocations to various asset classes by single employer plans with more than 100 participants (excluding assets held in pooled or separate accounts, trusts, and insurance company general accounts, for which asset allocation information is not given). The allocation to equities (not including employer stock) by defined benefit plans is nearly twice the equity allocation by defined contribution plans.

Will Current Investment Decisions Meet Retirement Goals?

Participation

Studies seem to indicate that the baby boom is not preparing adequately for retirement. Bernheim (1993) compared simulated savings requirements to actual savings and found that, not including housing wealth, baby boomers are saving at one-third the necessary rate. With housing wealth included, they are still saving at only 84 percent of the necessary rate. A study by Arthur D. Little, Inc. (1993) reached similar conclusions, estimating that even households with pension plans will fall far short of retirement goals. Those headed by women and those without private pensions will fare substantially poorer. Furthermore, since Social Security currently replaces a large proportion of pre-retirement income for these groups, any substantial alterations in that system will impact heavily on their financial well-being relative to the rest of the population.

It could be argued that one of the best ways to encourage participation by employees in an employer-sponsored plan is for the employer to offer a salary reduction plan with employer matching contributions. For an employee in the 28 percent tax bracket, a one dollar contribution, matched by the employer, is equivalent to receiving US $2.76 in current income. Thus, in the absence of liquidity constraints, it would be expected that employees would contribute up to the maximum percentage of compensation that is eligible for matching. However, the groups that are more likely to be liquidity constrained are also the groups that have shown lower levels of participation in the past. It is also possible that secondary funding objectives, such as the purchase of a house or saving for college tuition, will supersede retirement planning for younger families, thus reducing participation.

Although participation percentages are higher for plans that offer employer matches, the difference is not as great as one might expect (77.8 percent as compared to 71.8 percent). The April 1993 Current Population Survey data indicates that more than half of employers with salary reduction plans provide matching contributions with an average match rate of 65 percent for every dollar contributed by the employee. The average contribution rate by participants in plans without matching was slightly lower than those that provided matching (Yakoboski and Reilly 1994).

Salary reduction plans are another means by which employees can increase their overall savings level, and participation in these plans has been increasing over time. During the period 1988 to 1993, the fraction of workers participating in salary reduction plans, such as 401(k) plans, 457 plans, and 403(b) plans, increased from 15.3 percent to 23.8 percent, representing a 62 percent increase in the number of participants. Among workers with an employer offering a salary reduction plan in 1993, 64.4 percent actually participated in the plan as compared to 57.0 percent in 1988 (Yakoboski and Silverman 1994).

Lump-Sum Distributions

There is evidence that many individuals who receive lump-sum distributions spend some or all of the distribution rather than preserving it on a tax-deferred basis. Tabulations of the April 1993 Current Population

Survey indicate that over 11 percent of the experienced labor force aged 25 to 64 have received a lump-sum distribution from a pension or retirement plan. Of these, 29 percent spent all of the money received, 21 percent rolled it over into another form of retirement savings, and 35 percent saved or invested it in some other form. Although the percentage of recipients who save the entire distribution shows an upward trend, only 6 percent in 1980 and 15 percent for the years 1981 to 1986 did so. Nevertheless, the large percentage of distributions that are not rolled over is cause for concern. Myopic treatment of lump-sum distributions reduces the ability of individuals to meet their retirement income goals without substantial contributions in later years. The advantages normally attributed to defined contribution plans for individuals who switch jobs several times over their lifetime disappear without rollover of contributions to each plan.

With the increasing use of defined contribution plans, it is more likely that individuals will receive distributions several times. The United States Department of Labor (1993) estimates that, between the ages of 18 and 30, the average number of jobs held is 7.5 (with a median of seven). Although this number has increased over the last two decades, it is not clear whether this has been due to greater job mobility, more involuntary terminations, or some other factors. A recent examination of job tenure figures for prime age workers (25 to 64 years) revealed that tenure levels in the 1980s and early 1990s were actually higher than for comparable age workers in the three previous decades.[4] Whether the larger number of jobs held by younger workers will make it more likely that participants will spend lump-sum distributions is not clear but should certainly be watched closely for its potential impact on retirement income security. Provision of information regarding this issue should undoubtedly be an important element of any participant education program.

Asset Allocation in Defined Contribution Plans

Although it is not clear that defined benefit plans are being replaced with defined contribution plans, the increased prevalence of the latter type of plan shifts much of the burden of retirement planning from employers to individuals.[5] Available evidence indicates that, in the aggregate, defined contribution plan assets tend to be more conservatively invested than their defined benefit counterparts, an indication that individuals are making different allocation decisions than professional plan managers.

Greater conservatism by individuals could be due to a lack of knowledge regarding the risk and return characteristics of investment alternatives. The complexities of the economic and investment environment and the proliferation of different choices are confusing to even the best informed and, although the variety of investment options offered under salary reduction plans has increased, employers have shown reluctance specifically to advise participants on investments.[6] They recognize that even if they carefully explain the potential for short-term losses to participants, individuals do not have much patience in down markets. Evidence of this can clearly be seen in the large volume of shares sold at the bottom of the markets in 1987 and 1989.

Furthermore, financial experts are not in agreement regarding optimal investment strategies for individuals over their life cycle. Clearly, since individuals differ in time to retirement, level of income, home ownership, inheritance prospects, liquidity requirements for other major expenditures, and other characteristics, their investment portfolios must differ as well to satisfy their particular needs. The pension portfolio is only one part of the individual's wealth, which includes housing wealth, human capital, Social Security wealth, and other assets. If the pension allocation decision is made in the context of the individual's overall portfolio, ownership of other non-pension risky assets would imply that the pension's allocation to risky assets should be adjusted downward. Since managers of defined benefit plans are concerned primarily with meeting the employers' benefit obligations as opposed to balancing pension portfolio wealth with other participant investments, it is not surprising that their allocation decisions would differ from those made by individual participants.

Risk Versus Return

There is a general consensus based on historical data that, for long-term investors, returns on equity portfolios will exceed returns on all other asset classes. Average annual returns for stocks over the years 1964 to 1993 exceeded bond returns by more than 3 percent. If invested for 30 years at the average annual rates of return for that period of time, a one dollar annual contribution to a stock fund in 1964 would have accumulated to almost twice as much as the same investment in a bond fund by 1993.[7] Although this is a simplified example, it illustrates the powerful effect of long-term compounding. When inflation is taken into account the proportionate difference in accumulation is greater, since the "safe" investment returns do not always have positive real returns. Treasury bills generated negative real after-tax returns in fourteen of the years 1970 to 1991 (Williamson 1994).

If the higher returns on stocks are accompanied by higher risk, then lower allocations to stocks in defined contribution plans may be a reflection of greater participant risk aversion. Although Siegel (1994) argues that, for long holding periods, the risk of stock portfolios is lower than that of bond portfolios, there is strong disagreement on this point (Bodie 1995; Samuelson 1963 and 1989).

In Siegel's study of nearly 200 years of returns on different asset portfolios, he shows that even in the worst (meaning worst for stocks and best for bonds) post-1926 thirty-year period, stock investment accumulations were three times that of bond investments. He demonstrates that, for long-term investors (twenty-year holding periods), the risk as measured by standard deviation of holding period returns is even lower than that of T-bills. For shorter time horizons there is less time diversification and therefore the reductions in risk are lower but still substantial. Furthermore, the investment strategies commonly referred to as "low risk" may in fact be the highest risk. Siegel finds that, for longer holding periods, real returns on fixed-income assets become relatively less certain. Bodie (1995) argues that, although the probability of a shortfall declines over the long run, this ignores the potential size of the shortfall. He models insurance against shortfall risk as a put option and shows that the price of this option actually increases with the time to maturity, thus casting doubt on the conventional wisdom regarding long-run stock investment risk.

An interesting aspect of this debate is the different impact that long-run stock investment may have on defined contribution versus defined benefit pensions. If Siegel's observations of past historical patterns hold true for the future, then it would seem that participants would be better served by investing substantial portions of their retirement portfolio in equities, at least until they are closer to retirement, and in fact this is the strategy often recommended by investment advisors. However, for defined contribution participants, the success of this strategy is sensitive to the choice of retirement date and may necessitate delaying retirement if the stock market does particularly poorly in the years immediately preceding that date. In contrast, as long as employers have an age-diversified set of employees, they will be better able to take advantage of time diversification, a fact that may explain the greater stock allocations in defined benefit plans.

Evidence of Individual Risk Aversion and Myopia

It is a generally accepted principle that investors do not make decisions based solely on expected outcomes, but also consider the possibility of deviation from the mean. The way in which individuals trade risk and return is subject to dispute,[8] and decision theorists argue that behavioral decisions over uncertain outcomes are made with reference to a system of judgments and beliefs that are often based on faulty reasoning.[9] For individuals with high levels of risk aversion or loss aversion, a low-risk strategy will result in greater current utility. Unfortunately, over a long-term investment horizon, a short-term, low-risk investment strategy can result in negative real return. Although the available data regarding individual investment decisionmaking is not ideal for analyzing the issue of risk aversion, there have been several studies that provide evidence supporting the hypothesis that individuals exhibit some degree of risk aversion and myopia with regard to consumption. A recent study by Jianakoplos and Bernasek (1994) reports that, in the Surveys of Consumer Finances, when responses are sample weighted, 51.08 percent of all women in 1983, and 57.12 percent in 1989, indicated that they were not willing to take any financial risks at all. Compared to the men's responses of 36.4 percent for 1983 and 40.66 percent in 1989, and without controlling for other factors, women appear to be more risk averse than men. However, if women tend to have lower income and there is a correlation between income and risk-taking behavior, then the lower risk taking could be an income effect rather than a gender-related effect. In addition, if women are not the head-of-household, their risk aversion may not have as great an impact on household wealth.

The survey evidence of risk aversion in pension allocations is mixed. A Hewitt Associates (1993) survey found that where GICs were offered, they accounted for 47 percent of employee contributions, indicating fairly low risk tolerance. Employer stock accounted for 33 percent of employee contributions and 67 percent of employer contributions. Equity and balanced funds had much smaller average shares, accounting for only 21 percent and 13 percent respectively of employee contributions. Fidelity Investments, on the other hand, reports that, for companies with an employer stock option, 45.5 percent of plan assets were in equity (other than company stock), 16 percent in company stock, 28.7 percent in GICs.[10] Without a company stock alternative, the stock and GICs each had larger shares (52.4 percent and 34.2 percent). Goodfellow and Schieber (this volume) report 52.8 percent of assets in their sample invested in GICs.

Another potential explanation for participant allocations is that they have a shorter time horizon for decisionmaking. In early working years, savings may be targeted toward housing, then for college expenditures. Alternatively, individuals may simply have a strong preference for current consumption. Often termed "myopia," short-sighted decision horizons may not be irrational but may instead be evidence that prevailing life cycle theories are flawed. However, one of the reasons for passage of Social Security and, later, ERISA was the observed failure of individuals to save adequately for the future. Although it could be argued that alternative reasons for saving are legitimate, the fact remains that inadequate savings, or inadequate accumulation of savings due to overly conservative investment by a large segment of the population, can have serious implications for the future.

An additional observation regarding conservatism in investment allocations is that individuals tend to exhibit inertia (i.e., they do not change their allocations in response to changes in age or in the market). A study examining allocations between the TIAA fixed income alternative and the CREF equities fund found that the vast majority of individuals picked a 50–50 mix and did not alter their allocations in later periods. In some ways, this finding is consistent with a strategy of investing more in equities in later years, since the better performance of the equities account will increase the allocation to that account over time. However, failure to change allocations as retirement approaches would probably result in an overly risky portfolio in later years. Furthermore, in many fixed income alternatives, there are restrictions on changing allocations of balances, which makes large portfolio shifts impossible (for example, TIAA restricts movements out of their guaranteed contracts to 10 percent of the balance per year).

Investment in Employer Securities

Many defined contribution plans now offer the opportunity for participants to invest all or part of their pension contributions in the plan sponsor's stock. For example, in the Hewitt sample above, 40 percent of the plans offered employer stock as an investment alternative for employee contributions and 50 percent offered it for employer contributions. Although one of the arguments originally put forth in favor of Employee Stock Ownership Plans (ESOPs) was that stock ownership would give employees incentive to work harder for "their own company," empirical evidence has shown only a weak relationship between employee stock ownership and stock returns (Kruse 1992). Furthermore, Conte and Jampani (1996) find that, although ESOP returns are higher than diversified equity portfolios, they are substantially riskier and, on a risk-adjusted basis, are substantially lower than those of diversified plans.

There are several possible explanations for popularity of employer stock investments. In some cases, high allocations to this asset class are due to restrictions on the employer match, which can be entirely in employer stock. However, employees often choose employer stock on their own. This may be because they feel they have an informational advantage over other investors in their employer's stock. Ownership of employer stock may give employees an "illusion of control" (Kahneman, Slovic, and Tversky 1987) over the performance of their investment as compared to alternatives that appear to be more volatile. It is also possible that individuals consider investment in employer stock the least risky of the investment alternatives, offering equity-like returns without the same level of perceived risk. A past history of good performance may add to this misconception.[11] Finally, the negative signal inherent in company managers selling their employer stock might result in allocations that exceed employees' desired allocations to that asset category. This may be particularly the case where employer matches are given in the form of employer stock.

Regardless of the past and current performance of an employer's stock, the fact remains that investment of pension dollars in employer stock violates one of the most basic rules of investing. Not only is the pension undiversified, but the employee has both human and financial capital tied to the success or failure of a single business. In the extreme, the failure of the employer, particularly when retirement is imminent, could be disastrous. Even without failure, poor stock performance late in a person's working career could severely impact retirement wealth. For example, if the employer's stock dropped in value just prior to retirement, it would result in a percentage decline in pension annuity comparable to the percentage decline in total portfolio value. It is doubtful that plan participants fully realize the extent of the risk they assume in investing in employer stock and, for obvious reasons, it is even more doubtful that any employer is going to tell them not to do so.

Is Risk Aversion a Group Characteristic?

The usual argument regarding differences in risk aversion is that "in the small" they make little difference (Pratt 1964). However, if certain groups exhibit largely different levels of risk aversion, there may be important implications for pension policy that go beyond mere preferences. For example, if wealthy households exhibit less aversion to investment risk than their poorer counterparts, "in the large" the net effect will be a wider wealth gap in retirement.[12]

More perplexing are the implications of risk preferences across race and gender. There is an economics literature that links risk-taking behavior to economic success, which depends upon, among other things, the decisions made over the lifetime that affect wages, income, and wealth. Observed wealth and income differences by race and gender, although often argued to be the result of discrimination, are also potentially explainable as the result of greater risk aversion exhibited by these groups. If this is the case, then the recent trend toward giving individuals greater control over their retirement investments could be particularly detrimental to elderly women who will be supporting their longer retirement period with less accumulated wealth than their male counterparts.

In addition, although the wage gap has narrowed in the last two decades, women and racial minorities still tend to earn less than white males in equivalent jobs, a fact that implies even greater retirement income inequality.

Although there is historical evidence that elderly women have never been as well off as their male counterparts, this may be the result of years of lower wages and labor force participation as opposed to differences in risk tolerance. At least for older generations, it was common for a woman to enter the labor force after the children were in school and, with lower education and experience, her lower income was considered secondary to her husband's.

The evidence on investment risk taking is not clear. Jianakoplos and Bernasek (1994) were unable to show any significant gender- or race-related differences in risk preferences after controlling for other explanatory characteristics such as savings, home ownership, insurance, and other assets. Riley and Chow (1992) find that asset holdings of women exhibit greater risk aversion than those of men, but they do not control for other characteristics such as age, income, and wealth. However, Hinz et al. (this volume) analyze recent survey data from the Thrift Savings Plan for federal government workers and find that gender differences in investing persist even after controlling for demographic differences.

Evidence from Individual Level Data

Sample Description

The sample of 20,000 management employees used in this study is based on the information supplied by a large United States employer and includes demographic, wage, and pension information on the firm's employees for calendar year 1993. Table 2 provides descriptive statistics for

TABLE 2 Sample Descriptive Statistics ($n = 16,963$)

Variable	Mean	Minimum	Maximum	Standard Deviation
Age	43.88	22.95	64.98	8.53
Female	0.30	0	1	0.45
Tenure	17.58	1.91	46.97	9.06
Non-caucasian	0.17	0	1	0.37
Accumulated 401(k) balance (in US $1,000s)	73.84	0	892.49	78.08

Source: Authors' calculations based on sample firm's internal records for 1993.

TABLE 3 Portfolio Allocations for Sample, by Gender

	Beginning of Year 1993 Account Allocation		Allocation for 1993 Contributions	
Investment Choice	Men (n = 11,863)	Women (n = 5100)	Men (n = 11,863)	Women (n = 5100)
Employer Stock	41.0%	42.1%	42.4%	43.5%
Diversified Equity Portfolio	14.2%	12.9%	18.8%	16.7%
Fixed Income (Government Bonds and GICs)	44.8%	45.0%	38.8%	39.8%

Source: Authors' calculations based on sample firm's internal records.

this sample. There are nearly twice as many men as women and, as might be expected, men are overrepresented in the sample of employees nearing retirement and those in the higher salary ranges.

The employer provided five investment alternatives for the plan participants during this time period, including employer stock, a diversified equity portfolio, a government bond portfolio, a guaranteed interest fund (GIC), and a socially responsible equity fund. In order to better distinguish low-risk and high-risk strategies, the GIC and government bond allocations are consolidated in the following analysis and discussion. Given the nonfinancial objectives that may influence the social choice fund, we exclude this asset class from the analysis. The allocation percentages for the reweighted account balances as of the beginning of year 1993 and for the 1993 contributions are given in Table 3 by gender.

Empirical Methodology

The empirical hypothesis is that employee characteristics will have an affect on the likelihood of allocation to particular asset classes. As in Hinz et al. (this volume), we estimate the Tobit under the assumption that the data are censored (i.e., observation of bunching at the extremes of the allocation choices indicates that the participants might have preferred to invest in portfolios with lower or higher risk than those offered in the plan).

Allocation Decisions

Tables 4 and 5 report the results for three different dependent variables: percent allocation to fixed income (government bonds and GICs);

TABLE 4 Determinants of Investment Allocations for 401(k) Account Balances

	Dependent Variable					
	(1) Percent in Fixed Income		(2) Percent in Equities		(3) Percent in Employer Stock	
Independent Variables	Coeffic. (Std. Err.)	Prob > Chi	Coeffic. (Std. Err.)	Prob > Chi	Coeffic. (Std. Err.)	Prob > Chi
Intercept	0.3674 (0.1258)	0.0035	0.1476 (0.1029)	0.1513	0.2153 (0.1178)	0.0677
Age	−0.0205 (0.0063)	0.0042	−0.0066 (0.0052)	0.2071	0.0201 (0.0060)	0.0007
Age^2	0.0003 (0.0001)	0.0001	0.0001 (0.0001)	0.1762	−0.0003 (0.0001)	0.0001
Female	0.0330 (0.0109)	0.0026	0.0035 (0.0092)	0.7067	−0.0251 (0.0102)	0.0142
Tenure	0.0204 (0.0029)	0.0001	−0.0360 (0.0024)	0.0001	0.0105 (0.0027)	0.0001
Tenure^2	−0.0005 (0.0001)	0.0001	0.0007 (0.0001)	0.0001	−0.0002 (0.0001)	0.0004
Salary	0.0032 (0.0003)	0.0001	0.0023 (0.0002)	0.0001	−0.0052 (0.0002)	0.0001
Race	−0.0003 (0.0131)	0.9840	−0.0101 (0.0110)	0.3606	0.0056 (0.0122)	0.6468
401(k) Wealth	−0.0017 (0.0001)	0.0001	0.0012 (0.00012)	0.0001	0.0018 (0.0001)	0.0001
401(k) Wealth^2	2.0906E−6 (3.21E−7)	0.0001	−1.383E−6 (2.57E−7)	0.0001	−2.69E−6 (3.27E−7)	0.0001

Source: Authors' calculations.

TABLE 5 Determinants of Allocations for Current Contributions

	Dependent Variable					
	(1) Percent in Fixed Income		(2) Percent in Equities		(3) Percent in Employer Stock	
Independent Variables	Coeffic. (Std. Err.)	Prob > Chi	Coeffic. (Std. Err.)	Prob > Chi	Coeffic. (Std. Err.)	Prob > Chi
Intercept	0.1433 (0.1696)	0.3980	0.0715 (0.1324)	0.5884	0.3738 (0.1410)	0.0080
Age	−0.0188 (0.0086)	0.0270	−0.0076 (0.0067)	0.2598	0.0201 (0.0072)	0.0050
Age^2	0.0003 (0.0001)	0.0009	0.0001 (0.0001)	0.2742	−0.0003 (0.0001)	0.0002
Female	0.0457 (0.0148)	0.0020	0.0045 (0.0118)	0.7028	−0.0388 (0.0123)	0.0016
Tenure	0.0203 (0.0039)	0.0001	−0.0356 (0.0031)	0.0001	0.0060 (0.0033)	0.0656
Tenure^2	−0.0004 (0.0001)	0.0001	0.0007 (0.0001)	0.0001	−0.0001 (0.0001)	0.0777
Salary	0.0020 (0.0003)	0.0001	0.0031 (0.0003)	0.0001	−0.0058 (0.0003)	0.0001
Race	0.0088 (0.0177)	0.6208	−0.0285 (0.0141)	0.0438	0.0165 (0.0147)	0.2604
401(k) Wealth	−0.0022 (0.0002)	0.0001	0.0014 (0.0001)	0.0001	0.0009 (0.0001)	0.0001
401(k) Wealth^2	2.5656E−6 (4.41E−7)	0.0001	−1.569E−6 (3.36E−7)	0.0001	−1.902E−6 (4.28E−7)	0.0001

Source: Authors' calculations.

percent allocation to diversified equities; and percent allocation to employer stock. For each asset category, the allocation is measured in two ways. Table 4 reports the empirical results for the likelihood of allocation for the account balance, which is measured as the dollar value of assets in the category divided by the total account balance. The estimated model for allocation of current contributions, measured as the dollar investment in the category for 1993 divided by the total contributions for 1993, is reported in Table 5. Although it might seem that these would be highly correlated, if pension participants tend to modify allocations for new contributions without modifying allocations in account balances, then both specifications have informational value. The account balance allocation is obviously a better indication of overall riskiness of the portfolio, but the current contribution allocation is more likely to capture changes that are made in response to changing life circumstances, such as job tenure, age, and accumulated wealth.

Explanatory Variables

The data set includes valuable demographic information on plan participants that allows us to control for factors that are hypothesized to influence risk preference and thus the likelihood of certain investment choices. Gender and race (defined as Caucasian or non-Caucasian) are binary variables, whereas the age, length of employment (tenure), salary, and total defined contribution savings (401(k) wealth) are continuous. To control for expected non-linearities in age, tenure, and wealth, squared terms were also used as controls. The results for the account balance allocations and the current contributions do not differ substantially in that the same variables are found to influence both decisions. Therefore, the following discussion applies to the results in both Tables 4 and 5.

Gender Effects

Consistent with existing theoretical and empirical literature, we find that the women in this sample are more likely to invest in the fixed-income alternative than are their male counterparts. Although fixed-income investment is less risky than stock investment, we do not necessarily view this result as conclusive evidence of gender differences in risk aversion. Missing information on marital status and other household wealth and income make it impossible to draw such a general conclusion. Although gender does not have a strong influence on diversified equity allocation, the employer stock results show that women are less likely than men to invest in this asset class.

Age and Job Tenure. Money managers often recommend a life-cycle approach to investment allocation. Although specific allocations may differ, this type of strategy usually results in lower-risk portfolios in the early
years of work (when individuals have a greater need for liquidity), increasing allocation to equities during mid-work years, and reduced riskiness of the portfolio as retirement approaches. The coefficients on age
and age-squared for the fixed-income allocation tend to support the
non-linearity of the allocation decision over time. Age has a significant
negative effect on the fixed-income allocation, but the positive sign on
the squared term implies that the function has a minimum and that,
at higher ages, individuals begin increasing their allocation to fixed-
income securities. The age effect on allocations to employer securities is
also non-linear, but shows the reverse pattern: allocations increase with
age to a maximum, after which they decrease, a pattern that is consistent
with a reduction in risk as retirement approaches.

After controlling for age, the impact of job tenure on the allocation
decision was found to be one of considerable risk aversion for the first
few years of employment with the sponsor, followed by a more aggressive
asset allocation thereafter. Regression results (not included) with a series
of dummy variables for age and tenure provided significant differences
at all ages for the likelihood of investing in fixed-income assets between
short- and long-tenure employees.[13] In Tables 4 and 5, tenure has a significant positive effect on the fixed-income allocation, but the negative
sign on the squared term implies that the function has a maximum and
that, at longer tenures, individuals begin decreasing their allocation to
fixed-income securities. The tenure effect on allocations to equities is
also non-linear, but shows the reverse pattern: allocations decrease with
tenure to a minimum, after which they increase.

Wealth and Income

The participants' pension account balance is used as a proxy for the
missing household wealth variable and is shown to exhibit non-linearities
indicative of a concave (risk-averse) utility function. The allocation to
equities increases with wealth but at a decreasing rate, supporting the
hypothesis of decreasing relative risk aversion. This variable has a similar
impact on the employer stock allocation, showing that individuals are
treating this as they would other risky investments.

Although salary appears positively to influence allocations to both
fixed-income and equity securities, this effect is undoubtedly influenced
by the significant negative relationship between salary and employer
stock. This would be expected if the sponsor's stock options are positively
correlated with employee salary.

Conclusions and Policy Implications

The trend toward giving individuals more control over investment of their defined contribution accounts has caused concern among pension economists who fear that overly conservative investment by risk-averse individuals will translate into lower retirement income. If certain groups, particularly those that already have lower income and wealth, exhibit different risk preferences, income and wealth differentials in retirement will be even greater. Existing theoretical work suggests that higher levels of risk aversion are associated with lower wealth, but empirical studies related to pension investing have been hampered by inadequacy of available data.

In this study, we used a rich database of employee pension and demographic characteristics to examine the hypothesis that individual characteristics are important determinants of pension allocation decisions. The general results indicate that investment allocations for this sample are consistent with an assumption of decreasing relative risk aversion. However, allocations to stock and fixed-income alternatives show a life-cycle pattern that conforms to expectations. As expected, those with shorter time horizons for investment and those with alternative motivations for saving are more inclined to invest in fixed-income securities, an empirical finding that is largely consistent with our hypotheses. Although more than one-third of all of the plan assets are invested in low-risk, low-return assets, the fact that this strategy is being used primarily by younger employees and those approaching retirement does not imply, as some have suggested, that individuals are generally too risk averse in their investing behavior.

Our results also provide evidence that gender has a significant effect on allocation decisions. Specifically, the women in this sample are significantly more likely to invest in fixed-income securities and are less likely to invest in employer stock. However, since we are missing important information on household wealth and marital status, this result does not necessarily imply that elderly women will be worse off in retirement. Given the potentially serious consequences of inadequate retirement wealth for women, this is an issue that deserves further examination.

Notes

1. For a recent discussion of the issues related to retirement and longevity, see Munnell (1991).

2. It is not currently expected that longer lives will imply retirement at older ages. In fact, the trend is to earlier retirement. In the 1980s, two-thirds of all men over the age of 60 were retired from the labor force. See Ransom, Sutch, and

Williamson (1991). Fries (1991), however, shows that although life expectancies have lengthened over the last decades, the average age of disability has not changed substantially.

3. In 1990, for those retired households with income at or more than three times the government-determined poverty level (US $18,804 for a single person age 65 or over), Social Security benefits represented only 25 percent of retirement income. For higher income retirees, these benefits will be an even less important sources of income; see Yakoboski and Silverman (1994).

4. These figures are based on compilation by the Employee Benefits Research Institute of United States Department of Labor statistics and reported in Yakoboski and Silverman (1994).

5. Silverman (1993) reports that although the number of primary defined benefit plans declined over the period 1985–1989, two-thirds of the decline was in plans with fewer than nine participants, and the number of large defined benefit plans has remained stable. At the same time, there has been a large increase in the number of defined contribution plans across all plan sizes, indicating that the increases were not simply the result of shifts from one type to the other.

6. According to a Hewitt (1993) survey, 4.5 choices are offered on average, with equity options being offered by 89 percent of the plans. Other popular options are money market accounts, GICs, and employer stock.

7. See Ibbotson Associates, Chicago as cited in Blair and Sellers (1994). With annual compounding, an annuity of one dollar for 30 years at 10.5 percent (the thirty-year holding period return for stocks over that period) has a future value of US $180.88. The comparable bond investment with annual interest of 7.4 percent has a future value of US $101.54. Equivalently stated, the stock investor could have reduced their annual contribution to US $0.56 and achieved the same portfolio value as the one dollar annual contribution to the bond fund.

8. Mossin (1968) suggested that investors may exhibit partial myopia, having utility functions characterized as constant relative risk aversion (CRRA) or constant absolute risk aversion (CARA). With CRRA, they will choose portfolios each period as if that period were their last. With a risk free asset choice, the utility function will be CARA. Musumeci and Musumeci (1996) perform dynamic programming simulations under different utility assumptions and find that simulated outcomes with partial myopia utility is consistent with observed patterns of investing (i.e., greater proportions in the low-risk asset choices).

9. For a discussion of these generally invalid heuristics and biases, see Kahneman, Slovic, and Tversky (1987). As an example in the investment context, individuals may estimate the probability of a stock market crash by use of the heuristic called "availability" which essentially states that if you can remember a recent occurrence of an event, you will judge it more likely to occur in the future. A similar rule of thumb in judgments of unknown probability is that a short sequence of events is indicative of a pattern, so that a recent period of rising stock price will imply that, in the next period, the stock price will also rise.

10. The Fidelity data included over 1500 plans and 2 million participants as of June 30, 1994.

11. In a study of returns on ESOPs, Conte and Jampani (1996) found substantially higher returns in ESOPs than for the control group of diversified defined contribution plans, but this greater return was accompanied by greater risk. On a risk-adjusted basis, the returns to large ESOPs were similar to diversified plans but those of smaller ESOPs were substantially lower.

12. For example, Palsson's (1993) cross-sectional study of Swedish households

finds that wealthy households exhibit greater investment risk tolerance than do poorer households.

13. Alternative thresholds of three-, five-, and seven-year job tenures produced similar results.

References

Arthur D. Little, Inc. *America's Retirement Crisis: The Search for Solutions*. Final Report to Oppenheimer Management Corporation. June 24, 1993.

Bernheim, B. Douglas. *Is the Baby Boom Generation Preparing Adequately for Retirement?* New York: Merrill Lynch & Co., 1993.

Blair, Dennis T. and Andrea T. Sellers. *Retirement Planning More Than Investment Education*. New York: The Alexander Consulting Group, New York, 1994.

Bodie, Zvi. "Pensions as Retirement Income Insurance." *Journal of Economic Literature* 28, 1 (1990): 28–49.

———. "On the Risks of Stocks in the Long Run." *Financial Analysts Journal* 51, 3 (May/June 1995): 18–22.

Conte, Michael, and Rama Jampani. "Financial Returns of ESOPs and Similar Plans." *Pensions, Savings, and Capital Markets*. U.S. Department of Labor. Washington, DC: USGPO, 1996.

Fries, James F. "The Workspan and the Compression of Morbidity." In Alicia H. Munnell, ed., *Retirement and Public Policy*. Washington, DC: Kendall-Hunt, 1991: 159–71.

Gustman, Alan L. and Olivia S. Mitchell. "Pensions and Labor Market Activity: Behavior and Data Requirements." In Zvi Bodie and Alicia H. Munnell, eds., *Pensions in the Economy: Sources, Uses, and Limitations of Data*. Philadelphia: Pension Research Council and University of Pennsylvania Press, 1992.

Gustman, Alan L. and Thomas Steinmeier. "The Stampede Toward Defined Contribution Plans: Fact or Fiction?" *Industrial Relations* 31, 2 (1992): 361–69.

Hewitt Associates. *401(k) Plan Hot Topics*. Lincolnshire, IL: Hewitt Associates, 1993.

Hinz, Richard P., David D. McCarthy, and John A. Turner. "Are Women Conservative Investors? Gender Differences in Participant-Directed Pension Investments." This volume.

Ippolito, Richard A. "Encouraging Long-term Tenure: Wage Tilt or Pensions?" *Industrial and Labor Relations Review* 44, 3 (1991): 520–35.

———. "A Sorting Theory of Defined Contribution Pensions." Pension Benefit Guaranty Corporation Unpublished working paper, Washington DC, 1994.

Jianakoplos, Nancy and Alexandra Bernasek. "Are Women More Risk Averse?" Paper presented at Western Economics Association annual meeting, Vancouver, June 1994.

Kahneman, Daniel, Paul Slovic, and Amos Tversky. *Judgment Under Uncertainty: Heuristics and Biases*. Cambridge, MA: Harvard University Press, 1987.

Kruse, Douglas L. "Profit Sharing and Productivity: Microeconomic Evidence from the United States." *Economic Journal* 102 (1992): 24–36.

Kusko, Andrea L., James M. Poterba, and David W. Wilcox. Employee Decisions with Respect to 401(k) Plans: Evidence from Individual Level Data. NBER Working Paper No. 4635, 1994.

Lazear, Edward P. "Pensions and Deferred Benefits as Strategic Compensation." *Industrial Relations* 29 (Spring 1990): 263–80.

————. "Incentive Effects of Pensions." In David Wise, ed., *Pensions, Labor and Individual Choice*. Chicago: University of Chicago Press, 1985: 357–75.

Mitchell, Olivia S. "Worker Knowledge of Pension Provisions." *Journal of Labor Economics*. 61, 1 (1988): 21–38.

Mossin, Jean. "Aspects of Rational Insurance Purchasing." *Journal of Political Economy* 79 (1968): 553–68.

Munnell, Alicia H., ed. *Retirement and Public Policy*. National Academy of Social Insurance. Washington, DC: Kendall Hunt, 1991.

Musumeci, Jim and Joe Musumeci. "Optimal Diversification Strategies Given a Distant Planning Horizon." *Pensions, Savings, and Capital Markets*. U.S. Department of Labor. Washington, DC: USGPO, 1996.

Palsson, A. "Household Risk Taking and Wealth: Does Risk Taking Matter?" In Edward N. Wolff, ed., *Studies in the Distribution of Household Wealth*. Research on Economic Inequality 4. Greenwich, CT: JAI Press, 1993: 225–61.

Papke, Leslie E. Participation in and Contributions to 401(k) Pension Plans: Evidence from Plan Data. NBER Working Paper No. 4199, 1992.

Papke, Leslie E., Mitchell Peterson, and James M. Poterba. Did 401(k) Plans Replace Other Employer Provided Pensions? NBER Working Paper No. 4501, 1993.

Pratt, J. "Risk Aversion in the Small and the Large." *Econometrica* 32, 1–2 (1964): 122–36.

Quattlebaum, Owen M. "Loss Aversion: The Key to Determining Individual Risk." *Journal of Financial Planning* 1, 2 (1988): 66–68.

Quinn, Joseph F., Richard V. Burkhauser, and Daniel A. Myers. *Passing the Torch: The Influence of Economic Incentives on Work and Retirement*. W. E. Upjohn Institute. New York: Basic Books, 1990.

Ramaswami, Sridhar N., Rajendra K. Srivastava, and Thomas H. McInish. "An Exploratory Study of Portfolio Objectives and Asset Holdings." *Journal of Economic Behavior and Organization* 19 (1992): 285–306.

Ransom, Roger L., Richard Sutch, and Samuel H. Williamson. "Retirement: Past and Present." In Alicia H. Munnell, ed., *Retirement and Public Policy*. Washington, DC: Kendall-Hunt, 1991: 159–71.

Riley, William B., Jr. and Victor K. Chow. "Asset Allocation and Individual Risk Aversion." *Financial Analysts Journal* (November/December 1992): 32–37.

Samuelson, Paul A. "The Judgment of Economic Science on Rational Portfolio Management: Timing and Long-Horizon Effects." *Journal of Portfolio Management* 16, 1 (Fall 1989): 4–17.

————. "Risk and Uncertainty: A Fallacy of Large Numbers." *Scientia*, ser. 6, 5 (April/May 1963): 1–6.

Schmitt, Ray, ed. *The Future of Pensions in the United States*. Philadelphia: Pension Research Council and University of Pennsylvania Press, 1993.

Siegel, Jeremy J. *Stocks for the Long Run*. Burr Ridge, IL: Irwin, 1994.

Silverman, Celia. "Pension Evolution in a Changing Economy." *EBRI Issue Brief No. 141*. Washington, DC: Employee Benefits Research Institute, September 1993.

TIAA-CREF. "Replacement Ratio Projections in Defined Contribution Retirement Plans: Time, Salary Growth, Investment Return, and Real Income." *Research Dialogues* 41 (September 1994): 1–6.

U.S. Department of Labor. Bureau of Labor Statistics. Work and Family: Turning Thirty. Job Mobility and Labor Market Attachment. Report 862. Washington DC: USGPO, 1995.

Williamson, Gordon K. *Low Risk Investing*. Holbrook MA: Bob Adams, 1994.
Yakoboski, Paul and Annmarie Reilly. "Salary Reduction Plans and Individual Saving for Retirement." *EBRI Issue Brief No. 155*. Washington, DC: Employee Benefits Research Institute, November 1994.
Yakoboski, Paul and Celia Silverman. "Baby Boomers in Retirement: What Are Their Prospects?" *EBRI Issue Brief No. 151*. Washington, DC: Employee Benefits Research Institute, July 1994.

Chapter 5
Investment of Assets in Self-Directed Retirement Plans

Gordon P. Goodfellow and
Sylvester J. Schieber

There is a growing concern among some retirement policy analysts and employer-sponsors of retirement programs that the shift toward participant-directed investment of defined contribution plan assets in recent years is resulting in overly conservative investment of these assets. The real concern is that we are not realizing the economic horsepower from our defined contribution assets that we could realize and that, in the long term, the retirement security of many workers participating in self-directed plans will suffer accordingly. One recent survey suggests that nearly two-thirds of plan sponsors are concerned about the asset allocation decisions that their employees are making with their employer-sponsored retirement plan assets (Institute of Management and Administration 1995).

Recently there have been a number of articles in newspapers, general news magazines, and trade publications raising the consciousness of the general public about the concerns related to participant-directed investment of retirement plan assets. In some of the articles the focus is on the relative capabilities of professional asset managers who are generally involved in the asset placement decisions of defined benefit assets and those of individual plan participants in typical defined contribution plans. In other cases the focus is on the relative risk that large sponsoring organizations can assume in investing retirement assets in comparison to individual investors.[1]

Despite the growing concerns about participant-directed investment of retirement assets, there has been remarkably little research into the actual investment decisions made by the participants in these plans. To date, what limited research has been done mostly has focused on the comparative aggregate distribution of retirement assets in defined benefit and defined contribution plans. The conclusion from this research is quite straightforward—DC plan participants tend to invest more of their assets in fixed-income type assets and less in equities than do the investors of DB plan assets. By itself, this conclusion may be interesting but is not necessarily informative.

The reason that the conclusions drawn from prior research on the differences in the investment in DB and DC assets is not informative is that it generally fails to account for the underlying variation in investment behavior that is behind the conclusion. Much of the prior research also fails to consider the reasons for the variations between the investment styles of different types of plans and their legitimacy. In this chapter we attempt to expand on the prior research. First, we investigate the gradual shift from the organized management and investment of retirement assets to the current environment where the investment of these assets is increasingly being directed by the plan participants. Second, we take a brief look at the differences in the aggregate investment of defined benefit and defined contribution assets. Third, we analyze the investment of assets in a number of defined contribution plans across a range of worker characteristics based on actual investment records from a sample of defined contribution plans. In the final section of the chapter, we draw some conclusions based on the earlier sections of the chapter.

Background

Since the passage of the Employee Retirement Income Security Act (ERISA) in 1974, we have seen defined contribution plans assume an increasingly important role in the elements of the retirement security system sponsored by employers. In 1975 there were slightly more than 103,000 private defined benefit plans in operation in the United States. The number of defined benefit plans grew steadily until 1983, when there were just over 175,000 plans in operation. Since then we have seen a fairly steady decline in the number of plans, with just under 102,000 plans in existence in 1991, the last year for which we have published disclosure data. Over this same period the number of defined contribution plans grew steadily from slightly under 208,000 plans to nearly 600,000 plans (USDOL 1995:60).

The pattern of participation in defined benefit plans directly followed the pattern of plan growth between 1975 and the early 1980s as participation grew from 33 million workers in the prior year to about 41 million by 1984. Although there was a decline of nearly 42 percent in the number of private defined benefit plans in operation between the early 1980s and 1990s, participation in the plans only declined by about 2.5 percent from the peak and stood at 39 million workers in 1991. At the end of the 16-year period, participation was 18 percent higher in defined benefit plans than it had been at the beginning. In the case of defined contribution plans, the growth in participation was nearly as steady as the growth in the number of plans. In 1975, there were 11.5 million participants in plans, growing to nearly 35 million by 1985. Beyond 1985, the growth in defined contribution plan participants slowed somewhat. By 1991, participation in defined contribution plans had grown to 38.6 million workers, representing a 335 percent growth over the level in 1975 but only a 10 percent growth over the level in 1985 (USDOL 1995).

Participation in defined contribution plans grew rapidly immediately after the passage of ERISA because the benefit limits under section 415 of ERISA allowed greater tax-qualified retirement contributions in cases where employers were sponsoring both types of plans than in cases where they had only one or the other. This encouraged many employers that had traditionally offered only a defined benefit plan to introduce supplemental defined contribution programs. The growth in participation further accelerated during the early 1980s because of introduction of section 401(k) plans. Under these plans workers could voluntarily defer compensation on a pre-tax basis. Most employers that had sponsored profit-sharing or thrift-savings plans prior to the publication of section 401(k) regulations introduced 401(k) features into their defined contribution plans. Many employers that had not offered such plans in the past provided employees with a section 401(k) plan soon after the release of the regulations.

Through the end of the 1970s and into the early 1980s, the assets in defined contribution plans typically were held in a pooled trust, and each participant in the plan was credited with his or her vested pro rata share of the pool. The vesting periods during this era could range up to 10 years, although they tended to be somewhat shorter than that. Because of the vesting periods, however, significant amounts of the money in the plans at any point in time were not yet the property right of the individuals to whom they had been credited. With the establishment of 401(k) plans, however, workers were now contributing their "own" money to the plans to a much greater extent than they had before, and there was immediate vesting in their balances. The new realities of defined contribution plan structure changed perceptions about whose money was in the plans and how that money should be managed. With the evolution of 401(k) plans during the 1980s, sponsors of defined contribution plans increasingly offered participants the opportunity to direct the investment of their retirement accounts.

ERISA generally provides that a fiduciary of a benefit plan must discharge his or her investment responsibilities prudently, including diversifying plan investments to minimize the risk of large losses. To the extent these duties are breached, the fiduciary is liable to the plan for any losses. ERISA, however, includes an exception to this provision in section 404(c) where it provides that in cases where the participants can direct their own investments, the plan fiduciaries are not liable for any loss or breach that results from the participant's exercise of control. In the late summer of 1987, the Department of Labor released preliminary regulations under section 404(c) beginning to detail the rules under which employers could hand off some of the fiduciary obligations that they held when they controlled their defined contribution assets.

The precipitous decline in stock prices during October 1987 raised a number of fiduciary issues for plan sponsors still managing their defined contribution plan portfolios. For example, many plans at that time calculated the value of distributions on the basis of the last valuation date of assets in the plan prior to a worker's termination. Many valuations were done on a quarterly basis. Plans whose valuation dates coincided with the end of a calendar quarter were in the position of paying individuals who terminated prior to the end of 1987 considerably more than the value of their respective accounts at the date of termination. Paying someone terminating on October 31, 1987 the value of his or her account on the basis of a September 30, 1987 valuation would further drain the value of the remaining portfolio for those workers who remained in the plan. Thus, in addition to the restructuring of retirement plans and the changing perception about ownership of plan assets, there were practical developments that encouraged plan sponsors to allow participants to direct their own investments.

During September 1992 the Department of Labor finalized the section 404(c) regulations, which were somewhat less onerous than the initial proposed regulations had been. In order for a plan to meet the 404(c) requirements a plan must allow each participant to "exercise independent control" over the assets in his or her individual account. This means that the participant must be able to give investment instructions to a plan fiduciary, who must generally comply with such instructions. In addition, the regulations require that sufficient information to make informed investment decisions must be made available to participants in these plans. The regulations allow plans to restrict the frequency with which investment changes may be made, but require that participants be able to give investment instructions with a frequency which is appropriate for the expected market volatility of the investment. The regulations state general rules requiring that the available investment alternatives must be sufficient to give the participant a reasonable opportunity to affect materially both the potential return on assets in his or her account and the degree of risk to which the assets are subject. The regulations require that the participants be able to choose from at least three investment alternatives, each of which is diversified (thus an employer's securities cannot be one of the three), each of which has to have materially different risk and return characteristics, which allow the participant to achieve a diversified portfolio with desired risk and return characteristics, and so minimize overall risk. In return for setting up the 404(c) plan, the sponsor is not liable to participants for any loss or breach of fiduciary responsibility that may result from the participant's exercise of control.

The combination of factors that have evolved over the last 10 to 15 years means that most defined contribution plans today offer participants control over at least some part of their retirement accumulations. As we have made the transition from professionally managed pension portfolios to an increasing dependence on individual investment decisions, the relative level of assets in defined contribution plans has been increasing in comparison to defined benefit plans. In 1980, private defined benefit plans held slightly more than US $400 billion in assets. The balances had grown to US $1.1 trillion by 1991, reflecting an annual compound growth rate of 9.6 percent. By comparison, defined contribution assets grew from US $162 billion in 1980 to US $834 billion in 1991, with an underlying growth rate of 16.1 percent per year (USDOL 1995:70).[2]

Variations in the Investment of Retirement Plan Assets

A simple algebraic equation which captures the operations of both defined benefit and defined contribution plans is

$$\text{Benefits} = \text{Contributions} + \text{Asset Yield}$$

The relative interest of plan sponsors in the specific variables in this equation, however, are or should be vastly different between defined benefit and defined contribution plans. In a defined benefit plan the sponsor is responsible for delivering a set of benefits laid out in the benefit formula that defines the essence of the plan. In this case there is a direct inverse relationship between the yield on assets and the amount of contributions or cost of the plan to the sponsor. In a defined contribution plan the sponsor is responsible for delivering a set of contributions in accordance with the plan documents. In this case there is a direct positive relationship between the yield on assets and the benefits delivered to the participant.

Historically, one of the motivations for setting up defined contribution plans instead of defined benefit plans is that the plan sponsor can be freed of the investment risk faced when making the defined benefit promise. For example, one can argue that if private academic institutions, which now largely depend on defined contribution plans, were to shift to defined benefit plans they would face the prospect of required increases in retirement plan funding during down cycles in the investment markets which would coincide with the deterioration of the value of their endowments, which are generally invested in financial assets and on which they are dependent for operating income. In other words, if private academic institutions that rely heavily on endowment income were to shift to defined benefit plans, they would be hit with their heaviest benefit funding requirements at exactly the times they were least able to meet them. Thus, because of this timing problem, defined contribution plans may best meet the needs of private universities from the perspective of their larger financing considerations and the financial risk they face over the investment cycle.[3]

Employers' movement to 404(c) plans allowing the plan participants to direct the investment of their own accounts is a further effort to pass on the risk of negative market performance to the plan participants. The 404(c) regulations are quite specific: if the plan sponsor offers a diversified set of investment options, the participants are given the opportunity to move money among investment options with some frequency and are provided information on the investment options. The participants, not the plan sponsors, are at risk from negative investment outcomes. Presumably, sponsors of retirement programs have been aware that they are passing risk to the participants in their retirement programs as they have moved away from defined benefit plans and into 404(c) defined contribution plans.

Once risk is passed from the sponsor of a retirement program to the participants in the program, it should not be surprising that the risk that is assumed in the investment of the plan assets changes. One of the reasons that individuals have different investment preferences than plan sponsors relates to their respective time horizons. Especially for older workers, the time horizon over which they are considering the investment of their retirement assets may be extremely short. For a plan sponsor which is an ongoing entity, on the other hand, the time horizon might be almost infinite. The implications of the time horizon can be seen by considering the case of a worker who has US $100,000 to invest with the choice of investing it in a riskless asset with an annual rate of return of 3 percent or in a S&P 500 index fund with an expected return of 10 percent with a 15 percent standard deviation (Kritzman 1994). Table 1 shows the range of possible outcomes that the investor faces.

After one year the value of the fixed-income asset is US $103,000. The risky asset's value, on the other hand, will be between US $81,980 and US $147,596 95 percent of the time. There certainly is some upside po-

TABLE 1 Terminal Wealth from a Risky Versus Riskless Investment

	S&P 500 95% Confidence Interval		Fixed-Income Asset
	Lower Boundary	*Upper Boundary*	*Terminal Wealth*
1 Year	$ 81,980	$ 147,596	$103,000
5 Years	83,456	310,792	115,927
10 Years	102,367	657,196	134,392
15 Years	133,776	1,304,376	155,797
20 years	180,651	2,565,345	180,611

Source: Kritman (1994:15).

tential from investing in the risky asset, but there is also considerable downside risk. By comparison, after 20 years, the low-risk asset's value accumulates to US $180,611 while the 95 percent confidence interval range of values for the risky asset is from US $180,651 to US $2,565,345. This example seems to suggest that, over a longer time horizon, an investor's aversion to risk should be ameliorated.

Nevertheless Kritzman (1994) argues that some investors who prefer a low-risk asset to a risky one over a three-month time horizon would also prefer a riskless asset over a ten- or twenty-year horizon if three conditions are met: first, the investor's risk aversion is invariant to changes in wealth; second, the investor believes that risky returns are random; and third, the investor's future wealth depends only on investment income. The underlying logic in Kritzman's analysis is that risk aversion implies the standard economic model of declining marginal utility related to increases in wealth. Specifically, an investor is assumed to realize a greater increase in satisfaction as wealth increases from US $100,000 to US $150,000 than from a similar increase from US $150,000 to US $200,000. The problem with risky investments for some investors is that the slope of their utility curves is such that the potential disutility from losing even a small amount of value in their assets outweighs the added potential utility from substantially larger gains. While Table 1 suggests that a longer time horizon would make the more risky investment option the desirable one for our hypothetical investor, the table does not show the 99 percent confidence interval values of the risky investment outcomes. For some investors, the potential disutility of a loss in wealth is so large that, even considering its extremely small probability of occurring, it still is not worth the relatively smaller increases in satisfaction from large potential gains at a much higher probability of occurrence.

One of the conditions specified in the Kritzman analysis is that the investor must believe that risky returns are random. A recent Oppenheimer-*Money Magazine* poll indicated that nearly one-half of respondents believe that people who invest in the stock market get wiped out at least once during their investment careers (Oppenheimer Funds 1994). The conclusion that stock investors get wiped out periodically suggests that people believe the returns in the market are random, otherwise they would think investors would be able to anticipate downturns and get out of the market before being wiped out. On the other hand, most managers of pension assets believe that investing in a diversified equity portfolio pays a risk "premium" to the investor. Indeed, some prognosticators believe that all pension assets managed on a pooled basis might be fully invested in equities if it were not for liquidity needs to manage plan operations over the short term, and because of funding considerations over variations in the investment cycle—that is, the plan sponsor wants to avoid being thrown into an underfunding situation by a decline in equity values in the portfolio during the down portion of the investment cycle (Markland 1994).

Information on exactly where different types of investors put their retirement money varies somewhat from study to study. An Employee Benefit Research Institute analysis of 1989 Form 5500 filings suggested that defined benefit plans compared to 401(k) plans held nearly two-thirds more of their investment portfolio in stocks (Wyatt Company 1994). Greenwich Associates has estimated that participants in 401(k) plans invest only 39 percent of their assets in equities and the remainder in fixed-income investment options. They estimate that defined benefit plans, on the other hand, have just exactly the opposite mix of equities and fixed-income assets (Smith 1993).

Where Plan Participants Put Their Retirement Money

Today there is a growing sense that we need to change the investment allocation of the assets that are accumulating in defined contribution plans or, more specifically, 401(k) plans. The news media frequently runs stories about the need to invest retirement assets more wisely. There is a growing public policy awareness that there is a potential problem here, and we are even beginning to see calls for employers to take back the responsibility of investing and managing the assets in 401(k) plans (Rohrer 1994). In light of this, some employers have begun undertaking major education programs to change the investment behavior of plan participants. Yet remarkably little is known about how individual investors allocate their retirement resources and what we must do if we want to encourage alternative behavior.

In order to help explain the investment behavior of participants in self-directed retirement plans, we have pooled administrative records on slightly more than 36,000 participants drawn from 24 defined contribution plans holding nearly US $1.4 billion in total assets. The total number of participants in these plans ranged from around 150 to 6,000. We had some larger plan data that we chose not to include here because there were strong financial incentives encouraging investment in company stock which resulted in disproportionately heavy investment in that asset option. Table 2 shows a distribution of the total assets in the plans that are included in this analysis. We did not include approximately US $50 million in rollover money in these plans because such accounts were reported in only about 5 percent of the cases and because some plans may have more restrictive investment options for such money compared to money accumulated under their own programs.

Table 2 shows both the distribution of participants investing in various asset types and the total assets invested in each asset class. The fixed-income funds include bond, GIC, and money market funds and would generally be the classes of assets which have raised the concerns about where self-directed retirement money is being invested. The balanced fund class of investments are funds that hold a mixed portfolio of stocks and bonds. Company stock is the stock of the sponsor of the plan in which the individual participates. The domestic equity funds invest in a portfolio of stocks of companies issuing such stocks in the United States. The international equity funds invest in stocks of companies outside the United States.

The distribution of assets in the table suggests that between 35 and 40 percent of the total assets being analyzed here are in equity funds, which is comparable to other estimates of the aggregate allocation of self-directed retirement assets. Interestingly, consistently a larger share of the participants invest in each of the equity funds than the share of assets that are allocated to each of them. One of the things that is clear from Table 2 is that substantial numbers of investors are investing at least some of their assets in equity funds.

Self-Directed Investment of Retirement Assets and Age of Participants

The earlier discussion suggested that, for at least some participants in plans, the time horizon over which they are investing might be important in determining their investment allocations. While a longer time horizon might be insufficient to encourage some investors with a strong aversion to risk to move any of their assets into equities, for some, the prospect of moderate risk of loss over a longer time frame and the possibility of

TABLE 2 Assets Held in Defined Contribution Accounts by Type of Investment

Type of Asset	Participants with This Asset Type	Percent with This Asset Type	Total Assets (US $)	Percent of Total Assets	Average Asset Balance of Asset Holders (US $)
Fixed-Income Funds	24,825	68.9%	$ 799,457,499	58.1%	$32,204
Balanced Funds	7,647	21.2	107,432,387	7.8	14,049
Company Stock Funds	6,827	19.0	83,307,341	6.1	12,203
Domestic Equity Funds	24,801	68.9	348,221,176	25.3	14,041
International Equity Funds	3,730	10.4	38,464,729	2.8	10,312
Total	36,244		$1,376,883,132	100.0%	$38,234

Source: Authors' calculations.

TABLE 3 Percent of DC Participants Invested in Specific Types of Investment by Participant Age

Type of Investment	Age of Plan Participant					
	Under 21	21 to 30	31 to 40	41 to 50	51 to 60	61+
Fixed-Income Funds	65.1%	63.8%	67.3%	69.9%	73.8%	81.8%
Balanced Funds	27.4	21.4	22.8	20.8	19.9	21.2
Company Stock Funds	13.2	17.9	19.4	18.6	20.4	19.0
Domestic Equity Funds	59.4	70.8	73.0	69.5	61.2	68.9
International Equity Funds	0.0	8.6	11.2	11.2	9.8	10.4

Source: Authors' calculations.

substantial gain from a more aggressive investment posture suggest that young people would likely put more of their money into riskier assets than older workers.

Table 3 shows the percentage of workers by their ages who invest in each of the money classes being considered. The patterns there are consistent with what is expected. At each succeeding age in the table, increasing percentages of plan participants put money into the fixed-income option from youngest to oldest participants. We also see lower utilization of the various equity funds at older ages.

The allocation of assets in the plans by the age of participants is even more pronounced than the distribution of individual investors in each of the asset classes. Table 4 shows the relative allocation of assets into each of the fund options by the age of the participants. At the younger ages, under 40, the allocation of assets is probably fairly close to the 60 percent equity, 40 percent fixed-income combination that some analysts think is relevant for retirement assets. At the older ages, though, there is a marked shift away from the riskier asset options which many retirement planners would advocate. Within the context of the age distribution shown here, the investment of assets does not appear as unsophisticated as the aggregate data suggest.

While Table 4 suggests that the investment behavior of individuals is more reasonable than we often conclude by looking at the aggregate results, it also holds at least part of the key for explaining why the aggregate distribution of self-directed investment behavior looks so conservative. Table 5 holds the remaining part of the explanation. Table 5 shows the average balances of the participants holding various kinds of assets by the age of the participants. It is not too surprising that the balances at the older ages are significantly higher than they are at younger ages. The higher balances among the older participants in combination with their natural inclinations to invest more conservatively result in the overall conservative nature of the investment of self-directed accounts.

The data presented thus far suggest that there is considerable diversification in the selection of assets from the options available to plan participants. Another way to look more specifically at the diversification in the portfolios is to consider the concentration of investments in individual investment options. Table 6 shows the investment concentration for three elements of the investment portfolios offered to the plan participants: fixed-income, domestic equity, and international equity funds. The second column in the table shows the number of potential investors in each of the funds by the participant's age. The number of potential investors can vary from fund type to fund type because not every fund type is offered by each plan sponsor, although all offer fixed-income and domestic equity funds. The next column in the table shows the percent

TABLE 4 Percent of DC Assets Invested in Specific Types of Investment by Participant Age

Type of Investment	Age of Plan Participant					
	Under 21	21 to 30	31 to 40	41 to 50	51 to 60	61+
Fixed-Income Funds	52.6%	41.4%	43.4%	49.4%	61.5%	85.2%
Balanced Funds	8.4	5.7	8.2	11.0	8.3	1.3
Company Stock Funds	4.2	11.0	8.9	6.1	5.8	2.7
Domestic Equity Funds	34.8	39.1	36.4	29.7	22.0	9.5
International Equity Funds	—	2.8	3.1	3.8	2.5	1.2

Source: Authors' calculations.
Note: Some columns may not sum to 100 percent due to rounding error.

TABLE 5 Average DC Investment Balance (US $) in Specific Types of Investment for Those Holding the Investment by Participant Age

Type of Investment	Age of Plan Participant					
	Under 21	21 to 30	31 to 40	41 to 50	51 to 60	61+
Fixed-Income Funds	$400	$3,786	$12,974	$29,265	$65,131	$187,542
Balanced Funds	152	1,553	7,217	21,938	32,443	17,761
Company Stock Funds	156	3,584	9,238	13,517	22,068	29,246
Domestic Equity Funds	290	3,223	10,064	17,684	28,043	35,995
International Equity Funds	—	1,881	5,608	13,968	20,123	31,627
Total	$494	$5,836	$20,150	$41,387	$78,133	$179,955

Source: Authors' calculations.

TABLE 6 Concentration of DC Assets in Selected Investment Options by Participant Age

			Percent of Potential Investors with x Percent of Total Assets in This Investment					
Age of Workers	No. Potential Investors	Zero	0.01 to 20.0	20.1 to 40.0	40.1 to 60.0	60.1 to 80.0	80.1 to 100.0
Fixed-Income Funds							
Under 21	106	34.9%	6.6%	8.5%	10.4%	5.7%	34.0%
21 to 30	6,267	36.7	9.4	12.5	12.3	6.3	22.9
31 to 40	12,836	33.7	10.4	13.1	12.2	7.0	23.6
41 to 50	10,001	30.8	9.2	13.0	12.2	7.1	27.8
51 to 60	5,464	26.7	7.4	11.0	12.2	7.5	35.2
61 or over	1,338	18.7	5.7	8.1	9.6	9.4	48.5
Domestic Equity Funds							
Under 21	106	40.6%	6.6%	10.4%	15.1%	7.5%	19.8%
21 to 30	6,267	29.2	7.3	10.9	15.9	12.2	24.5
31 to 40	12,836	27.1	9.7	12.7	16.7	12.3	21.6
41 to 50	10,001	30.6	9.5	12.2	16.9	11.2	19.5
51 to 60	5,464	38.9	11.3	12.0	13.7	8.7	15.5
61 or over	1,338	52.3	9.6	9.0	10.2	5.2	13.6
International Equity Funds							
Under 21	14	100.0%	0.0%	0.0%	0.0%	0.0%	0.0%
21 to 30	2,277	76.3	11.3	7.7	2.5	0.9	1.3
31 to 40	5,742	74.9	11.9	8.1	3.0	1.0	1.1
41 to 50	4,533	75.3	12.0	7.4	3.2	0.8	1.3
51 to 60	2,487	75.8	11.5	5.7	2.3	0.6	1.3
61 or over	807	88.5	5.9	2.9	1.6	0.2	0.9

Source: Authors' calculations.

of the potential investors who have zero percent of their portfolio invested in the particular fund type. The right hand column of the table shows the percent of potential investors who have more than 80 percent of their total plan assets in the designated fund type. The table suggests that, even at the youngest ages, there are substantial numbers of participants who are investing their assets quite conservatively. The fixed-income funds seem to be particularly attractive to significant numbers of investors for most or all of their retirement assets. This would not be an investment strategy that most financial counselors would recommend for many of the plan participants who are investing their assets in this fashion.

Table 7 shows the concentration of investment in the company stock and balanced fund investment classes. Company stock is relatively popular with many of the participants who have an option to purchase it. The problem with buying company stock for the retirement portfolio is that it accentuates the risk that the worker already faces from the possibility of reduced lifetime income if the employer sponsoring the plan should have economic problems. It was this concern that led policymakers to limit the amount of a plan sponsor's stock that can be held in the asset portfolio of a defined benefit plan. While many plan participants undoubtedly feel secure and will do well in investing in a company where they work and in which they trust, this again is not an investment option in which most financial counselors would advise workers to invest significant amounts of their retirement assets.

The balanced fund option might be thought of as a "lazy" investor's way naturally to diversify the retirement portfolio between equities and bonds without having to do any of the asset allocation personally. Despite being an easy way to diversify risk, these investment funds do not attract the high concentration of investment that fixed-income and the company stock funds attract. There certainly seem to be some opportunities here for improving the allocation of retirement funds directed by plan participants.

Self-Directed Investment of Retirement Assets and Wage Level of Participants

Another way to consider the variations in the self-directed investment of defined contribution assets is to look at how investment behavior varies across different wage levels of workers. Table 8 shows the percent of participants investing in various classes of assets in comparison to their annual wage levels. Here again, there are some very clear differences in the investment behavior of workers at different wage levels. Other than at the very lowest wage level, there is a clear declining pattern of investment

TABLE 7 Concentration of DC Assets in Company Stock and Balanced Funds by Age of Plan Participants

Age of Workers	No. Potential Investors	Percent of Potential Investors with x Percent of Total Assets in This Investment						
		Zero	0.01 to 20.0	20.1 to 40.0	40.1 to 60.0	60.1 to 80.0	80.1 to 100.0
Company Stock							
Under 21	16	12.5%	6.3%	25.0%	18.8%	6.3%	31.3%
21 to 30	1,799	37.8	13.5	18.9	12.5	4.7	12.6
31 to 40	3,928	36.5	16.9	19.7	11.4	6.1	9.4
41 to 50	3,164	41.2	15.9	19.7	9.9	5.0	8.2
51 to 60	2,198	49.4	12.9	15.2	8.1	5.6	8.8
61 or over	447	50.3	14.5	18.1	7.4	4.7	4.9
Balanced Fund							
Under 21	83	65.1%	13.3%	8.4%	9.6%	2.4%	1.2%
21 to 30	4,284	68.7	11.1	10.2	6.1	1.6	2.4
31 to 40	9,102	68.0	11.3	11.2	6.6	1.2	1.7
41 to 50	6,813	69.5	10.7	10.7	6.3	1.1	1.7
51 to 60	4,120	73.6	9.8	9.1	5.3	0.9	1.2
61 or over	1,046	82.9	6.5	5.7	3.2	0.7	1.1

Source: Authors' calculations.

Table 8 Percent of DC Participants Invested in Specific Types of Investment by Participant Earnings (US $)

Type of Investment		Participant Annual Earnings						
	Less than $15,000	$15,000 to $24,999	$25,000 to $34,999	$35,000 to $44,999	$45,000 to $59,999	$60,000 to $74,999	$75,000 to $99,999	$100,000 or More
Fixed-Income Funds	63.5%	74.7%	72.4%	67.3%	61.5%	58.3%	56.0%	63.9%
Balanced Funds	31.8	19.6	19.7	22.4	21.3	19.8	17.9	18.1
Company Stock Funds	16.0	17.3	21.5	24.0	27.6	28.0	22.4	5.9
Domestic Equity Funds	68.5	59.0	65.7	74.5	81.5	84.2	86.7	86.4
International Equity	3.0	6.8	7.9	11.0	15.5	19.8	25.7	26.3

Source: Authors' calculations.

Table 9 Percent of DC Assets Invested in Specific Types of Investment by Participant Earnings (US $)

Type of Investment		Participant Annual Earnings						
	Less than $15,000	$15,000 to $24,999	$25,000 to $34,999	$35,000 to $44,999	$45,000 to $59,999	$60,000 to $74,999	$75,000 to $99,999	$100,000 or More
Fixed-Income Funds	62.1%	63.0%	61.6%	66.7%	53.2%	32.2%	26.0%	27.2%
Balanced Funds	5.9	7.2	9.0	6.5	12.0	11.1	14.7	8.4
Company Stock Funds	6.5	7.6	8.2	6.6	7.6	10.6	7.9	2.3
Domestic Equity Funds	24.6	21.5	19.5	18.6	25.3	42.2	45.4	52.0
International Equity	0.6	0.8	1.7	1.6	2.0	3.9	6.1	10.2

Source: Authors' calculations.
Note: Some columns may not sum to 100 percent due to rounding error.

in fixed-income funds. At the higher wage levels there is generally a greater prevalence of investment in the equity funds. The other fund category is particularly popular at the upper wage levels.

Table 9 shows the distribution of assets in the various asset classes by the wage levels of the participants. While we noted above that the percent of participants investing in fixed-income funds declined at higher wage levels, we see an ever greater drop-off in the concentration of assets in these funds among higher-wage workers, especially at wage levels above US $60,000 per year. Higher-wage workers appear to be pursuing higher rates of return and invest a greater percentage of their assets in equity funds than their lower-wage counterparts.

In the earlier discussion about aversion to risk, three conditions were posited as necessary for the short-term risk aversion carrying over into the longer term. One of these was that an investor's risk aversion was invariant to changes in wealth. Another was that future wealth depends only on investment results. The more aggressive investment pattern of the higher-wage workers suggests that these conditions may not apply evenly across the wage spectrum. Part of the reason might be because of the higher relative utility of accumulated wealth on the part of lower-wage workers than for those with higher wages.

Table 10 shows the average balances in each of the investment classes for the individuals with assets in the class. Interestingly, in each of the wage categories up to US $60,000 per year or more, the average fixed-income fund balance for the investors with some fixed-income holdings significantly exceeds the average balances in the other investment categories. In other words, at lower wage levels those with the most money tend to invest in fixed-income options. Another interesting aspect of Table 10 is that in the pay ranges up to US $35,000 per year, the participants in the plans appear to have accumulated an average balance that is roughly equivalent to a year's pay. Between US $35,000 and US $60,000 per year, they appear to have accumulated somewhat more than a year's pay on average. Above US $60,000 per year the average accumulation is significantly less than one year's pay.

Earlier we looked at the concentration of investment in certain of the investment funds on the basis of the age of the participants. Table 11 shows the concentration of investment by the wage level of the participants in the plans for fixed-income funds, company stock, and the balanced fund investment options. In each case there tends to be a much greater concentration of investment in the specific funds at lower-wage levels than at higher ones. For example, within the wage band of US $15,000 to US $24,999, 37.5 percent of the participants eligible to invest in fixed-income funds put more than 80 percent of their total

TABLE 10 Average DC Assets Investment Balance in Specific Types of Investment Classes for Those Holding the Investment by Participant Earnings (US $)

Type of Investment	Participant Annual Earnings							
	Less than $15,000	$15,000 to $24,999	$25,000 to $34,999	$35,000 to $44,999	$45,000 to $59,999	$60,000 to $74,999	$75,000 to $99,999	$100,000 or More
Fixed-Income Funds	$13,827	$13,173	$24,002	$52,605	$54,681	$28,608	$32,314	$31,943
Balanced Funds	2,615	5,753	12,901	15,382	35,517	28,890	57,133	35,023
Company Stock Funds	5,723	6,864	10,767	14,528	17,346	19,624	24,681	28,887
Domestic Equity Funds	5,082	5,685	8,394	13,281	19,592	25,952	36,472	45,158
International Equity	4,402	1,741	5,883	7,957	8,357	10,138	16,483	29,103
Total	14,147	15,624	28,220	53,105	63,252	51,738	69,673	75,104

Source: Authors' calculations.

TABLE 11 Concentration of DC Individual Asset Holdings in Selected Investment Funds by Participant Earnings (US $)

Participant Annual Earnings	No. Potential Investors	Percent of Potential Investors with x Percent of Total Assets in This Investment					
		Zero	0.01 to 20.0	20.1 to 40.0	40.1 to 60.0	60.1 to 80.0	80.1 to 100.0
Fixed-Income Funds							
Under $15,000	6,720	36.6%	7.0%	13.2%	14.2%	5.9%	23.2%
$15,000 to 24,999	8,827	25.6	7.4	11.2	11.2	7.1	37.5
$25,000 to 34,999	6,700	28.0	9.7	12.7	11.2	7.3	31.1
$35,000 to 44,999	3,820	33.2	10.4	13.2	13.4	7.9	21.9
$45,000 to 59,999	2,811	39.5	11.7	12.0	11.1	8.1	17.6
$60,000 to 74,999	1,433	43.6	13.1	14.2	9.4	6.4	13.3
$75,000 to 99,999	1,163	47.0	12.2	13.0	10.6	5.8	11.4
$100,000 or more	2,152	39.7	14.6	13.8	11.6	6.9	13.4
Company Stock							
Under $15,000	2,008	46.5%	9.0%	17.6%	10.4%	3.2%	13.3%
$15,000 to 24,999	2,777	45.0	13.2	17.0	9.7	5.4	9.7
$25,000 to 34,999	2,231	35.4	16.0	19.5	12.1	6.9	10.1
$35,000 to 44,999	1,436	36.3	16.9	18.5	11.7	6.8	10.0
$45,000 to 59,999	1,203	35.6	21.6	19.5	10.1	6.2	7.0
$60,000 to 74,999	660	39.2	22.9	18.6	9.8	4.7	4.7
$75,000 to 99,999	422	38.4	21.6	24.9	7.6	4.5	3.1
$100,000 or more	225	44.0	16.9	28.4	5.3	2.7	2.7
Balanced Fund							
Under $15,000	4,901	56.4%	11.5%	16.7%	10.5%	2.0%	2.9%
$15,000 to 24,999	6,208	72.2	10.4	8.8	5.7	1.0	1.7
$25,000 to 34,999	4,592	71.2	10.8	9.7	5.2	1.5	1.6
$35,000 to 44,999	2,795	69.5	11.7	10.2	6.2	0.9	1.6
$45,000 to 59,999	2,116	71.7	12.3	8.5	5.3	0.8	1.4
$60,000 to 74,999	1,152	75.3	10.8	7.5	4.3	1.1	1.0
$75,000 to 99,999	954	78.4	8.8	7.7	3.9	0.6	0.6
$100,000 or more	225	79.3	9.4	8.4	2.0	0.2	0.6

Source: Authors' calculations.

retirement plan assets in those types of funds. By comparison, only about 10 to 15 percent of workers at higher wage levels do so.

Participants are much less likely to bet most or all of their retirement assets on the stock of the companies for which they work than they are to put it mostly in fixed-income options. Where company stock is available as an investment option, workers at the lowest wage levels are three to five times as likely to have 80 percent or more of their retirement plan savings in company stock than at the highest wage levels. It is somewhat ironic that the workers who generally have the least potential to control the operations of the employers for which they work are the most willing to fully commit their long-term retirement security to the successful performance of those organizations.

The concentration of assets in the balanced fund class of investments is interesting because of the relative lack of use of the accounts across the wage spectrum. At the bottom of the wage distribution, only about 45 percent of plan participants with a balanced fund option put any money into the funds. In the middle of the wage distribution, generally less than 30 percent use these fund options, and at the top of the wage distribution it falls to only about 20 percent. For those using these options, most are putting less than half their retirement assets in them. Never as many as 5 percent of those who have an option to use a balanced fund put more than 60 percent of their savings into these accounts. At the highest wage levels, not even 1 percent of the participants put more than 60 percent of their assets into them. Much of the recent commotion about repackaging balanced funds under the rubric of "life stages" funds may result in their greater utilization, but the data here suggest that they do not attract many retirement savers faced with a number of alternative investment options.

Self-Directed Investment of Retirement Assets and Plan Sponsor

Thus far we have focused on variations in investment patterns of participants in retirement savings plans on the basis of the age and wage levels of the participants. A completely different way to look at variations in participants' investment patterns is to consider how these patterns vary across the plans included in the analysis. For this segment of the analysis we are only looking at the concentration of assets invested in fixed-income funds. While this may provide a somewhat incomplete picture, it is instructive because it suggests that plan sponsors can affect the investment behavior of the participants in their plans.

Table 12 shows the percentage of investors with varying concentrations of their total retirement plan assets in the various fixed-income funds. The variation in the distributions is quite remarkable. The percentage of

TABLE 12 Concentration of DC Individual Asset Holdings in Fixed-Income
Funds by Plan Sponsor

	Percent of Potential Investors with x Percent of Total Assets in This Investment					
Plan Sponsor	*Zero*	*20.0 or Less*	*20.1 to 40.0*	*40.1 to 60.0*	*60.1 to 80.0*	*80.1 to 100*
A	22.0%	8.0%	10.5%	15.4%	8.5%	35.7%
B	23.4	11.3	12.2	11.9	13.0	28.2
C	25.7	6.3	9.4	10.5	8.6	39.4
D	35.3	12.5	14.7	15.0	6.5	16.0
E	28.4	13.4	21.8	23.8	5.4	7.2
F	5.8	0.7	3.6	5.1	0.0	84.7
G	30.5	11.4	14.9	11.7	6.7	24.8
H	29.0	4.2	8.1	15.1	6.8	36.8
I	69.5	8.0	11.8	3.2	1.6	5.9
J	11.4	7.2	15.4	15.7	17.9	32.4
K	28.6	11.9	27.6	17.2	5.3	9.3
M	19.1	3.8	12.6	21.4	15.1	28.1
N	32.8	5.2	7.8	2.2	0.0	51.9
O	0.6	0.3	0.0	1.6	0.8	96.8
P	5.4	2.3	3.4	4.0	1.9	83.0
Q	42.4	4.7	13.2	15.2	6.7	17.8
R	49.2	6.0	15.8	14.4	3.1	11.5
S	30.7	5.5	14.8	17.5	8.4	23.2
T	35.9	12.3	16.3	11.5	6.9	17.2
U	49.2	7.3	15.2	12.8	3.6	11.9
V	44.5	19.3	13.1	7.3	4.8	11.1
W	8.8	2.4	2.3	5.9	3.7	76.9
X	45.4	18.4	11.5	9.8	2.9	11.9
Y	43.8	10.0	12.5	11.5	8.9	13.4

Source: Authors' calculations.

participants who have no fixed-income investments in their plans range
from a low of 0.6 percent to a high of 49.2 percent. The percentage holding 80 to 100 percent of their assets in fixed-income funds ranges from
7.2 percent to 96.8 percent. In the latter case, the plan sponsor also offers the participants a domestic equity fund, an international equity
fund, and a balanced fund. The participants in plans O and P are relatively old, which may account for the heavy concentration of investment
in fixed-income funds. Plan W has only recently offered participants investment options other than a GIC, and it may simply take some time for
participants to become familiar with their other opportunities to invest.
Even taking these explanations for high concentration of assets in some
of the fixed-income funds into account, the variations in the table suggest that there is something about the plans being offered by the sponsors, or in how they are being communicated, that is having a very

significant effect on the investment behavior of the participants. At this stage of the analysis we have not yet begun to understand more fully what may be causing the variations that we have found. That will be an issue to be pursued in further research.

Conclusions

The research presented here is merely a beginning assessment of the factors behind the investment behavior of retirement plan participants who manage the allocation of their own retirement plan assets. As the immediately preceding section suggests, there is a great deal of additional work to be done. Still there are several conclusions that we can draw from the current effort. First, we find a pattern of investments that suggests younger workers are generally more aggressive in their investment behavior than older workers. There are some clear exceptions to this general pattern, however, as even some of the youngest workers are totally invested in fixed-income investment options. Second, we find that higher-wage workers are somewhat more aggressive in their investment behavior than lower-wage workers. Again, there are clear exceptions to this conclusion. Some high-wage workers are very conservatively investing their retirement assets. Among lower-wage workers with an option to invest in the stock of their employers, we find that there is some substantial number who are investing virtually all of their retirement money there which is probably inappropriate, or even undesirable, in a diversification sense. We believe that better education programs may lead to somewhat different investment patterns than we now find in self-directed defined contribution plans. We do not believe, however, that any amount of education would result in self-directed defined contribution assets being invested in accordance with the investment style that prevails among defined benefit plans.

Putting these results into the framework of the larger discussion about self-directed retirement investment issues leads back to consideration of the motivations that employers have in setting up and administering their retirement savings programs. Traditionally, employers have thought about retirement programs as target savings vehicles that have certain human resource incentives built into them. In the context of the replacement rate model often utilized in designing or analyzing retirement programs, plans are designed so participants can accumulate retirement assets during their working careers sufficient to generate income during their retirement that allows them to maintain their pre-retirement disposable income levels.

More specifically, within the context of sponsoring a defined benefit plan, the replacement rate model has often been used to design plans which deliver benefits in conjunction with Social Security and personal savings that allow retirees to maintain pre-retirement living standards. Once the defined benefit plan is specified, the sponsor is on the hook for delivering the benefits as stipulated. In this environment the plan sponsor is interested in pursuing investment policies which minimize contributions to the plan over time, or at least coordinate contributions with business operations, and over time periods that exceed the earning or accumulation periods of individual employees.

Within the context of sponsoring a defined contribution plan, sponsors are pushing investment risk onto plan participants. But for a variety of reasons discussed above, workers may have completely different risk preferences than their employers in investing retirement assets. It should not be a surprise to anyone that risk preferences or tolerances vary across individuals and for workers in comparison to their employers. Returning to the replacement rate model used in designing retirement programs, if self-directed defined contribution plans tend to generate lower rates of return, as we believe they generally will on average, then the overall saving in the defined contribution plans will have to be greater in order to generate the same replacement of pre-retirement income than if a defined benefit plan was being used. If employers' motivation in setting up retirement plans is to deliver a targeted level of retirement income at a minimum contribution cost, then self-directed defined contribution plans are not the optimal way to achieve their goal. If employers' motivations in setting up their defined contribution plans is to hand off investment risk, minimize the liability for bad investment outcomes, and give workers some flexibility in meeting their own retirement income needs, then self-directed defined contribution plans are probably the optimal way to achieve that goal. No matter which goal is pursued, there is a price to be paid in each case.

The authors' comments and opinions expressed in this paper are solely their own and do not necessarily represent the opinions of Watson Wyatt Worldwide or any of its associates.

Notes

1. The headlines and tone of the articles has become alarmist in some cases— such as a recent Panel Publishers piece "When Employees Choose, They Lose" (1995).

2. The asset amounts exclude funds held by life insurance companies under allocated group insurance contracts. These funds make up roughly 10 to 15 percent of total private pensions plan assets.

3. Of course there are other motivations for choosing a defined benefit or defined contribution plan than assumption or diversification of investment risk.

These include the ability to attract, retain, and motivate workers during their working years and to retire them on an orderly basis at the end of their useful careers. These considerations are not dealt with in the current context.

References

Institute of Management and Administration. Defined Contribution Plan Investing. Washington, DC, April 25, 1995.

Kritzman, Mark. "What Practitioners Need to Know About Time Diversification," *Financial Analysts Journal* (January–February 1994): 15.

Markland, Judith. "Defined Benefit Approach Doesn't Always Suit Defined Contribution Investors." *Pension World* (February 1994): 24–26.

Oppenheimer Funds. *Restoring the Dream of a Comfortable Retirement.* New York: Oppenheimer Funds Distributor, 1994.

Panel Publishers. "When Employees Choose, They Lose." *401(K) Advisor* 2, 1 (April 1995).

Rohrer, Julie. "Putting Responsibility Above Liability?" *Institutional Investor* (May 1994): 157–58.

Smith, Roger. "DC Plans Accepted, Assets Growing . . . What's the Problem?" *Pension World* (February 1993): 28–30.

United States Department of Labor (USDOL), Pension and Welfare Benefits Administration. Abstract of 1991 Form 5500 Annual Reports. Private Pension Plan Bulletin No. 4, Winter 1995, Washington DC: USGPO, 1995.

Wyatt Company, *Wyatt Insider* (October 1994): 8.

Chapter 6
Are Women Conservative Investors? Gender Differences in Participant-Directed Pension Investments

Richard P. Hinz, David D. McCarthy, and John A. Turner

The rise in United States private-sector pension coverage during the 1980s and early 1990s was primarily attributable to the growth of 401(k) plans. In 1983, 401(k) plans covered 6 percent of participants in private pension plans; ten years later they covered 46 percent (USDOL 1994). Participation declined in both defined benefit plans and non-401(k) defined contribution plans during this period.

A common feature of 401(k) plans, and increasingly of other defined contribution plans, is that participants may direct the investment of some portion of their account.[1] In 1991, medium and large firms reported that 91 percent of participants in savings and thrift plans could direct the investment of participant contributions and 62 percent could direct the investment of employer contributions.[2]

Investment funds managed by individual pension participants allow participants to consider a range of investment strategies, selecting portfolios suited to their time horizon and risk tolerance. The shift toward individual management may, however, have adverse effects. Individuals may be too conservative, allocating to short-term, fixed-income assets a share of their portfolio inconsistent with specialists' views as to the optimal mix for a pension portfolio (EBPR 1993). In a survey, 69 percent of working Americans said that if they had to choose how to invest their pension money knowing that their benefits would go up with investment gains and down with investment losses, they would prefer low-risk, low-return investments (EBRI 1993). An increasingly prominent interpretation is that this preference results from financial naiveté. This study uses a new data set on the federal Thrift Savings Plan (TSP) to explore these and other hypotheses.

Prior Studies on Gender Differences in Investments

Investment decisions may differ by sex for several reasons. One possibility is that women know less and are less confident about their knowledge of investments as compared to men (New York Life Insurance Company 1993). Other surveys suggest that women are also more conservative investors than men. One study of business students found females less likely to take business risks than males (Zinkhan and Karande 1991). Using the 1989 Survey of Consumer Finances, a different team reported that 57 percent of women said they were unwilling to take any financial risks, compared to 41 percent of men (Jianakopolos and Bernasek 1994). That study found no significant gender differences, however, after controlling for savings, home ownership, and other assets. A different analysis of investor styles based on a questionnaire sent to clients of a large brokerage firm concluded that investor age, income, and sex in descending order were the primary determinants of investor style, with women being more conservative (Lewellen, Lease, and Schlarbaum 1977). Finally, a recent nationally representative survey concerning willingness to take a job with the potential for higher earnings but the risk of lower earnings found that women were more risk averse (Barsky, Juster, Kimball, and Shapiro 1995).

One caveat to these conclusions is that individuals' responses to questionnaires may differ from their actual behavior, with men and women being distinguished by what they consider a "socially acceptable" response. Nevertheless, a recent exploration of individual asset allocation and risk aversion patterns concluded that women are overall slightly more risk averse than men (Riley and Chow 1992). That report speculated that this could be due to differences in age, income, and wealth rather than gender, but they did not test that hypothesis in a multivariate framework. In a companion piece to the present one, VanDerhei and Bajtelsmit (this volume) found that women were more likely to invest in fixed-income securities and less likely to invest in employer stock than men.

If women invest in lower-risk pension portfolios than men, growing reliance on participant-directed individual account plans could worsen existing retirement income disparities by gender. For new pensioners in 1993 to 1994 the median of women's benefits was 50 percent less than men's (USDOL 1995:20).

Explanations for Gender Differences in Risk Preferences

To explore further possible explanations for why women and men differ in the amount of financial risk they hold, we consider a range of arguments. First, women and men may differ in their underlying attitudes or utility functions for risk. For example, cultural factors may cause men to bear more risk than women. Second, gender differences in risk bearing might be due to differences in economic status. For example, women often have lower earnings than men. If higher income workers were more willing to bear risk, a gender difference in risk bearing could be due to a difference in income. A third hypothesis is that differences in risk bearing could be due to gender differences in information. To the extent that males are better informed about investments, this might explain their willingness to bear more risk. Fourth, women's longer life expectancy and greater probability of outliving their spouses could affect their willingness to accept financial risk. If individuals with a longer time horizon have a greater ability to bear risk, women would be expected to hold riskier portfolios than men.

Testing the Hypotheses

To pursue these hypotheses in an empirical setting, we use data from a 1990 survey of participants in the federal government's Thrift Savings Plan (TSP) for federal employees. This plan had assets of approximately US $27 billion as of January 1995, making it one of the 20 largest pension funds in the nation after less than ten years' existence (USGAO 1995, *Pensions and Investments* 1995). With 2 million participants, the TSP is projected to become the largest pension fund in the United States (Chernoff 1990).

Created during the 1986 reform of the federal retirement system, the TSP covers most federal employees hired after January 1, 1984. Participants in the preexisting Civil Service Retirement System were also given the option of joining the new system. Workers covered under the new TSP system also participate in the Federal Employees Retirement System (FERS), which is a defined benefit pension plan, and in the national Social Security system.

The federal government automatically contributes 1 percent of salary to the Thrift Savings Plan for all FERS employees. For workers who also contribute additional pre-tax amounts from their salary, the federal government matches these contributions up to 5 percent of pay—dollar for dollar for the first 3 percent and 50 cents per dollar for the next 2 percent, for a maximum government contribution of 5 percent. In 1990, three quarters of male and 62 percent of female FERS employees contributed part of their salary to the Thrift Savings Plan.[3]

The TSP has three funds in which participants may invest. First, the G fund holds short-term nonmarketable United States Treasury securities specially issued to the plan. By law, the interest rate on these investments equals the average of market rates of return on United States Treasury marketable securities outstanding with four or more years to maturity. Because of the longer maturity and greater interest rate risk than on Treasury bills, the G fund earns a higher rate of return than Treasury bills.

The second fund available to TSP participants is the F fund, a fixed-income index fund of government and corporate bonds. Over the period of 1988 to 1990 this fund invested primarily in a commingled Shearson Lehman Hutton Government/Corporate bond index fund. In dollar terms, the United States Government sector comprised 74 percent of the index and corporate bonds the remaining 26 percent. This fixed-income fund has greater risk than the government securities G fund because of its longer maturity (and thus greater interest rate risk) and because it includes corporate bonds with default risk.

The third option open to TSP participants is the C fund that invests in common stocks in the form of a Standard & Poor's (S&P) 500 index fund. The C fund invests passively, closely matching the performance of the S&P 500 index. Over the period of 1980 to 1989, rates of return were 11 percent for the government bond fund, 12.2 percent for the fixed-income fund, and 17.4 percent for the stock fund.

The agency managing the TSP, known as the Thrift Savings Board, conducted a survey in 1990 to learn more about the effectiveness of the Board's publications informing employees about the plan. This survey was also matched with administrative records on covered employees.[4] These data have not been used previously to analyze differences across workers in risk bearing. Because the data on the investment of pension contributions and worker earnings are based on administrative records, they are highly reliable. Unfortunately, the survey lacks information on worker educational attainment and family asset holdings.

Turning to the evidence, we note that FERS employees could allocate a maximum of 60 percent of their own contributions to the common stock and fixed-income funds in 1990.[5] Our tabulations (see Table 1) indicate that women and men differed greatly in the probability of investing in common stock during that year. Only 28 percent of women, compared to 45 percent of men, participated in the common stock fund under the TSP. Of those respondents participating in that fund, the gender difference in the percentage of contributions allocated to common

TABLE 1 Descriptive Statistics on TSP Participants

Description	Women	Men	Total
Percent Contributing to:			
C or F	33%	48%	44%
C but not F	28	45	40
F but not C	12	20	18
Fraction of Funds in C Fund			
All Participants	8.9%	15.3%	13.4%
	(16.7)	(21.2)	(20.2)
Contributors Only	31.2	34.4	33.7%
	(16.8)	(18.9)	(18.5)
Fraction of Funds in F Fund			
All Participants	2.6%	8.8%	3.4%
	(7.7)	(8.8)	(8.5)
Contributors Only	21.1	18.5	19.0
	(10.2)	(10.6)	(10.5)
Fraction of Funds in G Fund	88.6%	81.0%	83.2%
	(19.8)	(23.3)	(22.6)
Average Salary (US $)	$35,614	$46,706	$43,410
	(19,681)	(19,995)	(20,520)
Other Income	$19,582	$14,768	$16,198
	(19,222)	(13,383)	(15,489)
Married (%)	0.58	0.81	0.74
Average Age (years)	38.9	40.9	40.3
	(10.2)	(11.1)	(10.8)
Sample Size	148	350	498

Notes: Statistics given for the regression sample (unweighted); they do not represent population statistics. All participants required to contribute to the G fund, so statistics on the percentage contributing to that fund not presented. Standard deviations in parentheses.

stock was slight—on average 31 percent for women and 34 percent for men. All agency automatic and matching contributions were restricted to the government bond fund.

It is next of interest to ask whether the observed gender difference in portfolio allocations persists after controlling for economic and demographic variables available in the survey. That is, one might hypothesize no pure gender difference in risk bearing—the observed differences are due to differences in economic and demographic characteristics. The particular controls available here are salary, other family income, age, gender, and marital status (married/not married).[6] However our analysis decisively rejects the hypothesis. That is, holding constant the worker's salary and other family income, men are still more likely to invest in the common stock and fixed-income funds than women. The analysis also shows that rising salary and other family income increases the likelihood that a worker invests in the common stock or fixed-income funds. However, the effect of own salary is 10 times greater than other family income. This result is similar to results reported by Bernheim and Garrett (1995) concerning participation in 401(k) plans. They found that spouse's earnings had little effect on the respondent's own participation, and that the respondent's earnings had little effect on the spouse's participation.

Because Social Security replaces a higher percentage of earnings for low-paid workers than for high earners and because Social Security presumably is viewed as low risk, it might be thought that low earners would be more willing than high earners to accept risk. In fact, the reverse was found among TSP participants. Higher earners were significantly more likely to contribute to the common stock fund than lower earners. Our survey did not supply information on the workers' entire portfolios, but most Americans hold no financial assets outside their pension plans, so we believe that we have not omitted important controls from the analysis. Even among households with income of US $50,000 or more, only 49 percent owned stocks (Kennickell and Shack-Marquez 1992).

Because marriage provides insurance through income pooling, with the employment possibilities of husbands and wives generally subject to different risks, married couples might be thought willing to take greater risk even after holding constant family income. Complicating factors are that married people have longer life expectancies than do nonmarried people and are more likely to have child dependents, but the direction of these effects is unclear.[7]

When we use the TSP sample to compare investment decisions by marital status, we compare people who are currently married to people who are single for whatever reason (divorced, never married, widowed). The results clearly show that marriage has a significantly negative effect; that is, married people were much less likely to invest either in stock or the fixed-income portfolio. The effect of marriage on differing individual risk bearing for men and women was also investigated, on the view that perhaps marriage might reduce gender differences in risk bearing, oppositely affecting the risk bearing of men and women. This investigation, however, shows that married men and unmarried women take similar investment risks. Married women are the most conservative, and unmarried men are the least conservative. In other words marriage appears not to reduce the gender gap in risk bearing. An alternative interpretation would view the married couple as a unit, finding that the combined husband-wife portfolio is intermediate in risk between the portfolios of the two people acting as single individuals. Thus by this interpretation, marriage bridges the gender gap in financial risk bearing.[8]

The estimated effect of marriage on risk bearing may shed light on the gender gap in risk bearing. The gender gap in risk bearing that remains after holding constant demographic and economic variables is unexplained in our data; however, a major gender difference that has not been measured directly is the gender difference in mortality risk. The gender difference in mortality risk is roughly equal to the marital status difference in mortality risk, and both gender and marital status have roughly the same magnitude of effect on risk bearing. This pattern suggests the interpretation that the gender difference in risk bearing is caused by the gender difference in mortality risk, with people that have lower mortality risk taking less financial risk.

Age differences could also affect willingness to bear financial risk. One argument is that those nearing retirement should place more retirement in fixed income. However Bodie (1995) argues that young workers with a long time horizon should not invest a large share of their portfolio in stocks. Another issue is that financial sophistication may increase with age and experience. In our analysis of the survey (see Table 3 below), we find that age generally is not a good predictor of asset allocation preferences except in investment in fixed-income securities where its effect is negative.[9]

One interesting fact discerned in the TSP survey is that a large percentage of the sample, 65 percent of women and 52 percent of men, invested only in the government bond fund. Several factors may explain this investment behavior. First, the Thrift Savings Plan statute required that all employee contributions had to be invested in the G fund in 1987. This requirement decreased each year by 20 percent through 1990 and was eliminated in 1991. Some employees who were invested entirely in the G fund may have not taken advantage of the opportunity to move out of the bond fund merely due to inertia. For other employees, the initial restrictions may have had a chilling effect on their willingness to invest in other funds. Second, by 1990, workers who had been in the Thrift Savings Plan only a short time may have invested in the least risky portfolio, preferring a conservative approach initially. As they learned more about the different funds through information provided them by the Thrift Savings Board, they would have had the chance to move to riskier investments. Nevertheless, when we investigated these hypotheses, none of them were borne out.[10]

An alternative explanation for why many participants invested in the minimum-risk portfolio is that some would have preferred a fund with even lower risk, for example, a fund with no real interest rate risk. This possibility is explored using a statistical technique known as a Tobit estimation procedure, and we posit that some workers fully invested in the government bond fund might have preferred an even more conservative fund had one been available. In results not explored in detail here, this appears to be true for women in that more women than men would appear to prefer even less risky assets.[11] On the whole, we find that women would be predicted to have held 15 percent less in stock funds than men using this Tobit approach, double the estimate using simpler statistical techniques.

It should be noted that some TSP participants bunch at the opposite extreme, selecting the most risky portfolio available. Specifically 11 percent of men and 5 percent of women invested the maximum percentage in common stock, suggesting that some would have preferred an even riskier portfolio had that been available.[12] For workers having the maximum or minimum risk portfolio within the plan and for whom their pension portfolio is their entire financial investment portfolio, the restrictions on risk bearing within the plan are therefore likely to be binding. By contrast, workers who also had financial investments outside their pension portfolio could adjust the risk of their overall portfolio by offsetting outside investments.

In order to decide whether "right censoring" of this sort affects our results, we reestimated a Tobit model allowing for both left and right censoring. This analysis suggests an even larger estimate of the gender effect—a 19 percentage point differential.[13] This effect is large, equaling in magnitude that of a woman having 48 percent less salary than an otherwise comparable man!

This finding is probably too large to be credible, based on additional evidence supplied by the survey. In particular, workers were asked whether they would prefer another investment option. Overall, about a quarter of all participants said "yes" with the same fraction of "yes" responses for those contributing only to the least risky fund, while 32 percent of workers contributing to the most risky portfolio said "yes." A better question for our purposes would have been, "Would you have invested in a less (more) risky option had that been available?" Nonetheless, the relatively low percentages of positive responses suggest few workers at the extremes were truly constrained in their investment portfolio options.

The economic importance of our findings is ascertainable using the data in Table 2. We calculate how much larger would be a man's pension account at retirement than a woman's, assuming equality of all relevant factors except the percentage of their two pensions held in stock. Among women who invested part of their pension portfolio in stock, the modal percentage of their contributions invested in stock was 20 percent. We use the estimated difference in the percentage of contributions invested in stock for men and women of 14 percentage points. We assume

TABLE 2 Pension Assets at Retirement Resulting from Gender Differences in the Percentage of Pension Contributions Allocated to Stock

Years in the Plan	Male/Female Portfolio Size
10	1.04
20	1.08
30	1.13
35	1.16

Source: Authors' calculations.

a 5 percent nominal wage growth over the career, no portfolio rebalancing, and that each year the stock and bond portions of the portfolio earned the average rate of return received over the period 1926 to 1994 on large company stocks (10.4 percent) or on long-term corporate bonds (5.4 percent) (Ibbotson 1995).

The effect on the plan's account balance of the gender difference in portfolio allocation increases with the number of years in the plan as shown in Table 2. With 20 years' participation in such a plan, the pension accumulation is about 8 percent larger for men; after 35 years of plan participation, the man's plan would be 16 percent larger.

Conclusions

Using a survey of TSP participants, we confirm that women appear to invest their pension assets more conservatively than men. A large percentage of women invested in the minimum-risk portfolio available to them. A portion of the pattern is explained by women's lower incomes, but the result persists after controlling for economic and demographic variables. Nonetheless, married women also invest less in common stock than married men, holding constant age and income. Because lower risk portfolios have lower expected return, the findings imply that women's pension accumulations will exacerbate the gender gap in retirement income over time.

Although examining evidence from a single pension plan somewhat limits the generality of our findings, we believe that data from a single plan avoids the possibility that unobserved plan or firm characteristics are confounding our interpretation of individual behavior.[14] Also, by using data on a single plan we can incorporate the plan rules in our analysis. Nevertheless, it is possible that federal workers are more conservative in their investments than private-sector workers would be. On the other hand, federal workers face less risk of layoff, and hence might be more willing to accept financial risks. In either case, as long as government employment affects risk taking similarly for both males and females, the gender comparisons found in our study remain unaffected.

The authors gratefully acknowledge comments from Vickie Bajtelsmit, Veda Charro, Marcia Goldstein, Olivia Mitchell, Mark Warshawsky, and Paul Yakoboski. The views expressed here are solely the responsibility of the authors and do not represent the position of the United States Department of Labor or of the above acknowledged persons.

Notes

1. A 1992 Department of Labor regulation relieves employers sponsoring participant-directed plans from fiduciary liability related to selection of investments when specific conditions are met.

2. There is a large overlap between 401(k) plans and savings and thrift plans. In 1991, 98 percent of participants in savings or thrift plans in medium and large firms were in 401(k) plans, and 64 percent of participants in 401(k) plans were in savings or thrift plans (USDOL 1993).

3. The information reported in this section is taken from Federal Retirement Thrift Investment Board (1991: B-69). Even and Macpherson (1993) also found lower participation rates for women than men in 401(k) plans in the private sector.

4. The full survey included part-time workers, postal service workers, and federal workers in the Civil Service Retirement System, but we restrict the analyses below to full-time federal workers in the FERS who contributed part of their salary to the Thrift Savings Plan.

5. The ceiling has since been lifted and FERS employees can now direct 100 percent of their contributions to any of the funds.

6. A Chow test on OLS regressions indicated it is appropriate to pool the male and female samples.

7. The association between mortality risk and marital status is particularly strong. For ages 20 to 49, the unmarried/married mortality factor exceeds the male/female factor, indicating that the death rate for unmarried women exceeds that for married men (Trowbridge 1995).

8. There may also be assortative mating if people seek spouses with opposite risk preferences. In this event, husbands and wives would specialize within the marriage, with women selecting conservative aspects of the family portfolio and men selecting more risky assets. A full understanding of gender differences in risk bearing within the family clearly requires data with information on the characteristics of spouses and on other family investments. Because of the complicating factor of marriage in interpreting gender differences in risk bearing, it might be thought that gender differences would best be estimated for a sample of unmarried workers. However, such a sample would likely be subject to selectivity bias, with single men and single women differing from married men and married

women in their attitudes toward risk. To evaluate this possibility, we also interacted gender with marital status in a multivariate model, but that variable was not
statistically different from zero.

9. Other variables were entered in regressions (see Table 3) but were insig-
nificant, including age at hire, tenure with the government, years to eligibility for
retirement, years to eligibility for a retirement supplement (generally requiring
more years of service), and dummy variables for being within five or ten years of
eligibility for either type of retirement benefit.

10. We investigated the effect of short tenure in the plan by entering dummy
variables for one or two years of tenure. We also interacted the tenure term with
gender under the hypothesis that women might be more likely to enter the plan
lacking knowledge, but then would increase their risk bearing as they became
more knowledgeable. In a separate regression, we entered a variable for participation in the plan in 1987, and thus having faced the requirement that all contributions be invested in the G fund. None of these variables was statistically
significant.

11. The Tobit estimation procedure assumes that some of the women's zero
allocations to the stock fund would have been negative, if this were possible (see
Table 4).

12. An additional constraint is that no more than 60 percent of the portfolio
can be invested in the C or F funds. In the analysis sample, 14 percent of the men
and 7 percent of the women were affected by this constraint.

13. See Table 4. The Tobit procedure assumes that errors are normally distributed. We relaxed this assumption by reestimating the model assuming first a Wei-
bull then a Gamma distribution. The parameter estimates proved insensitive to
the distributional assumption and are presented only for the familiar Tobit
model.

14. This point was made for age differences in the analysis of single-plan data
by Kusko, Poterba, and Wilcox (1994).

TABLE 3 Estimates of the Effect of Gender on Portfolio Investment Decisions

Variable	Stock or Fixed Income	Stock Only	Fixed Income
Male	.411	.584	.616
	(.19)	(.23)	(.30)
Ln (Salary)	.584	.931	.252
	(.18)	(.21)	(.27)
Ln (Other Income)	.060	.057	.054
	(.02)	(.03)	(.03)
Age	.002	−.011	−.030
	(.01)	(.01)	(.01)
Married	−.544	−.520	−.237
	(.21)	(.24)	(.30)
−2 Log Likelihood	850.07	669.33	450.81
N	617	498	498

Note: Asymptotic standard errors in parentheses for Logit models, standard errors for OLS.

TABLE 4 Multivariate Estimates of TSP Participants

Variable	OLS	Tobit, Left Censored	Tobit, Left and Right Censored
		Dependent Variable: *% of Contributions to Stock Fund*	
Male	4.659	14.855	19.424
	(2.03)	(4.99)	(6.51)
Ln (Salary)	8.928	22.769	29.718
	(1.85)	(4.61)	(6.08)
Ln (Other Income)	.553	1.438	1.764
	(.23)	(.55)	(.72)
Age	−.071	−.281	−.368
	(.08)	(.20)	(.26)
Married	−4.847	−13.276	−18.493
	(2.19)	(5.24)	(6.89)
−2 Log Likelihood		2349.00	2068.34
R^2	.08		
F	8.12		
N	498	486	486

Note: Asymptotic standard errors in parentheses for Tobit, standard errors for OLS. The sample size in the second and third regression is reduced because participants who do not invest in the C fund but do invest in the F fund were excluded from those regressions.

References

Barsky, Robert, Thomas F. Juster, Miles Kimball, and Matthew Shapiro. An Experimental Approach to Preference Parameters and Behavioral Heterogeneity in the Health and Retirement Study. Health and Retirement Study Working Paper No. 94-019 (rev.), July 1995. University of Michigan Institute for Survey Research, Ann Arbor.

Bajtelsmit, Vickie L. and Jack L. VanDerhei. "Risk Aversion and Pension Investment Choices." This volume.

Bernheim, B. Douglas and Daniel M. Garrett. The Determinants and Consequences of Financial Education in the Workplace: Evidence from a Survey of Households. Stanford University working paper, August 1995.

Bodie, Zvi. "On the Risk of Stocks in the Long Run." *Financial Analysts Journal* 51 (May/June 1995): 18–22.

Chernoff, Joel. "Federal Fund Sits in Cash." Pensions and Investments. January 22, 1990, p6.

Employee Benefit Plan Review (EBPR). "Conservative Players Should Seek Balance with Common Stocks" (January 29–30 1993).

Employee Benefit Research Institute (EBRI). *Public Attitudes on Investment Preferences.* Washington, DC: Employees Benefit Research Institute, 1993.

Even, William E. and David A. Macpherson. The Pension Coverage of Young and Mature Men. Report submitted to the US Department of Labor, Pension and Welfare Benefits Administration, March 1993.

Federal Retirement Thrift Investment Board. Thrift Savings Plan: Report on 1990 Survey of Federal and Postal Employees. Report by the Office of Communications, Washington, DC, November 1991.

Ibbotson, R. *Stocks, Bonds, and Inflation: 1995 Yearbook*. Chicago: Ibbotson and Associates, 1995.

Jianakopolos, Nancy and Alexandra Bernasek. "Are Women More Risk Averse?" Paper presented at the Western Economics Association annual meeting, San Diego, California, June 1994.

Kennickell, Arthur and Janice Shack-Marquez. "Changes in Family Finances from 1983 to 1989: Evidence from the Survey of Consumer Finances." *Federal Reserve Bulletin* 78 (January 1992): 1–18.

Kusko, Andrea L., James M. Poterba, and David Wilcox. Employee Decisions with Respect to 401(k) Plans: Evidence from Individual-Level Data. NBER Working Paper No. 4635, February 1994.

Lewellen, Wilbur G., Ronald C. Lease, and Gary G. Schlarbaum. "Patterns of Investment Strategy and Behavior Among Individual Investors." *The Journal of Business* 50 (July 1977): 296–333.

New York Life Insurance Company. "Most 401(k) Participants Are Well Informed. And Now for the Bad News." New York: New York Life Insurance Company, 1993.

New York Stock Exchange. *Shareownership 1990*. New York: New York Stock Exchange, 1991.

Pensions and Investments. "The Top 200 Pension Funds/Sponsors" (January 23, 1995): 25.

Riley, William B., Jr. and Victor K. Chow. "Asset Allocation and Individual Risk Aversion." *Financial Analysts Journal* (November/December 1992): 32–37.

Trowbridge, Charles L. "Marriage, Sex, and Mortality." *Contingencies* 7 (November/December 1995): 25–29.

United States Department of Labor (USDOL), Bureau of Labor Statistics. Employee Benefits in Medium and Large Firms. Washington, DC: USGPO, 1993.

United States Department of Labor (USDOL), Pension and Welfare Benefits Administration. Abstract of 1991 Form 5500 Annual Reports. Private Pension Plan Bulletin No. 4, Winter 1995. Washington, DC: USGPO, 1995.

———. *Pension and Health Benefits of American Workers*. Washington, DC: USGPO, 1994.

United States General Accounting Office. *Federal Pensions: Thrift Savings Plan Has Key Role in Retirement Benefits*. Washington, DC: USGPO, October 1995.

Zinkhan, George M. and Kiran W. Karande. "Cultural and Gender Differences in Risk-Taking Behavior Among American and Spanish Decision Makers." *Journal of Social Psychology* 131 (October 1991): 741–42.

Part II
Emerging Pension Issues

Chapter 7
Funding of Defined Benefit Pension Plans

Mark J. Warshawsky

Funding of defined benefit pension plans has long been an important topic to financial analysts and government policymakers. Knowing the funded status of sponsored plans is often an essential part of knowing the financial health of a corporate sponsor. Similarly, the funded status of plans is relevant to the financial prospects of the Pension Benefit Guaranty Corporation (PBGC) and to the necessary level of tax expenditures for the private pension system.

This chapter has three specific goals: (1) to explain fully the evolution of the complex minimum funding requirements imposed by the federal government on plan sponsors by highlighting three legislative eras; (2) to give a short history of financial accounting standards for pension sponsors, focusing on the current regime of measurement, recognition, and disclosure; and (3) to present statistics on funding from plan sponsors' financial statements. This chapter also discusses the broad motivations of government and accounting policymakers in adopting various rules, as well as the impact of these rules on the current and future funding of private defined benefit plans in the United States. Finally, a simple set of minimum funding requirements and maximum limits, akin to financial accounting standards, is recommended here to partially replace the complex requirements currently in place.

Defined Benefit Plans, Funding, and the PBGC

There are two main categories of qualified retirement plans offered in the United States, defined benefit (DB) and defined contribution (DC) plans. In a DB plan, the employer promises to pay the worker a specified retirement benefit that generally increases with each additional year of work. In a DC plan, the employer, and sometimes the worker, contributes an amount of money every year into the worker's account, available, with accrued investment earnings, upon retirement. Although DC plans, particularly 401(k) plans, expanded greatly during the 1980s as both primary and secondary plans, DB plans still provide most of the retirement benefit coverage to workers at large private and public employers.

In order to provide the benefits, the DB plan sponsor must have assets on hand when workers retire and benefit payments start. If the sponsor were to default on its obligation and did not set aside enough assets, retirees and workers will have lost hard-earned benefits important to their financial security. Despite generous tax incentives adequately to fund their pension obligations, through the 1960s some private employers defaulted without sufficient pension assets, and retirees and workers lost promised benefits.

With the passage of the Employee Retirement Income Security Act (ERISA) in 1974, Congress established minimum funding requirements and a federal government agency—the PBGC—to insure retirement benefits, up to a maximum level, earned through most private DB plans. When compliance with the minimum funding requirements is poor, or the requirements themselves are either inadequate or incomplete, a terminating plan sponsor in distress will probably have insufficient assets to fund its plan. In such cases, the PBGC will step in and pay the promised, but unfunded, benefits.

Through the 1980s, the financial situation of the PBGC worsened considerably. Successive legislative actions in the mid-1980s to tighten minimum funding requirements and raise premiums charged by the PBGC apparently did lead to some stabilization of PBGC finances. Nevertheless, concerns about the PBGC in the media, Congress, the administration, and among plan participants continued to mount in the late 1980s and early 1990s. One measure of the risk exposure of the PBGC—the liabilities less assets of underfunded plans—began to increase after several years of decline, and projections indicated that the long-term financial health of the PBGC was in jeopardy. The 1990–1991 recession weakened some plan sponsors and caused the value of some assets held by plan sponsors, particularly real estate, to fall. Moreover, during this time there have been very few new DB plans, and numerous DB plan terminations, thus lowering the premium base of the PBGC.

Actuarial Valuations

The funded status of a DB pension plan is determined by comparing the plan's assets with its liabilities. Assets are generally measured at market value. The liabilities are measured as the actuarial present value of the plan's benefits. Such a valuation reflects the probability that the various benefits will become payable and the discounting effect of the time value of money. Therefore, among the important actuarial assumptions involved in a valuation are rate of investment earnings, mortality, retirement, future salary increases, and employee turnover.

The purpose of the valuation can influence the calculation of liability by changing the relative importance of the various actuarial assumptions or even in some cases by changing the actuary's best estimate of a particular actuarial assumption. For example, in a forecast valuation, the open group technique is used, that is, it is assumed that the plan sponsor will hire additional workers in the future. Moreover, other actuarial assumptions reflect the plan as an on-going entity. By contrast, in a termination valuation, the closed group technique is used. Moreover, in such a valuation, there will be no assumption necessary concerning future salary increases, and the relevant interest rate and mortality tables should reflect the cost of annuitizing benefits.

In practical terms, the most important valuations are those mandated by federal law (ERISA) for purposes of determining a plan's minimum funding requirements and those mandated by generally accepted accounting principles for purposes of the recognition and disclosure of pension expense in the financial statements of the plan sponsor. Neither type of valuations allows an open group technique. Beyond this consideration, however, these valuations employ different blends of ongoing versus termination assumptions. Indeed, as will be explained in detail below, the funding requirements and financial accounting standards over time have increased the relative weight given conceptually to the likelihood that the plan will terminate.

The Evolution of Funding Requirements

Federal law requires that defined benefit plans sponsored by private employers be funded before benefits are due to be paid to plan participants. In particular, contributions of cash or, within strict limits, other employer securities must be made within a range specified in the law. The evolutionary history of these requirements can be divided into three distinct periods: first, that of the original ERISA rules; second, the Omnibus Reconciliation Act (OBRA) of 1987 was enacted; and finally, the Retirement Protection ACT (RPA) of 1994 was passed. As will be shown, the scope of plan sponsor discretion in funding has been narrowed over time and the consideration given to termination has become more prominent.

ERISA's Original Minimum Funding Requirements

In the years prior to the passage of ERISA, thousands of DB pension plans, mostly small and only in operation for a few years, terminated with some loss of benefits to participants. The failure in 1962 of the Studebaker plan, a large plan with sizable losses to many participants, however, particularly focused attention on plan benefit security. In order to protect participants against losses and to make feasible the federal pension insurance programs administered by the PBGC, Congress, when passing ERISA in 1974, added section 412 to the Internal Revenue Code to require minimum funding.

Under section 412, a funding standard account is set up to determine a DB plan's minimum funding requirement for a plan year. The requirement is the net sum of charges and credits, including (1) a normal cost charge, (2) any funding deficiency charge (or credit balance) carried over from the prior year, (3) an amortization charge for the initial unfunded accrued liability, (4) amortization charges (or credits) for increases (or decreases) in liabilities owing to plan amendments, (5) amortization charges (or credits) due to experience losses (or gains), and (6) amortization charges (or credits) for losses (or gains) resulting from changes in actuarial assumptions.

Excise taxes are imposed on the funding deficiency of a plan until the minimum required contribution is made. For plans unable to meet the minimum funding requirement because of the substantial business hardship of the plan sponsor, ERISA provided that a waiver of the requirement could be requested. If the IRS granted the request (subject to the satisfaction of certain conditions on the plan), the amount waived became a charge base to be amortized over the next 15 years in the funding standard account. If the request were denied and the plan sponsor failed to make the required contribution, excise taxes would be levied on the funding deficiency until the contribution is made.

ERISA listed six actuarial cost methods as acceptable for calculating normal costs and accrued liabilities. Each cost method has a unique way of calculating normal cost, related either to the actual accrual of benefits (unit credit method) or to the projected costs funded in the form of level annual payments. The accrued liability is defined as the present value of future benefits minus the present value of future normal costs; for the same plan and participant groups, the accrued liability differs depending on the cost method chosen. The unfunded liability is that part of the accrued liability in excess of assets. A plan can have an initial unfunded accrued liability if, when it is created, benefits are given based on the past service of current workers.

Gains and losses result from changes in actuarial assumptions and/or are the differences between the actual experiences of the plan and those expected in accordance with the actuarial assumptions. Depending on the cost method, experience gains and losses are amortized either over 15 years (as originally enacted in ERISA) (immediate gain methods) or as part of the normal cost (spread gain methods). ERISA also required that the actuarial assumptions used in determining plan costs be reasonable in the aggregate.[1]

For determining the minimum funding requirement, the amortization bases giving rise to the amortization charges and credits in the funding standard account are amortized over a specified number of years generally at the valuation interest rate. ERISA provided that the initial unfunded past service accrued liability be amortized over forty years for plans already in existence on January 1, 1974, and over thirty years for plans formed after January 1, 1974. If a plan is amended and the amendment results in a change in the unfunded accrued liability, such change is amortized over thirty years. (Most amendments increase benefits, and hence result in charges.) As originally enacted in ERISA, gains or losses resulting from changes in actuarial assumptions were also amortized over 30 years and, as already indicated, experience gains and losses and waivers were amortized over 15 years.[2]

The funding requirement is capped by the full-funding limitation. The limitation is the sum of the accrued liability and normal cost (both brought to the end of the year with interest) minus the lesser of the fair market value or actuarial (smoothed) value of plan assets (also brought to the end of the year with interest). The assets are also decreased for any credit balances in the funding standard account. When a plan has a funding requirement in excess of the full-funding limitation, a credit is given in the funding standard account for the amount of the excess, and all amortization bases are considered fully amortized.

Scope of Allowable Discretion Under Original ERISA

ERISA allowed implicitly for a range of funding levels in pension plans. It is possible for a plan to satisfy the minimum funding requirements and yet be underfunded if the plan should terminate. Alternatively, a plan may be well funded on a termination basis and still have a substantial required contribution for the plan year under section 412. Under original ERISA, the plan sponsor had considerable discretion to choose the funding scenario it desired.

The plan sponsor is allowed a choice of funding methods and, furthermore, is allowed, subject to IRS requirements, to switch funding methods.[3] Some methods amortize past service liabilities over 30 years, while other methods fund these liabilities over the average working lifetime of plan participants. In most plans, average working lifetime is shorter than thirty years; therefore, choosing a method that amortizes past service liability over thirty years reduces the rate at which the plan accumulates assets.

Among immediate gain methods, for the same group of employees and in a plan where benefits accrue ratably to retirement age, annual plan costs under the unit credit funding method are lower in earlier years and higher in later years than those under the entry age normal method. Even with the entry age normal method, a level dollar approach will fund more quickly in early years than a level percent of pay approach when contributions increase as overall participant compensation increases.[4]

There are two other sources of variability in funding status within the context of sponsor choice within the funding rules. First, subject to the full funding limitation, plan sponsors could contribute on a tax-deductible basis by amortizing unfunded accrued liabilities over no fewer than ten years. Second, it has been alleged that actuarial assumptions were sometimes manipulated to effect smaller or larger contributions, notwithstanding the requirement that the actuary use assumptions reflecting his or her best estimate of anticipated experience.

Despite the wide discretion given plan sponsors, there are certain correlations of funding levels with plan types in which the funding rules seem to play an important role. A plan with a flat dollar formula provides a specified dollar amount for each year of service. In order for this plan to provide a benefit equivalent to a consistent percentage of compensation, the flat dollar benefit must be increased periodically to keep pace with inflation and compensation increases. The plan cannot fund for these increases before the plan amendment is negotiated but, under most funding methods, instead funds the resulting increases as unfunded liabilities over 30 years. This problem generally does not exist in a plan which bases benefits on compensation because funding for such plans is required to be based upon the projected benefits at retirement, including expected increased compensation.

OBRA '87 Minimum Funding Requirements

When ERISA was passed, plan sponsors had quite a bit of latitude in their funding decisions before they approached either the Scylla of exceeding maximum allowable contributions or the Charybdis of failing the minimum funding requirements. To a large extent, this latitude was the intent of Congress in order to encourage the formation of DB plans and the granting of new benefits. If the funding decision was too narrowly circumscribed, existing plan sponsors would lack flexibility and could even be forced into bankruptcy or other forms of financial distress. Of course, the PBGC was left exposed, but it was probably hoped at the time that the PBGC would confront minimal plan failures.

The experience of the 1980s, however, forced changes. Some small DB plans sponsored by highly paid professionals were claiming very large income tax deductions. At the same time, losses at the PBGC were mounting as certain industries declined and some large plan sponsors failed, leaving large unfunded pension liabilities. Congress responded in 1987 with a tightening of limitations on deductions and attempts to strengthen the minimum funding requirements. In 1987 and again in 1989, Congress raised the premiums DB plan sponsors paid to the PBGC.

The most important concept introduced by OBRA '87 was the "current liability." It is the sum of the present values of accrued benefits for each participant, calculated as if the plan purchased annuities for these benefits, using an interest rate within a permissible range of rates. The permissible range is defined as an interest rate not more than 10 percent above or below the weighted average of the thirty-year Treasury bond yields for the preceding four-year period. Current liability is therefore determined independently of the actuarial cost method of the plan and is related to the termination liability.[5]

OBRA '87 uses this concept to establish the "current liability full funding limitation," which prevails if it is less than the old limitation based on the accrued liability. The new limitation equals 150 percent of the current liability plus the expected increase in current liability due to benefits accruing during the year (brought to the end of year with interest, using the current liability interest rate) minus the lesser of the fair market value or the actuarial value of assets (also brought forward with interest).[6] When the new limitation applies and the plan has a funding deficiency (prior to contributions) in excess of this limitation, a ten-year amortization charge base is established for the amount which would have been a required contribution except for application of the new limitation.

The lower current liability limitation can make funding less smooth over time due to the deferred amortization payments, particularly for plans using funding methods other than unit credit. The new limitation also may defer funding for a compensation-based plan covering relatively young employees. In particular, the accrued liability (even when calculated using the projected unit credit method) for a new group would reflect a significant amount of benefits based on projections of increased future compensation; 150 percent of the current liability (wherein such increases cannot be anticipated) may be less than the accrued liability. Schieber and Shoven (1994) claim that this limitation as well as other legislative and regulatory changes of the 1980s and 1990s will lead to a delay in the funding of the baby boom generation's defined benefit plans. It is unclear, however, how the fact that a smaller percentage of the baby boom generation is covered by the private DB plan system than in the prior generation is included in their model.

OBRA '87 tried to improve funding in underfunded plans as well as to limit overfunding. It provided that the deductible limit for non-multiemployer plans with more than 100 participants would not be less than the plan's unfunded current liability. For all DB plans other than multiemployer plans, OBRA '87 required that a plan's minimum funding requirement be paid in quarterly installments, rather than the previously permitted situation where sponsors could delay contributions until 8½ months after the end of the plan year.[7]

OBRA '87 also shortened the length of several of the amortization periods used in determining a non-multiemployer plan's minimum funding requirement. Experience gains and losses arising in plan years after 1987 are amortized over five years, gains and losses arising from changes in actuarial assumptions are amortized over 10 years, and funding waivers granted after 1987 are amortized over five years. The interest rate applied to the amortization of the waiver is related to current market rates rather than the valuation interest rate. The conditions for granting waivers were also tightened.[8]

OBRA '87 did not shorten the amortization periods for initial liability created on the granting of past service credit in a new plan or for increases in liability due to benefit increases. Rather, it introduced an additional funding scheme in new section 412(l) to reduce underfunding in addition to the old ERISA minimum funding rules. This scheme—the additional funding charge—applies only to single-employer plans with 100 or more participants and whose current liability exceeds the value of assets reduced by any credit balance in the funding standard account. The additional funding charge equals the "deficit reduction contribution" (DRC) offset by certain amortization payments.

The DRC equals the unfunded old liability amount plus the unfunded new liability amount. The unfunded old liability is the current liability less the actuarial value of assets reduced by the credit balance as of the 1988 plan year. (Plans formed after 1988 have no old liability.) The unfunded old liability *amount* is the payment amortizing the unfunded old liability over 18 years beginning in 1989. The unfunded new liability is the unfunded current liability in the current plan year less the outstanding balance of the unfunded old liability. The unfunded new liability *amount* is the "applicable percentage" of the unfunded new liability. The applicable percentage is 30 percent if the funded current liability percentage is less than 35 percent; it decreases by .25 of one percentage point for each percentage point by which the plan's funded current liability percentage exceeds 35 percent. An applicable percentage of 30 percent is equivalent to an amortization period of about four years.

To arrive at the additional funding charge, the DRC was reduced by the net of amortization charges and credits for the initial unfunded liability, waivers, and increases and decreases in the unfunded liability due to amendments. Because these offsets to the DRC did not include amortization charges and credits for changes in actuarial assumptions or experience losses and gains, it was entirely possible for an underfunded plan to have no additional funding charge. In particular, old flat dollar benefit plans which started funding under ERISA with low interest rate assumptions (resulting in large amortization charges) would have a large offset to the DRC. In addition, if the plans increased their interest rate assumptions in the 1980s, they would have large credits in their funding standard accounts. By contrast, newer plans established with high interest rate assumptions which then lowered their assumptions would experience the contribution burden in extra measure.

RPA '94 Minimum Funding Requirements

Although the immediate financial situation of the PBGC had not changed much since the passage of OBRA '87, there were indications that the underfunding of plans was a growing problem. Following intense scrutiny of the FSLIC-savings-and-loan debacle and the resulting review of other government-sponsored insurance programs, Congress, in the RPA, significantly altered the minimum funding rules. These changes were passed in December 1994 as part of the legislation implementing GATT and are generally effective beginning in the 1995 plan year.

The RPA makes three important changes to the formulas used to calculate the DRC and the additional funding charge. First, the applicable percentage of 30 percent for calculating the unfunded new liability amount now holds if a plan's funded current liability percentage is less than 60 percent (rather than 35 percent as before). The applicable percentage decreases by .40 of a percentage point for each percentage point by which the funded current liability percentage exceeds 60 percent, to a minimum of 18 percent for a plan that is 90 percent funded. For example, a plan which is 70 percent funded would now have an applicable percentage of 26 percent rather than 21.25 percent, as under OBRA '87. Second, the DRC now includes as a component the expected increase in current liability due to benefits accruing during the plan year. Third, all amortization charges and credits are now included as offsets to the DRC in computing the additional funding charge, including experience gains or losses, changes in liabilities due to changes in actuarial cost methods, and gains and losses due to changes in actuarial assumptions. Thus, the minimum required contribution for underfunded plans, in general, is the greater of the amount determined under the normal funding rules or the DRC.

The RPA gradually narrows the interest rate corridor used to calculate current liability for purposes of the DRC and specifies a mortality assumption. More specifically, for the 1999 plan year and beyond, the maximum interest rate used to calculate current liability is 105 percent of the weighted four-year moving average yield on 30-year Treasury bonds. Until then, the maximum is reduced by 1 percent per year from 110 percent, that is, the maximum is 109 percent in 1995, 108 percent in 1996, and so on. For the 1995 plan year, the mortality table used to determine current liability (to be prescribed by the Secretary of Treasury) will be based on the 1983 Group Annuity Mortality (GAM) Table.[9] The underlying logic of this requirement is that, in recent years, when pricing group annuities for terminating pension plans, life insurers typically use the 1983 GAM table.

The combined impact of these changes in the minimum funding rules probably would have increased substantially the required contributions of many plans, especially compared to the very low level of additional contributions induced by section 412(l) introduced in OBRA. Furthermore, the required changes in actuarial assumptions would have drawn in plans heretofore untouched by the special funding rules for underfunded plans.[10] Hence, Congress designed numerous permanent and transitional items in the RPA that exempt some plans from the strengthened funding rules and limit the immediate impact of the rules.

There are two permanent exemptions from the additional funding charge for underfunded plans. First, the charge will not apply for a plan year if the plan has a "funded current liability percentage" of 90 percent or greater. Second, the charge does not apply for a plan year if (1) the plan's funded current liability percentage is at least 80 percent, and (2) the plan had been 90 percent or better funded for any two consecutive years of the previous three plan years. For purposes of these thresholds, the funded current liability percentage is calculated using the highest allowable interest rate, and assets are *not* reduced by credit balances.

There are also two transition rules exempting plans in near years. The first rule is that a plan is exempt from the additional funding charge in the 1995 and 1996 plan years if the plan's funded current liability percentage is at least 80 percent and the plan meets one of three special tests in each of any two of the 1992, 1993, or 1994 plan years.[11] The second transition rule is that a plan is exempt from the additional funding charge in the 1996 and 1997 plan years if (1) the plan's funded current liability percentage is at least 80 percent, (2) the plan's funded percentage was at least 90 percent in 1995, and (3) the plan met one of the special tests in 1994.

The net effect of these permanent and transitional exemptions is probably to remove most plans with a funded percentage of at least 80 percent in the 1995 and 1996 plan years from the application of the strengthened additional funding charge. Some, but progressively fewer, 80 percent-funded plans will be exempted in the 1997 plan year and beyond.

For those plans not exempted from the additional funding charge, the charge is limited into the next century under various other transition rules. The RPA permits a plan to amortize over twelve years the increase in current liability in 1995 due to the mandated interest rate and mortality table (as compared to the relative interest rate and mortality table actually used in the 1993 plan year). This amortization is called the "additional unfunded old liability amount." Alternatively, the plan sponsor can make an irrevocable election to amortize over twelve years the entire unfunded post-1987 increase in current liability. If this alternative is chosen, however, the additional funding charge cannot be less than if the OBRA '87 version of the law remained in effect. This election may prove to be popular with many severely underfunded plans.

For plan years 1995 to 2001, the RPA limits the additional funding charge, at the option of the plan sponsor in any year, to the amount necessary to achieve certain funding ratio targets.[12] Under this optional rule, however, the additional funding charge must be at least that required under OBRA '87.

In its 1987 Annual Report, the PBGC stated the following: "Companies such as Allis-Chalmers Corporation terminated plans with large liabilities but virtually no assets, yet the companies had satisfied the existing minimum funding requirements" (PBGC, 1987:4). In response to these situations, the RPA added a solvency requirement to minimum funding as a third independent element. This requirement applies to non-multi-employer plans less than 100 percent funded for current liability, and requires these plans to maintain cash, marketable securities, or other liquid assets equal to three years' worth of disbursements, generally calculated based on payments made from the plan during the prior 12 months. If the necessary assets are not maintained in any quarter, either additional contributions must be made to achieve the necessary level or excise taxes are imposed and the plan is prohibited from making payments (such as lump-sum or annuity purchases) to participants in excess of the amount payable as a single life annuity.[13]

The PBGC justified the complexity of its initial legislative proposal by stating that it was carefully crafted to reach only problem areas. The final funding requirements passed as RPA became even more complex as a result of the political legislative process. The question remains, however, whether essentially the same goals and expected outcomes could have been accomplished in a much less complex manner. Complexity, of course, translates into large administrative burdens, particularly for small- and medium-size plans.

Financial Accounting Standards for Pension Obligations of Single-Employer Plan Sponsors

The link between the funding status of plans and financial accounting standards for pensions can never be as direct as the link of funding status with the minimum funding requirements for contributions. The former reflects accounting transactions, while the latter represents requirements for actual cash outlays. Moreover, initially financial standards were quite amorphous, and then were changed to match the range of actuarial funding practice eventually refined and reflected in the original version of ERISA. More recently, however, financial accounting standards for pensions have been standardized and may serve as an influence, independent of the funding requirements, on the funding decisions of plan sponsors. Unlike the evolution of funding requirements, where older conceptual elements coexist with newer ones, the history of accounting standards is more revolutionary, being characterized by the disappearance of past conceptual structures.

The financial statements of plan sponsors (including income statements, balance sheets, and accompanying notes) are examined intensively by financial analysts on behalf of investors and creditors for a view of the overall long-term profitability of the company as well as for any signs of financial weakness. Through their influence on the flow of investment funds to plan sponsors, it is likely that financial accounting standards also have an influence on the funding decisions of plan sponsors. In particular, these standards may provide a cynosure for financial analysts, in turn establishing a funding goal for the community of plan sponsors.

Accounting Standards Under ARB No. 47, APB No. 8, and FAS No. 36

Accounting Research Bulletin (ARB) No. 47 was issued in 1956 and called simply for pension costs to be spread over the current and future service of employees in a systematic and rational manner. It was discovered, however, that under ARB No. 47 there were wide ranges in amortization periods, and past and prior service costs were sometimes charged to retained earnings instead of current income.[14] Other problems included lower pension expense being recorded when profits were low, and instances of pay-as-you-go and terminal accounting.[15]

The accounting treatment of pension costs was stabilized somewhat when the Accounting Principles Board (APB) issued Opinion No. 8 in 1966; the opinion was operative until 1987. Annual charges of pension expense to current income were required regardless of actual funding practices. Despite a desire for standardization, however, APB No. 8 only specified minimum and maximum allowable pension cost accruals.[16] It allowed the charge to expense to be based on reasonable actuarial assumptions and any reasonable actuarial cost method (other than pay-as-you-go and terminal accounting) chosen by the plan sponsor. The methods eventually allowed by ERISA were allowed by APB No. 8.

Because the minimum and maximum charges, with few exceptions, bracketed the contributions allowed by ERISA, pension expense for accounting purposes usually equaled actual contributions to the plan. If, however, contributions to a plan during a given year were less than pension expense, the difference was a liability for accrued pension cost shown on the balance sheet. If contributions exceeded pension expense, an asset for prepaid pension cost was established. A required disclosure was the unfunded vested benefit.

In 1980, the Financial Accounting Standards Board (FASB) issued Statement No. 36 requiring additional disclosures by plan sponsors. In particular, Financial Accounting Statement (FAS) No. 36 required that the notes to the financial statement include listing the vested and non-vested accumulated plan benefit obligations (and the interest rate used to determine them) and net assets available for benefits. The accumulated benefit obligation is essentially the accrued liability calculated under the traditional unit credit method, that is, without salary projections. All plans of the employer could be aggregated. No other changes were made to APB No. 8 until an entirely different accounting approach was promulgated in 1985.

Accounting Standards Under FAS No. 87

Beginning in 1987 (earlier application was encouraged), new accounting standards for the recognition of pension expense and the disclosure of funding status by plan sponsors were required by the FASB. Statement No. 87 reduced considerably the discretion of plan sponsors in their accounting choices for pensions and, moreover, completely broke the link with federal funding requirements. As will be explained below, FAS

No. 87 reflects at least two views of the economic exchange between plan sponsors and employees: termination and on-going plan views. (See also DeBerg, Mittelstaedt, and Regier 1987.) FAS No. 87 does consistently reflect the principle, however, that amortizations should occur over the remaining service lifetimes of active plan participants, rather than arbitrary fixed periods.

Pension Expense

Under FAS No. 87, pension expense is generally not materially different from "net periodic pension cost." Such cost is the combination of the following six components: (1) service cost, (2) interest cost, (3) actual return on plan assets, (4) amortization of unrecognized prior service cost, (5) gain or loss to the extent recognized, and (6) amortization of unrecognized net transition obligation (asset). Certain components will be positive, and others usually negative; the sum will usually be positive. Each component will now be explained in turn.

Service cost is the normal cost calculated under the projected unit credit method for compensation-based plans and under the traditional unit credit method for flat-dollar plans. No other actuarial cost methods are allowed. Generally, therefore, the cost for the year for a compensation-based plan would be the actuarial present value of the participants' anticipated benefits attributed to that year of service. By using projected benefits, FAS No. 87 reflects the ongoing plan view, whereby it is assumed that the plan will continue in existence beyond the year, and, therefore, the plan sponsor's obligations will generally be greater than if the plan were to terminate in the current year.

The interest assumption used to calculate service cost (and pension benefit obligations) must reflect the rates at which the pension benefits could be effectively settled. These discount rates can be based on yields on high-quality bonds or those implicit in group annuity contracts. (In September 1993, the SEC stated that high-quality bonds are those receiving one of the two highest ratings given by a recognized rating agency.) This requirement reflects the termination view, whereby it is assumed that the plan can be terminated immediately and that the termination liability represents the sum total of the sponsor's obligation. All other actuarial assumptions must be individually reasonable and chosen on the premise that the plan will continue into the future.

Interest cost is the amount by which the projected benefit obligation (the accrued liability calculated under the projected unit credit method) is expected to grow during the year because of interest. The actual return on assets is investment income for the year, including realized and unrealized depreciation and appreciation of assets. The return component is subtracted from expense; if the return on assets has been positive for the year, pension expense is reduced.

Amortization of unrecognized prior service cost is the amortization of the unfunded initial accrued liability for a new plan and of the increase in accrued liability due to plan amendments, both adopted after the implementation of FAS No. 87. The amortization period is the expected future period of service of active plan participants.

Gain or loss to the extent recognized is a change in the amount of the projected benefit obligation or plan assets resulting from experience different from that expected or from changes in assumptions. It is negative if a gain, and positive if a loss. It includes two main subcomponents: the difference between the actual return on plan assets and the expected return on plan assets, and amortization of the unrecognized net gain or loss from previous periods. The expected return on plan assets is based on the expected long-term rate of return (potentially different from the discount rate) and the market-related (actuarial) value of plan assets. The first subcomponent essentially neutralizes which the volatility would have been induced by the second component of plan expense—the actual return on assets. Amortization of unrecognized net gain or loss (excluding asset gains and losses not yet reflected in market-related value) from previous periods occurs at a minimum rate of one divided by the average remaining service life of active participants.[17]

The sixth component of expense is the amortization of the excess of the projected benefit obligation over the market value of assets (at the date of adoption of FAS No. 87) plus previously recognized unfunded accrued pension cost or less previously recognized prepaid pension cost. The amortization period of the net obligation (loss) or the net asset (gain) is the average remaining service period of employees; if this period is less than fifteen years, the plan sponsor may choose fifteen years.

Recognition and Disclosure of Liabilities and Assets

Like APB No. 8, FAS No. 87 requires the recognition in the balance sheet of unfunded accrued pension cost or prepaid pension cost. If the accumulated benefit obligation exceeds the market value of assets, FAS No. 87 requires the recognition of a liability (including unfunded accrued pension cost) that at least equals the unfunded accumulated benefit obligation. This is called the "additional minimum liability."[18]

Required disclosures under FAS No. 87 include the amount of net periodic pension cost showing separately the service cost, interest cost, actual return on assets, and net total of the other components. Also FAS No. 87 requires separate disclosure for underfunded and overfunded plans (where funded status is defined on basis of the accumulated benefit obligation) of the market value of assets and the projected benefit obligations, also identifying the vested and non-vested accumulated benefit obligations.

A Comparison with Minimum Funding Requirements

The FASB engendered much controversy when it first proposed an accounting standard for pensions like FAS No. 87. Discretion was taken away from accountants and actuaries, and the link to the funding requirements was being broken; two entirely different actuarial valuations would now need be done. Although the funding requirements themselves were changed at the same time (and continue to change) to limit discretion, the new accounting standard has come to be viewed as a success and no changes are contemplated. Unlike the current funding requirements, which result from layer after layer of legislative and regulatory changes, the current financial accounting standard represents a fairly consistent logical construct. In addition, by standardizing the actuarial cost method, by limiting somewhat the choice of actuarial assumptions, and by tying most amortization periods to the expected remaining service life of active participants, the accounting standard has succeeded in making possible the reporting and comparative analysis of the funded status and expense of DB plans on a realistic economic basis. Indeed, as will be proposed at the end of this chapter, the accounting standard represents a good model for a reform of the minimum funding requirements.

Statistics on the Current Funded Status of Plans

Two primary sources of information on the funded status of defined benefit pension plans are the pension notes to the financial statements of sponsors of (single-employer) plans, as required to be reported under FAS No. 87, and the Schedule B (Actuarial Information) of the Form 5500 filed with the IRS and Department of Labor. Databases from these two sources, representing nearly all private large DB plans, were collected, edited, and analyzed for statistical evidence on funded status and analysis of the impact of the funding requirements. The results are presented below.

FAS No. 87 Database (1987–93)

The database came in a fairly uniform manner for corporate fiscal years 1987 through 1993 from Standard and Poor's Compustat Services and includes information about the general, financial, and pension characteristics of single-employer DB plan sponsors who filed annual financial statements with the SEC (generally those whose equity was traded on the national stock exchanges). The Compustat computer data files for the fiscal years 1987 through 1993 were searched for United States-domiciled companies reporting, under the framework of FAS No. 87, the sponsorship of one or more DB pension plans. Companies filing annual statements in 1992 and 1993, and companies currently bankrupt or merged but filing annual statements in prior years, were included in the search. Subsidiary companies, even if they filed their own annual statements, however, were excluded. Because FAS No. 87 requires separate reporting of underfunded and overfunded plans, but otherwise allows the combination of all plans sponsored by a corporation, information on funding status on a group basis for each plan sponsor is available from the FAS No. 87 database. In contrast, information on the funded status of individual single-employer plans, any multiemployer plans, or any plans sponsored by privately held companies is only available from the Schedule B databases.

As shown in Table 1, the number of corporate sponsors with underfunded plans rose over the period 1987 through 1993, the number of sponsors with overfunded plans declined, and the number of sponsors with defined benefit plans declined slightly. These results should be caveated, however, because it is likely that for the 1987 year, as defined by Compustat, some plan sponsors still had not adopted FAS No. 87. The large increase in the number of underfunded plans from 1992 to 1993

TABLE 1 Number of Corporate Sponsors of Defined Benefit Plans: All Funded Statuses, with Underfunded, and with Overfunded Plans

Year	All Funded Statuses	With Underfunded Plans	With Overfunded Plans
1993	1,781	755	1,416
1992	1,752	589	1,517
1991	1,814	603	1,602
1990	1,788	651	1,544
1989	1,848	599	1,627
1988	1,892	593	1,681
1987	1,767	531	1,573

Source: See text. Author's computations from Compustat data only include those United States-domiciled corporations reporting under FAS No. 87 the sponsorship of at least one defined benefit plan. All subsidiaries reporting separately are excluded. For 1987, some plan sponsors may still not have adopted FAS No. 87.
Note: In each year, the number of corporate sponsors with underfunded and overfunded plans combined exceeds the number of sponsors of plans with all funded statuses because some sponsors have both underfunded and overfunded plans.

TABLE 2 Ratio of Assets to Accumulated Benefit Obligation (Funded
Ratio of ABO) of DB Plans Sponsored by Corporations

Year	All Plans	Underfunded	Overfunded
Simple Averages			
1993	1.13	.73	1.34
1992	1.23	.71	1.43
1991	1.29	.71	1.51
1990	1.27	.72	1.50
1989	1.36	.68	1.61
1988	1.38	.70	1.62
1987	1.47	.71	1.73
Weighted Averages			
1993	1.13	.69	1.28
1992	1.22	.71	1.35
1991	1.28	.69	1.40
1990	1.26	.71	1.40
1989	1.40	.78	1.54
1988	1.37	.78	1.52
1987	1.39	.73	1.51

Source: See Table 1.

may be explained by the dramatic fall in market interest rates in 1993. An additional possible explanation may be the spotlight shown during 1993 by the SEC on corporate compliance with the requirement to compute benefit obligation with an FAS No. 87-mandated discount rate. Also there are plans hovering around funded ratios of 100 percent flipping between underfunded and overfunded status; this fact explains some of the year-to-year volatility in the statistics.

Table 2 shows the funded status of plans sponsored by these corporations, measured by the "funded ratio (ABO)," that is, the market value of plan assets divided by the accumulated benefit obligation (ABO). The ABO is closely related to the OBRA current liability, although different actuarial assumptions are sometimes used for each. Simple averages of funded ratios are shown in the upper panel of Table 2, while weighted averages are shown in the lower panel. By definition, the funded status of plans with larger ABOs are given more prominence in the lower panel.

The simple average of the funded ratio of all plans declined from 1.47 in 1987 to 1.13 in 1993. Among underfunded plans, the funded ratio remained quite steady over the period, at around .71, while among overfunded plans, the funded ratio declined significantly from 1.73 in 1987 to 1.34 in 1993.

The weighted averages of the funded ratio also showed declines, although at different levels and with different patterns. The weighted-average funded ratio for all plans declined from 1.39 in 1987 to 1.13 in 1993. Among underfunded plans, the funded ratio declined somewhat over the period, from .73 to .69; the ratio, however, rose to .78 in 1988 and 1989 before declining to .71 in 1990, following the general pattern of stock market returns experienced in those years.[19] Among over-funded plans, the funded ratio declined from 1.51 to 1.28. The differences between simple and weighted averages in level and pattern can be explained by larger plans generally having lower funded ratios and a higher proportion of assets in equities.

The period of examination here—1987 to 1993—coincides with the period just prior to and following the implementation of OBRA. As explained more fully above, the pension provisions of OBRA were intended to enhance the funding status of underfunded plans and to trim the funded status of overfunded plans to no more than 150 percent of current liability. Apparently, the law change was very successful in accomplishing the latter, while it failed in the former. (More evidence of the failure of OBRA to improve funding in underfunded plans is given below.) At the beginning of 1993, plan sponsors were limited to fund up to 150 percent of current liability, computed using an interest rate no lower than 7.27 percent at a time when all interest rates were declining rapidly and group annuity contracts were yielding around 6½ percent.[20]

The top panel of Table 3 shows the dollar amount of the unfunded liability (ABO less assets) reported for all underfunded plans. Over the period, the unfunded liability increased by US $44 billion, from US $16.6 billion in 1987 to US $60.4 billion in 1993. The increase is, in part, explained by a rapid deterioration in the funding status of the General Motors hourly plan indicated on GM's public financial statements (US $22.2 billion in unfunded liability in 1992). By mathematical identity, because the overall weighted-average funded ratio declined only somewhat, while the amount of unfunded liability more than tripled over the period, the aggregate ABO for underfunded plans must also have more than tripled. This is the case; the ABO for underfunded plans increased from US $61.8 billion in 1987 to US $193.7 billion in 1993.

The lower panel of Table 3 shows the unfunded accrued and prepaid pension cost for underfunded and overfunded plans, respectively. As explained above, an unfunded accrued pension cost is recognized in the financial statements of the plan sponsor if the net periodic pension cost (expense) exceeded amounts the employer had contributed to the plan since implementation of FAS No. 87. By 1992, sponsors of underfunded plans had contributed US $33 billion less than what generally accepted accounting principles deemed a reasonable rate of pension expense accrual. This can be mostly attributed to the fact that the Internal Revenue

TABLE 3 Corporate Defined Benefit Pension Obligations and Costs over Time

	Unfunded Accumulated Benefit Obligation of Corporations (US $ M)	
Year		Underfunded Plans
1993		$60,397.7
1992		39,615.3
1991		33,902.5
1990		32,997.0
1989		20,768.4
1988		20,205.2
1987		16,589.5

	Prepaid (Unfunded Accrued) Pension Cost of Corporations (US $ M)	
Year	With Underfunded Plans	With Overfunded Plans
1993	($28,269.1)	$42,747.1
1992	(33,276.2)	33,353.5
1991	(29,976.5)	27,859.7
1990	(26,648.9)	27,002.2
1989	(17,425.9)	17,591.8
1988	(11,902.3)	11,989.6
1987	(11,006.7)	6,226.1

Source: See Table 1.

Code allows a thirty-year amortization of the cost of amendments increasing benefits. In contrast, FAS No. 87 requires amortization over the future period of service of each active employee or over the average remaining service period of employees expected to receive benefits under the plan—generally less than 15 years for mature plans. It is also possible that some plan sponsors used a lower interest rate for FAS No. 87 than for funding purposes; a lower interest rate increases the relevant pension expense amounts. The decline in 1993 in the net aggregate unfunded accrued pension cost may be attributed to the sudden (and probably temporary) movement of many plans with prepaid pension cost into the underfunded plan category.

By 1993, sponsors of overfunded plans had contributed about US $43 billion more than they had recognized as pension expense in their financial statements. This is probably mostly explained by plans substantially overfunded in 1986 recognizing large credits owing to the amorti-

TABLE 4 Ratio of Assets to Projected Benefit Obligations
(Funded Ratio [PBO]) of DB Plans Sponsored by Corporations
(Weighted Averages)

| | Weighted Average | | |
Year	All Plans	Underfunded	Overfunded
1993	.99	.63	1.10
1992	1.05	.65	1.14
1991	1.09	.63	1.18
1990	1.06	.64	1.16
1989	1.18	.73	1.27
1988	1.14	.73	1.24
1987	1.16	.66	1.24

Source: See Table 1.

zation of the net transition obligation. It also may be due either to plan sponsors using Internal Revenue Code provisions allowing amortization of the cost of amendments increasing benefits as rapidly as over ten years, or to using higher interest rates or lower rates of future salary increases for FAS No. 87 than for funding purposes.

Table 4 shows the weighted-average funded ratio calculated using the projected benefit obligation (PBO) as the denominator. For final-pay and career-average plans, the PBO exceeds the ABO because the former concept includes a projection for the effect of future salary increases. The funded ratio (PBO) is therefore uniformly lower than the funded ratio (ABO). This, however, is less notable for underfunded plans, which are more likely to be flat benefit plans and therefore do not usually require salary projections under FAS No. 87. Overall, in 1993, plans had assets just below the projected benefit obligation.

Results from more recent financial statements were not available at the time of the writing of this chapter. Market conditions in 1994, however, indicate that the funded status of plans improved. As Bader and Ma (1995) calculate, the discount rate soared 130 basis points over 1994, and pension liabilities therefore would plummet. Even the poor investment returns of most pension funds generated large gains relative to their falling liabilities, strengthening their funded ratios. They estimate that the funded ratio of a typical plan rose by 9.1 percent during 1994.

Schedule B Data Base (1990)

Form 5500 series returns for all DB plans are required to be filed with an accompanying Schedule B under the mandate of ERISA. For better comparison with financial accounting data, however, only DB plans with more than 100 participants for the 1990 plan year were included in the analysis of this section of the chapter. There were about 19,400 such plans, of which 18,300 were single-employer and 1,100 were multiemployer plans. More than four-fifths of the plans were overfunded. This 1990 Schedule B database includes plans with over 39 million participants. Compared to earlier years, a higher portion of the participants in 1990 were non-active, a reflection of the continued aging of participants in the defined benefit plan system.

Statistics on funded ratios and unfunded liability from the database are shown in Table 5. The funded ratio and unfunded liability are calculated using the market value of plan assets and current liability, as reported on line six of the Schedule B. For all plans, the funded ratios in 1990 were 1.39 (simple average) and 1.35 (weighted average). For underfunded plans, the funded ratios (simple averages) were .77 for single-employer plans and .84 for multiemployer plans. For overfunded plans, the funded ratios were 1.56 for single-employer plans and 1.29 for multiemployer plans.[21] The unfunded liability (in aggregate) was US $30.3 billion.

One can compare the (beginning-of-plan-year) 1990 numbers on a (single-employer) plan basis from the Schedule B data base (Table 5) to the (end-of-fiscal-year) 1989 numbers on a sponsor basis from the FAS No. 87 data base (Tables 2 and 3). The funded ratios (weighted average) for underfunded and overfunded plans are approximately the same, and the unfunded ABO on a sponsor basis (US $20.8 billion) is not much lower than the unfunded liability on a plan basis (US $23 billion). It is unlikely that actuarial assumptions differ much between the two data sources. Any remaining differences can probably be explained by the

TABLE 5 Funded Ratios by Entity Type and Funded Status, 1990

| Plan Type | Funded Ratio | | Unfunded Liability (US $ M) |
	Simple Average (%)	Weighted Average (%)	
All plans	1.39	1.35	30,303
Single employer			
Underfunded	.77	.75	23,094
Overfunded	1.56	1.52	0
Multiemployer			
Underfunded	.84	.86	7,209
Overfundedd	1.29	1.23	0

Source: See text. 1990 Form 5500/Schedule B returns filed with the IRS of DB plans with more than 100 participants.

TABLE 6 Distribution of DB Plans by Actuarial Cost Method Number of Plans

	Plan Cost Method (# of plans)							
	A	B	C	D	E	F	G	Missing
All Plans	46	4379	6632	1665	4483	11	2097	99
Single Employer Underfunded	6	674	1746	120	746	2	282	21
Single Employer Overfunded	23	2902	4753	1512	3611	9	1806	67
Multiemployer Underfunded	8	167	52	6	35	0	5	5
Multiemployer Overfunded	9	636	81	27	91	0	4	6

Source: See Table 5.
Note: Key to actuarial cost methods: A = Attained age normal; B = Entry age normal; C = Accrued benefit (unit credit); D = Aggregate; E = Frozen initial liability; F = Individual level premium; G = Other.

fact that the Schedule B database represents more plans than the FAS 87 database.

The distribution of plans by actuarial cost method is shown in Table 6. The "other" actuarial cost method usually denotes the projected unit credit method. The three most popular cost methods are unit credit (traditional and projected), frozen initial liability, and entry age normal. Compared to earlier years, more plans are using unit credit methods (see Applebaum 1992). This may reflect a desire to match pension accounting expense more closely with contributions or may owe to the introduction of tighter funding limits. Underfunded plans are more likely to use unit credit and less likely to use the aggregate method than overfunded plans. Multiemployer plans, whether underfunded or overfunded, prefer the entry age normal method.

IRS Underfunding Study Sample (1990)

In 1993 and 1994, a random sample of 360 underfunded plans underwent comprehensive examinations for the 1990 plan year conducted by IRS Employee Plans revenue agents and field actuaries as part of an Underfunding Study by the Office of Assistant Commissioner for Employee Plans and Exempt Organizations of the IRS. Single-employer and multi-employer plans with at least 100 participants were included in the sample. As part of the study, the complete Schedule B for each of the 360 examined plans was carefully transcribed in the National Office; in the (universe) Schedule B database described above, transcription of only certain items was done by the IRS Service Centers. Some information on the study plans is presented here.

There were over 1.5 million participants in the examined plans, and over US $30 billion in asset holdings. The overall funded ratio (weighted average) was 80 percent and the unfunded liability was US $7.6 billion for these plans. The examined plans can be described as aging—there were only 1.3 active workers for every non-active participant—and expected benefit payments far exceeded the increase in liability owing to the accrual of new benefits. Although employers contributed US $1 billion to the plans, the aggregate credit balance declined by US $400 million over the 1990 plan year. The decline would have been greater but for significant actuarial gains. The additional funding charge (discussed in more detail below) made only a drop in the bucket—US $15 million more in charges to the funding standard account.

The distribution of funded ratios of underfunded plans examined for the study (not shown) is now described. More than one-third of the plans approach fully comfortable levels of funding, with funded ratios in excess of 90 percent. In contrast, about one-seventh of the plans were rather poorly funded (funded ratios below 60 percent), with a few plans containing almost no assets. Thirteen plans held assets (of any type) at a level less than three times expected annual benefit payments.

Plans in the study employed a panoply of mortality tables, with a tendency toward tables based on mortality experience of, or projected through, the 1960s and 1970s. The average assumed retirement age was 63.6, and many plans assumed 65. Most studies of retirement show that a majority of plan participants retire on or before the earliest age for receipt of Social Security benefits, 62. Hence, the mortality and retirement age assumptions for these examined plans can best be described as liberal. The assumed interest rates "for all other calculated values" (used in calculating normal cost and accrued liability), by contrast, tended to be conservative (averaging 8.2 percent), particularly when viewed in comparison to the experience of the 1980s and reasonable expectations in the 1990 plan year. In fact, a majority of the plans assumed an interest rate of 8 percent or less for all other calculated values.

The interest rate used in current liability calculations averaged 8.5 percent for the sample of plans examined for the study. The actual interest rates used by plans to calculate current liability were cross-tabbed against the highest interest rate allowed for a plan with its year beginning in a certain month. Because most plans use calendar years, the highest rate allowed for calculating current liability for the 1990 valuation for most plans was 9.42 percent. About 10 percent of the underfunded plans examined chose the highest allowable interest rate. Most plans, however, chose a rate lying somewhere between 8 and 9 percent—generally the rate identical to the one these plans assumed for calculations in the funding standard account.

TABLE 7 Extent and Characteristics of Underfunded Plans with Additional Funding Charges as Required Under OBRA

Number of Plans	Total	Plan Creation Date		Actuarial Cost Method		Funded Ratio (Current Liability)	
		After 1980	Before 1980	Aggre-gate	Other	≥90%	<90%
(1) With Actual Additional Funding Charge	111	41	70	5	106	29	82
(2) Indicated Potentially Subject to Additional Funding Charge	301	98	203	6	295	60	241
Percent [(1) ÷ (2)]	36.9%	41.8%	34.5%	83.3%	35.9%	48.3%	34%

Source: See text. IRS Underfunding Study for the 1990 plan year. 360 randomly selected underfunded single-employer and multiemployer plans with at least 100 participants were included in this sample.

The calculation of the additional funding charge is now analyzed in more detail. Of the 360 plans, 59 did not do the calculation. Most of these 59 plans are multiemployer plans—explicitly exempted by the Internal Revenue Code from the additional funding requirement in section 412(l)—but others incorrectly skipped the calculation. The calculated deficit reduction contribution was large—nearly US $1 billion—but the offsets reported were even larger. Hence, the additional funding charge was quite small. Further information about additional contributions is shown in Table 7. Just more than one-third of the plans made any additional contribution; plans with more recent creation dates, using the aggregate cost method and with higher funded ratios, were more likely to be required to have an additional funding charge.

Some Speculation About Future Trends in Funding

The first issues in evaluating the impact of the new minimum funding requirements on future trends in funding are identifying the class of plans potentially affected by the new rules and calculating the average funded ratio. In particular, which plans will be less than 90 percent funded in 1995 and beyond when their current liability is calculated with an interest rate at the top of the permissible corridor and the 1983 GAM mortality table? What will be their funded ratio?

For those plans with a plan year beginning in January 1995, the mandated value of the current liability interest rate is 109 percent of 7.27, that is, 7.93 percent. Only 10 percent of plans in the 1990 plan year were at the top of the interest rate corridor (9.42 percent). The average current liability interest rate was 8.5 percent at a time when corporate bonds were yielding about 9 percent. That is, the average rate used for current liability was about 50 basis points below the prevailing corporate bond yield. It is therefore likely that most plans will not have to move down much from the interest rates chosen from a corridor of 6.68 to 8.17 percent for their 1994 calculations of current liability, at a time when corporate bonds were yielding 7 percent, to meet the requirement of 7.93 percent for 1995, when bonds were yielding 8½ percent.

The requirement to use the 1983 GAM mortality table is probably more significant. A majority of underfunded plans in 1990 used the 1971 GAM or 1984 Unisex Pension tables, based on mortality experience of the 1970s. At 8 percent, an immediate annuity for a male age 62 is about 5 percent less if calculated using the 1984 Unisex Pension table rather than the 1983 GAM table. Hence, conversion to the required 1983 GAM table is likely to cause a general, but modest, increase in current liability and therefore a modest decline in funded ratios. The decline in funded ratios coming from both mandated changes in interest rates and mortality table, however, is unlikely to be more than 10 percent.

In summary, the plans potentially affected by RPA (those less than 90 percent funded with mandated actuarial assumptions) are generally the same plans that were subject to the OBRA minimum funding requirements (those less than 100 percent funded). Assuming that these are also the same plans indicated by the FAS No. 87 database as being underfunded in 1993 (see Table 2) and that the same assumptions were used for current liability and FAS No. 87 purposes, the average funded ratio in 1995 of plans to which the new rules will apply is probably around 65 percent.

The next issue in evaluating the impact of the new minimum funding rules is the effect of the strengthened rules relating to the additional funding charge. In the near term, it is difficult to predict the net impact because of the complexity of the various transition rules and the uncertainty of plan sponsor elections. In the long run, however, average funded ratios will inevitably rise above 80 percent owing to the faster amortizations of the amounts of underfunding outstanding or newly created for most plans with funded ratios below 90 percent. Whether the dollar amount of underfunding will be much reduced in the long run depends on whether the improvements in funded ratios occur faster than the increases in liability owing to periodic plan amendments.

There were only minor changes in RPA affecting the funding rules for overfunded plans. There is some evidence that the decline in funded ratios of these plans should soon stop and then level off, probably at around an average of 120 percent. According to the FAS No. 87 database, in 1987 over 56 percent of the companies with overfunded plans had funded ratios in excess of 150 percent. By 1993, however, the proportion of these "excess funded" plans had dropped to 21 percent. Because there are no incentives and some potential penalties to being excess funded and because, if they are able, plan sponsors will generally try to avoid having underfunded plans to avoid the higher PBGC premiums and the complex web of funding and other rules applying to under-funded plans under RPA, sponsors of overfunded plans probably have a target funded ratio of 120 or 125 percent.

A Funding Reform Proposal

A proposal to reform the minimum funding requirements and maxi-mum contribution limits is now outlined. Each element of the proposal will be described briefly, along with a short justification. The proposal applies only to single-employer plans because concerns about com-plexity and PBGC financial exposure are concentrated there.

Eliminate the Special Funding Rules for Underfunded Plans

The current rules applying to underfunded plans with more than 100 participants (additional funding charge and solvency requirement) are extremely complex and therefore administratively burdensome and costly, particularly for small and medium-size plans. In addition, extra volatility is introduced in required funding, as changes in asset values may move plans among various funded statuses, and therefore different funding requirement regimes, over short time periods. The solvency re-quirement, while applying to all underfunded plans, will actually cause very few plans to increase their funding. The current funding rules cre-ate the requirement to fund unfunded past service liabilities over short time periods, thereby increasing the cost of starting a DB plan. When the suspicion, lack of understanding of sometimes complex provisions, and general dislike of many workers (especially young mobile ones) is also factored into the new plan sponsor's decision calculus, it is no wonder that relatively few DB plans are created nowadays. Concerns about plans with endemic underfunding can be addressed more simply, as proposed below.

Eliminate the Current Liability Full Funding Limitation

As explained in the section on OBRA, this limitation introduces extra volatility to funding patterns and discriminates against plans with young workforces expecting large wage increases. The full funding limitation would be based on accrued liability, as under original ERISA. Concerns about excess funding and the loss of federal tax revenues can be addressed more simply, as proposed below.

Change (Generally Shorten) the Amortization Period for the Creation of New Plan Liabilities

As under FAS No. 87, the amortization period for the creation of new plan liabilities, either for past service for a newly created plan or owing to plan amendments increasing benefits, should be the expected future period of service of active plan participants. Thus, the amortization period will be long for young workforces and short for older workforces. In nearly all conceivable cases, however, it will be shorter than the currently allowed 30-year period. This change should reduce future underfunding, particularly among flat benefit plans that continually increase benefits to keep pace with wage inflation.

Restrict the Actuarial Cost Method to Be (Projected) Unit Credit

As under FAS No. 87, the only allowed cost methods should be the traditional unit credit method for flat benefit plans and the projected unit credit method for compensation-related benefit plans. This restriction will eliminate the technique of changing actuarial cost methods to influence the pattern of funding. Compared to other cost methods, use of the unit credit method generally reduces the level of funding in newly created plans and increases funding in older plans. In most instances, this restriction will also create economies in actuarial work, and perhaps eliminate the need for separate actuarial valuations for financial accounting and ERISA purposes. Any increase in accrued liability resulting from the mandated change in cost method should be amortized over no less than 15 years.

Amortize the Existing Unfunded Accrued Liability over 15 Years

Similar to some of the funding options available under RPA and the requirement of FAS No. 87 at the time of adoption of the new accounting standard, underfunding in existence at the time of adoption of the reform proposal should eventually be eliminated. A simple fifteen-year amortization period would not increase funding requirements for most underfunded plans too much.

Limit the Choice of Actuarial Assumptions

In order to control the outlay of federal tax revenues, as well to reduce underfunding, the ability to "game" the calculation of the accrued liability should be limited. In addition to the current restrictions on interest rate and mortality assumptions, legislative restrictions on the choice of other actuarial assumptions (particularly, the retirement age) should be imposed, or the ability of the IRS to police the choice of assumptions should be enhanced.

Conclusions

This chapter shows that the funded ratios of underfunded plans declined slightly and the amount of underfunding increased greatly over the 1987 to 1993 period, despite the intent of minimum funding requirements imposed by OBRA. The funded ratios of overfunded plans declined significantly over the same period, probably owing to the impact of a new full funding limitation. Changes in the minimum funding requirements in 1994 should cause an increase in funded ratios for underfunded plans over the long run. If the current regime of funding requirements can be simplified, this would contribute to an even greater reduction in underfunding.

Opinions expressed in this chapter are those of the author and not necessarily those of TIAA-CREF or of his former employer, the IRS. The author was senior economist with the Employee Plans Division of the IRS when he wrote the bulk of this chapter; he thanks the actuaries there, particularly Kathryn Marticello, for their comments and assistance. Lawrence Bader and Professor H. Fred Mittelstaedt also provided helpful comments.

Notes

1. In computing funding requirements and for certain reporting purposes, actuaries are allowed to use either the market value of assets or an "actuarial value" of assets. Actuarial asset valuation methods are used to smooth fluctuations in investment performance, by recognizing such fluctuations in a more gradual manner. The regulations originally required that allowable asset valuation methods must be applied on a consistent basis, take into account fair market value, and lie within a corridor of a minimum and a maximum of either market or average value. Guaranteed investment contracts issued by life insurance companies, however, are allowed to be carried at book value.

2. ERISA originally provided multiemployer plans longer amortization periods over which to amortize the initial unfunded liability and changes in liability

due to plan amendments (40 years) and experience gains and losses (20 years). The different amortization periods for multiemployer plans were removed by the Multiemployer Pension Plan Amendments Act of 1980 (MPPA), except for liabilities created before enactment of MPPA.

3. Prior to 1995, the IRS gave automatic approval to most changes in funding methods if done no more frequently than once every three years.

4. Yet another choice within some funding methods is whether normal cost is computed separately for each active employee and then summed together (individual basis) or calculated for the plan as a whole (aggregate basis). Although hardly utilized, ERISA also allows plans using the entry age normal cost method to elect to employ an alternative minimum funding standard. In particular, alternative funding standard account (ASA) charges are the sum of (1) normal cost (the lesser of those computed under the entry age normal or unit credit methods), (2) the excess, if any, of the present value of accrued benefits over the market value of assets, and (3) the excess, if any, of credits over charges to the ASA for all prior years. Also, for some collectively bargained plans, the shortfall method is allowed. This method allows contributions at a rate, expressed as cents per hour worked or dollars per units produced, *estimated* by an actuary as able to satisfy the minimum funding requirements.

5. The value of any "unpredictable contingent event benefits," such as plant closing benefits, however, are not included in current liability until the contingent event actually occurs.

6. For non-multiemployer plans, OBRA eliminated the minimum and maximum corridor for permitted actuarial value of assets around an average value of assets; only the corridor around market value remains.

7. Failure to make the required quarterly contribution results in an additional interest charge in the funding standard account on the unpaid amount and in excise taxes if still not paid 8-1/2 months after the end of the plan year. Liens are imposed when unpaid required installments exceed US $1,000,000 and are not made within specified time periods.

8. The waiver must now be based on *temporary* substantial business hardship, each member of the sponsor's controlled group must experience hardship, the PBGC must be consulted on large waivers and security may be required, and plan participants must be notified of the initial request.

9. This table will remain in effect at least until the 2000 plan year and until the Secretary of Treasury issues a new mortality table based on the actual experience of pension plans and projected trends. Plans are permitted to use special mortality tables for disabled participants. Certain large underfunded plans cannot change other actuarial assumptions, such as retirement age and turnover rates, to cause a substantial decrease in the current liability unless the new assumptions are approved by the Secretary of Treasury.

10. Moreover, for large non-multi-employer underfunded plans, the heretofore largely dormant requirement under Code Section 401(a)(29) to post security upon adoption of a plan amendment increasing the current liability may become more relevant as current liabilities are increased by the mandated change in interest rate and mortality table.

11. The transition tests are met (under the law then in effect) if (1) the plan did not have an additional funding charge (or would not have had such a charge if the plan had used the highest allowable interest rate and did not reduce assets by the credit balance), (2) the plan's full funding limit was zero, or (3) the addi-

tional funding charge did not exceed the lesser of 0.5 percent of current liability or US $5 million.

12. The target funding ratio is calculated by increasing the initial funding ratio (as of the beginning of the 1995 plan year) by a fixed number of percentage points each year. If the initial ratio is less than 75 percent, the target percentage is increased by three percentage points per year for plan years 1995 through 1999, four percentage points for 2000, and five percentage points for 2001. If the initial ratio is greater than 75 percent, the annual increments in the target percentage are somewhat smaller. The operation of this limit is independent of the limits tied to the permissible amortizations of old unfunded current liability described above.

13. Other changes directly relevant to funding made by the RPA include the repeal of the interest charge on quarterly contributions for plans funded in excess of current liability, an adjustment to the full funding limit to conform to the new minimum funding requirements, and relief from excise taxes on certain types of nondeductible contributions.

14. Past service cost is the unfunded initial accrued liability created when a new plan credits employees for service rendered before the initiation of the plan. Prior service cost is the addition to the accrued liability created when plan amendments increase benefits owing to service rendered prior to the effective dates of the amendments.

15. Terminal accounting refers to waiting until the participant is entitled to receive a benefit at retirement or termination before recognizing the expense.

16. The minimum charge to expense was the sum of (1) the normal cost, (2) interest on any unfunded past and prior service costs, and (3) for underfunded plans with a declining funding status, the lesser of (a) the amount of needed to bring about a 5 percent reduction in the unfunded vested benefit obligation or (b) the amount needed to amortize the unfunded past and prior service cost over 40 years. The maximum charge was the sum of (1) the normal cost, and (2) 10 percent amortization of any initial past service cost and any prior service cost arising from plan amendments (until fully amortized).

17. In the amortization, it is permitted to recognize only the gain or loss exceeding 10 percent of the greater of the projected benefit obligation or the market-related value of assets. In FAS No. 110, issued in 1992, the FASB revoked the former permission to value guaranteed investment contracts at contract value.

18. The additional liability generally may be offset in the balance sheet by an intangible asset rather than a reduction in equity.

19. One might challenge the explanation that the higher weighted-average funded ratios for underfunded plans in 1988 and 1989 were caused by financial market conditions by citing the decline in funded ratio in 1991 despite the strong stock market returns experienced that year. As will be noted below, however, the accumulation by 1991 of a very large unfunded liability by the General Motors hourly plan overwhelms the general pattern.

20. The decline in the funded ratio for overfunded plans in 1987 and 1988 can perhaps also be explained by continuing reversion activities.

21. Although employer securities and property are less helpful to benefit security than other assets, excluding employer securities and property from plan assets would change funded ratios very little in 1990 because, at US $4.2 billion, employer securities and property represent a small portion of total net assets.

References

Applebaum, Joseph. "Trends in Actuarial Assumptions, Cost Methods, and Funded Status of Defined Benefit Pension Plans." In John A. Turner and Daniel J. Beller, eds., *Trends in Pensions 1992*. U.S. Department of Labor, Pension and Welfare Benefits Administration, Washington, DC: USGPO, 1992.

Bader, Lawrence and Y. Y. Ma. "The Salomon Brothers Pension Discount Curve and the Salomon Brothers Pension Liability Index: 1995 Update." New York NY: Salomon Brothers, January 1995.

DeBerg, Curtis, H. Fred Mittelstaedt, and Philip Regier. "Employers' Accounting for Pensions: A Theoretical Approach to Financial Accounting Standards No. 87." *Journal of Accounting Education* 5 (1987): 227–42.

Pension Benefit Guaranty Corporation. *Annual Report to the Congress. Fiscal Year 1987*. Washington DC: USGPO, 1987.

Schieber, Sylvester and John Shoven. "The Consequences of Population Aging on Private Pension Fund Saving and Asset Markets." Cambridge, MA: NBER Working Paper No. 4665, March 1994.

Chapter 8
Corporate Governance and Pension Plans

Robert A. G. Monks

. . . the large funds are beginning to learn what Georg Siemens, founder of Deutsche Bank and inventor of the Hausbank system, said a hundred years ago when he was criticized for spending so much of his and the bank's time on a troubled client company: *If one can't sell, one must care.* (Drucker 1991: 318, emphasis added)

Institutional investors, especially pension funds, are the largest holders of equity securities. This chapter discusses what their role should be in the governance of the companies in which they invest. In the past, their involvement has been indirect, through the buying and selling of shares, but their very size now makes it almost impossible for them to beat the market—they *are* the market. More and more, they are "indexed," that is, invested in the market as a whole, rather than in a selected group of portfolio companies.

In light of evidence about the "value" of shareholder activism, this "permanent holder" status gives institutional investors additional opportunities as well as additional obligations as fiduciaries obligated to act "for the exclusive benefit" of the beneficial holders, which is best effected by evaluating ownership options with the same focus and risk-benefit analysis traditionally used in making buy-sell decisions. As a matter of law, ability, and policy, they cannot become involved in "ordinary business," but they can improve corporate value by encouraging governance structures that promote accountability and therefore responsiveness to the market and competitiveness. A number of possible models for shareholder involvement in governance are proposed.

Pension Fund Equity

Pension funds make up 48.1 percent of institutional capital in the United States and 29.6 percent of the total outstanding equity.[1] The pension system as a whole owns such a large percentage of the total equity capital of the country that "selling" its holdings is no longer a feasible method for dealing with underperforming companies. As of the end of the third quarter 1994, the pension systems aggregated US $4.6 trillion of assets, of which US $1.18 trillion were public funds, US $2.51 trillion were private trusteed funds, and the balance were managed as insurance assets; 43.8 percent of the assets of private plans and 48.7 percent of the assets of public ones were invested in equity.[2] Institutional investors owned 51.5 percent of the total outstanding equity and 55.8 percent of the equity of the 1,000 largest United States corporations at year end 1993. By mid-1994 the five largest institutional investors owned 11.2 percent of the largest 25 companies (Brancato 1993, 1995).

Defined Contribution and Defined Benefit Plans

There are two categories of pension plans with regard to benefits. The first, with a rapidly shrinking plurality (45.3 percent of assets) is the "defined benefit" plan. In these plans, the employer is committed to a specific payout, no matter what level of contribution is made by the employee and no matter what the performance of the investments. The employer, whether corporate or government, bears the risks; to an extent, the employer is guarantor of a specific defined benefit. In defined contribution plans (42.4 percent of assets), on the other hand, the employee bears all the risks. 40.1 percent and 32.1 percent of plan assets are invested in equities by defined benefit plans and defined contribution plans respectively.

In each type of pension plan there is an incentive to achieve superior investment results. The plan sponsor of a defined benefit plan, whether public or private, clearly wants to reduce its obligation to make additional payments into the pension scheme. Defined contribution beneficiaries are entitled to those funds comprising their plan assets, so the incentive to maximize values is personal and direct.

Obviously, everybody cannot achieve "superior" results. This has resulted in an increasing percentage of plan assets either advertently or de facto being invested in "index" funds that match the market's performance. Some have argued that the exercise of ownership rights, including voting proxies, becomes less important in an indexed fund because there is no commitment to hold the stock. If the company is managed badly, the stock will fall, and the index formula will require that it be sold—a self-activating variation on the Wall Street rule which says that investment managers should vote with management or sell the stock. Others have argued that, as a matter of economics, index fund managers cannot compete by taking an active interest in voting the shares. The costs of evaluating each proxy issue will outweigh the return to investors because index fund managers who do not vote will become free riders, benefiting at no cost to themselves from the work done by those who exercise the ownership rights. Those who do not incur the costs of exercising ownership rights will be more competitive by charging lower fees because they do not provide the additional service of active proxy review, although the returns are the same.

On the contrary, a fiduciary whose trading choices are self-activating must avail itself of every other mechanism, whether through the proxy system or a shareholders' derivative suit, to protect the assets it manages for others. In fact, index fund managers have a greater obligation to monitor and analyze proxy issues than managers of other funds. Indexed funds provide no discretion for asset managers with regard to trading. Index fund managers do not have the option of selling the stock if they do not agree with management's proposals; they must wait until it sinks far enough to fall off the index. Studies have shown that the adoption of devices that entrench management depresses share value. Therefore, to ensure the maximum return to shareholders, the asset fund managers acting as fiduciaries must vote against their adoption and for shareholder proposals to rescind them. Certainly a fiduciary cannot stand by and allow a firm in which it holds shares to siphon off corporate assets with no return in value to beneficiaries just because the mechanism used is the proxy vote rather than cash.

But, indexed or not, institutional shareholders can act against their interest when they are presented with options that benefit each of them marginally while harming the group as a whole significantly. They will accept the economic harm because, under the current proxy system, shareholders do not work together to maximize the return to all of them. It is thus clear that shareholders, by working together, can work to the benefit of all of them, and it is clear that failing to do so will work to the detriment of all of them.

Fiduciaries are obligated to act, actively and diligently, in the interests of those whose trust they hold. They are obligated to be on notice of others similarly situated and, by common action, lower their costs. As the institutions become larger, the free-rider problem diminishes. Furthermore, if this obligation is clearly understood, either through a regulatory or judicial interpretation of the fiduciary standards or through adoption of industry requirements by an organization like the Council of Institutional Investors, there will be no free-rider problem. Institutional investors, both indexed and managed, can work together to hold corporate management accountable to ensure that corporate management gives shareholders, the plan beneficiaries, the highest return.

Public and private plans have many similarities but certain important differences. For purposes of this paper, the one important difference lies in the tendency of plan sponsors to dominate administration of private plans, whereas public plans are more apt to function in a political mode.

The Role of the Government

The commitment of the state (or its subdivisions) to pay a "defined benefit" is in most cases guaranteed by the state constitution. Whether or not there are adequate funds in the pension trusts, the state is obligated to make the promised payments. Funding of pension systems is essentially a matter of intergenerational fairness, and public defined benefit plans are designed with the intention (though not always the reality) that the generation that receives the benefit of services pays the taxes to provide the pensions related to those services. Therefore, decisions about the appropriate investment policy for pension assets are essentially political because in the final analysis the electorate should decide on the levels of risk and reward thought appropriate for one time period or another.

The commitment of corporations to pay defined benefits is ultimately guaranteed by the federal Pension Benefit Guarantee Corporation (PBGC). But, in the first instance, it is promised and collateralized by the assets of the "plan sponsor" employer corporation. A medley of considerations underlies the investment policy of private companies. They can pursue high risk policies (in the manner of the airlines and steel companies in the 1980s) knowing that the PBGC will ultimately "bail out" the beneficiaries, or they can pursue the "conservative" path of assuring that their actuarial returns are achieved and the corporation has the highest assurance that it will not have to divert more than the planned payments into the system. Lawyers and courts can and will argue which alternative more closely achieves the statutory mandate that all trust assets be managed "for the exclusive benefit" of plan participants.

Investment Horizons

In general, plan sponsors, both public and private, benefit from maximum long-term growth in pension assets. Plan participants benefit to the extent that funding of their benefits requires decreased commitments from employers or taxpayers.

A common stock-based investment policy for pension funds raises two separate problems. First, there are drawbacks to public ownership of private enterprise. Pension fund holdings of common stock are viewed as "back door socialism." This is especially problematic when it leads to politically based initiatives from public pension funds that are unrelated to (or even contradictory to) economic returns. Some examples have included South Africa divestment and bailing out insolvent city governments. Second, active management—market timing, industry choice, stock selection—has not been able, over time, to produce consistently better results than those of the market itself (Ellis 1989; Nesbitt 1992, 1994). The level and profitability of fees to managers, consultants, trustees, custodians, and all manner of service providers to the pension industry is so high that it eliminates any advantage of active management and creates conflicts of interest that make it virtually impossible to receive unbiased advice about investment alternatives. The "indexation" of equity holdings is therefore as a policy and an investment matter compelling for public plans[3] and competitive for private ones.

Public funds are entirely funded by taxpayers, and private plans, significantly subsidized through tax incentives, are thus funded by the taxpayers as well. Because it is the taxpayer who is at risk, it is not only appropriate but essential for government to assure that the funds are administered consistent with the public interest. This particularly includes the responsibilities of pension fund trustees as owners of portfolio companies.

Pension Plan Fiduciaries in the United States

Public plans are administered subject to the laws of the sponsoring state. Private plans are regulated by the Pension and Welfare Benefit Administration (PWBA) of the United States Department of Labor (DOL) under the Employee Retirement Income Security Act of 1974 (ERISA).

Trustees of public plans are either appointed by a designated political official or they are elected by a particular constituency of plan participants; trustees of private plans under ERISA are appointed by the plan sponsor. In both cases, pension funds are administered by trustees who are subject to the highest standard of care developed by our legal system, the fiduciary standard. The fiduciaries of public and private pension plans have an unenviable role. By law and tradition they cannot personally benefit from favorable consequences through incentive payments and bonuses (with some exceptions), but they can be held liable for unfavorable ones by being fired (if they are in-house), losing the account (if they are outside), and even being prosecuted if there is an allegation that fiduciary duty has been violated.

ERISA requires fiduciaries to consider only the interests of plan participants in their decisionmaking—not their interest as employees or members of the community. But this provision has not been administratively enforced or judicially defined with sufficient conviction to mitigate the crippling conflict-of-interest problem that hobbles trustee behavior. Fiduciaries under ERISA are subject to strong industry pressures in the performance of their duties, and it is clear to individual and institutional trustees that their continued employment is at the discretion of the plan sponsor. To the extent that they exercise their discretion in a manner perceived as inimical by plan sponsors, they can be sure of not being reappointed and of being "blacklisted" for new business by other employers.

The trustees of public plans do not need to fear commercial reprisal, but they are subject to political pressures (Romano 1993, 1994). Although on occasion public plans such as Public Employees Retirement System of California (CalPERS) have been willing to oppose the managements of local corporations, including Occidental Petroleum and Lockheed, this is a very rare exception.

While the pension system as a whole "owns" almost one-third of the total equity in the United States, no individual plan has sufficiently large holdings to make it economically rational to find and pursue opportunities to increase the value of portfolio companies through the use of such shareholder activism initiatives as shareholder proposals, withholding votes for director candidates, or proxy contests (all with significant attendant costs of soliciting support). For example, TIAA-CREF and CalPERS, the largest pension systems, each hold approximately 1 percent of the total market equity. For either of them to take the lead as shareholder activists means that their beneficiaries bear all the costs of failure and stand only to be rewarded with 1 percent of the gains. This "collective action" or "free-rider" problem challenges the question of trustee prudence. It certainly presents an unattractive alternative to the individual fiduciary who personally cannot benefit from the fruits of his or her decision, but can be adversely affected if such a decision is unsuccessful as an investment or as a political matter.

United States employee benefit plans have almost no system for informing and being instructed by plan participants. ESOP plans often provide that the trustees will administer "ownership rights (tendering, voting)" in accordance with the instruction of beneficiaries, but there are a number of issues that make that process complicated. In one case, for example, "Bank of America was supposed to administer the plan according to the sole interests of the [Carter Hawley Hale] stockholder-employees. But it was simultaneously in the active, highly paid service of CHH management with a life or death interest in seeing that the shares of the plan were voted against the tender offer" (Drucker 1976:92). Given the perverse incentives for pension beneficiaries to refrain from becoming actively involved in monitoring corporate management, no matter how great the failure, enormous conflicts of interest create an all but insurmountable obstacle.

An Ownership-Based Economy

"Ownership" of the commercial sector of the economy by the approximately 100 million Americans having beneficial interest in the various public and private employee benefit systems provides a stable and "legitimizing" base for the power exercised by the leaders of the vast business aggregations. As Peter Drucker said, "Pension Fund Socialism should make it possible for management to regain legitimacy precisely because it re-establishes a genuine, socially anchored ownership" (Drucker 1976:92).

The pension system represents a financial foundation for public corporations that is both widespread and long term. Furthermore, pension fund "owners" have interests exactly congruent with those of the overall society; they are the overall society. Drucker notes that "The shift to the pension fund as a radically new kind of 'owner' is a truly profound change in social and economic power and structure . . . the shift is far too great a challenge—equally great as a threat and an opportunity—to wait for accident or insurgence. How the United States responds will largely decide whether it faces rapid decline as both an economy and a society" (Drucker 1991).

The Pension System as "Owner"

The owners of large, publicly held corporations cannot make "ordinary business" decisions. They have no right to do so, and they have no expertise in these areas. Even if they did have the right and the ability to become involved, they would have conflicts of interest with almost any company, as they invariably hold at least some of its competitors, its customers, and its suppliers. Shareholders elect the board, which in turn hires management to perform these functions. Likewise, owners should not interfere with those questions appropriate for boards of directors. If board questions are not being appropriately addressed, the remedy is through replacement of the board.

The fact that the role of shareholders is limited does not mean it is unimportant. Owners should organize themselves to have the expertise necessary to evaluate portfolio companies and to determine the appropriate level and form of their involvement. Many, indeed most, of the holdings of pension funds may be perceived as performing so well that the only involvement required by shareholders is thoughtful voting of the proxy. When owners determine that change is necessary, owners are obligated to commit the resources to be informed, to deal directly with management (in the very rare cases where discussions are not availing) to determine what kinds of individuals are needed for the board, and to nominate and elect these new board members. This means, of course, that they must also commit the resources to be able to determine when their involvement is appropriate or, in other words, "a good investment."

There will be situations where the "emergency" intervention of owners is necessary. These will occur when monitoring is inadequate, but even with the best system of prevention circumstances will inevitably arise requiring immediate and direct attention. One such example was the direct involvement of the "blue chip" shareholder of American Express to force out Jim Robinson as chairman in 1992 after the board of directors had approved a succession scheme confirming him in that role.

During the past decade, owners have begun to create a structure of cooperation with other owners. This is of particular importance as a way of mitigating the classic "prisoner's dilemma" collective choice problem, whereby otherwise appropriate shareholder initiatives are not pursued because, while doing so would benefit all shareholders, only one or a small group have to pay all the costs. The Council of Institutional Investors has been very effective in providing a way for large institutional shareholders to share information and resources and develop responses to issues like stock option accounting and legislative and regulatory proposals, but its ability to underwrite and organize company-specific initiatives is limited. One useful model for these efforts is used in the development and operation of huge energy projects and venture capital investment, where the parties will act as "managing partners." Over time, this permits a "fair" sharing of the "ownership" burden, all the while assuring that a motivated and highly competent management is actually doing what needs to be done.

Based on this model, I submitted a shareholder resolution (Appendix 1) at the Exxon Annual Meeting of 1993 calling for the creation of a shareholder advisory committee comprised of the holders of large blocks of stock. Because it provided that the company would pay the modest expenses of the committee's meetings (including the costs of the requisite information), this approach was designed to provide a way for shareholder involvement without unfair allocation of the expenses of "ownership responsibilities." The proposal received a small but significant vote (8 percent), and has since been submitted by other shareholders at other companies. While some companies have voluntarily agreed to the formation of some kind of shareholder committee, none has been created yet as the result of a shareholder proposal.

The problems of "commercial reprisal" for private fund trustees and "political reprisal" for public fiduciaries can only be solved through a government commitment that pension fund responsibilities transcend all other considerations despite the strong temptation to use pension money to solve other economic and financial problems. Without effective and evenhanded enforcement, however, this message will not be received. A vigorous and visible enforcement effort will remove the burden from those many trustees who want to carry out their statutory responsibility but are inhibited by competitive commercial realities. To the extent that government "draws a line in the sand" and puts all on notice of the priority of fiduciary obligations to beneficiaries, pension fund trustees can begin the process of becoming effective owners.

Value Added Through Shareholder Activism

Similarly, options for shareholder activism —vigilant exercise of ownership rights, ranging from careful evaluation of proxy issues to submission of shareholder resolutions and solicitation of support from other shareholders, to a proxy contest for one or more board seats— should be evaluated by fiduciaries and law enforcers on strictly economic grounds. Empirical data are beginning to be evaluated by consultants and academics. For example, Wilshire Associates and the Gordon Group are consultants who are retained by clients who are themselves "activist investors." It is, therefore, neither surprising nor convincing that both should assure CalPERS that its activist commitments have been beneficial to plan participants. Academic studies like one by Sunil Wahal are more equivocal, recognizing that there have in fact been relatively few examples of shareholder activism and that no orthodoxy has emerged as to an appropriate way of measuring its impact. A recent and extensive survey by Wahal (1994) of activism by nine public pension plans over a seven-year period (1987 to 1993) concludes:

Targeting announcements are associated with a small but significant wealth effect for a subset of firms. However, there is no evidence of improvement in the long-term stock price performance of targeted firms. In fact, performance continues to decline even three years after targeting. Moreover, in contrast to other institutions, pension funds do not appear to significantly reduce their holdings in underperforming firms in general, or in firms that they target. Collectively, the results cast doubt on the effectiveness of public pension fund activism as a substitute for an active market for corporate control. (Wahal 1994)

Another study by Gillan and Starks (1995) reaches a similar conclusion:

We examine whether institutional investor activism by public pension funds is effective in achieving its stated goal of increasing shareholder value. An investigation of the short-term stock market performance indicates that, during certain periods, there are significantly positive abnormal returns surrounding the targeting of firms for governance reform. In contrast, in any analysis of long-term stock market performance we do not find evidence of statistically significant positive returns. This leads us to question the overall effectiveness of this form of shareholder activism. (Gillan and Starks 1995:2)

Activism by Public and Private Pension Funds

These studies are particularly useful in making clear what is reasonable and what is unreasonable to expect from public pension funds. Public pension funds are governed by trustees who are either elected directly or appointed by elected officials. They are therefore sensitive to politics. They will be most involved in "fairness" issues and will be limited by concerns about "overreaching" by government as well as more particular concerns about their involvement with companies that have local connections. Public pension funds, therefore, are well situated to raise "fairness" issues, like management entrenchment, excessive compensation, and other areas of corporate governance. Beyond this, they are limited. They are led most often by people with backgrounds in government, not in business. Their own compensation does not increase as a result of initiatives that enhance shareholder value. Their political sensitivity can lead to initiatives designed more for political gain than for investment returns. Only continuing pressure will create change in targeted companies, and the adverse risk/return ratio for public trustees' activism makes such constancy improbable. Public funds have been and will continue to be invaluable leaders on a limited range of issues and allies for activism initiated and maintained by others on a broader range.

Another way of understanding "reasonable expectations" for public pension plan activism is to consider how much they spend and what they purchase. By and large, the entire expenditure of public plans consists of two items: the time and expense of key personnel, and items that can be purchased with "soft dollars."[4] Great discretion is needed in the use of soft dollars because of the omnipresent fear that the state legislature will decide to exercise control over these public funds. The highly publicized initiatives of CalPERS frequently amounted to the time and travel expense of CEO Dale Hanson, General Counsel Rich Koppes, and some home office back-up plus a variety of consulting services, limited to those that happened to be eligible for soft-dollar payment. For political and budgetary reasons, no money was ever spent for outside proxy solicitors, advertisement, or the panoply of professionals needed for a full-scale shareholder effort, and victory was declared on the basis of small steps forward. For example, CalPERS issued widely publicized corporate governance "report cards" for the 200 or so largest companies in 1994 and 1994. The grades were based on the responses to their requests for the boards to consider and react to the corporate governance guidelines issued by General Motors. The grading system was very process oriented. Anyone who did not respond got an F; any company that did respond fully to the letter from CalPERS, noting that their board had reviewed the GM guidelines and discussed them, got an A. One company, whose response was signed by every director, got an A+. The grades were not in any way based on the substance of the companies' governance provisions, only their willingness to raise the issues and inform the shareholders that they had done so.

As for the private pension funds, it is pertinent to consider Peter Drucker's prescient warnings of two decades ago:

> The new institutions that we have created—the pension funds and their "assets managers," who administer and invest the pension moneys—must have adequate management and be legitimate. Further, they must represent the beneficiaries and bear a clear-cut relationship to them. The pension funds have to be autonomous institutions. . . . By and large, however, the corporate pension funds have not yet even begun to organize themselves for either accountability or legitimacy. These new institutions must be free from any suspicion of conflict of interest. They must be set up to serve their beneficiaries and no one else. . . . What matters is that being both commercial banker and pension fund manager puts the bank into an inherent conflict of interest. . . . Pension funds are much too important to be run as a side line, which is all they can or should be in a commercial bank. Pension fund management requires and deserves an independent institution. (1976:85–87)

Twenty years later we are no closer to beginning to answer the question. As a result there is no shareholder activism emanating from the private pension fund system.

"Relationship Investing"

In a sense, all investing is "relationship investing," but the term is most often used to describe the involvement of a significant shareholder. One form, epitomized by the great investor Warren Buffett, has demonstrated massive positive returns from appropriate shareholder involvement in the governance of the companies in which he invests. In several cases, he or one of his colleagues joined the boards of directors. In the case of Salomon Brothers, he stepped in to take over the day-to-day operations of the firm to save it from going under entirely.

A different form is exemplified by our own LENS fund. Before LENS began, the companies in which we had become active consistently underperformed the market averages. Following our initiatives, LENS, investing in very large companies—Sears, American Express, Westinghouse, Eastman Kodak, Scott Paper, Stone & Webster, and Borden— achieved annual total returns approximating 23 percent over a period when the S&P index has done only half as well. The characteristics that LENS marshals in aid of profit are our own money, our business backgrounds (which make it possible for us to select portfolio companies that can be changed and develop the recommendations for change), our commitment, and our unwillingness to be distracted. And yet we could not achieve these results without the support of many of the public funds and private money managers. We had an explicit working arrangement with CalPERS in 1989 in successfully opposing Honeywell's effort to amend its charter to provide for staggered directors' elections; CalPERS and several other prominent institutions publicly supported our initiative with Sears Roebuck. In other cases, we were able to obtain a broad base of support by communicating our concerns to the shareholder community. Companies with confidential voting[5] give us the opportunity, at affordable cost, to secure up to 45 percent of the total vote for shareholder resolutions. This has given us credibility and leverage with both the shareholder and management communities.

A number of developments have made it easier to obtain support for shareholder initiatives. For example, in 1992 the SEC amended the rules governing shareholder communications. Until that time any communication to more than 10 other shareholders had to be reviewed, edited, and approved by the SEC before it could be circulated. The revisions to these rules sharply decreased the costs (and the risks) of activism. The increase in the adoption of confidential voting, most often at the urging of shareholders, has limited the real and perceived problems of commercial and political reprisal.

Pension Plan Impact on International Corporate Governance

Pension plans in the United Kingdom, the Netherlands, Canada, and Japan as well as the United States are becoming massive investors in the equity securities of companies outside their borders. The liberalization of investment restrictions all over the world has conferred economic and political power on those countries having liquid investable funds.

Countries such as France without a funded pension system have be-latedly recognized their disadvantage. Carolyn Brancato estimates that United States institutional investors increased their foreign equity hold-ings to a total of US $236 billion in 1993, of which the largest pension funds (those with assets over US $1 billion) are the major holders, con-trolling 88.8 percent of all institutional holdings of foreign stocks (Bran-cato 1993).

In many instances, institutional investors are a more vigorous force for change of the governance of corporations domiciled elsewhere. This was dramatically the case with Harris Associates of Chicago taking the lead late in 1994 in ousting Maurice Saatchi. CalPERS has been prominent in Germany, and Fidelity in the United Kingdom. Apparently the fear of commercial reprisal is less severe outside one's home base. This institu-tional pressure may predictably have a leveling effect on the governance structures of large companies irrespective of the country of their domi-cile. Capital costs may be lower in markets where governance standards are highest and information is most transparent. Thus, Daimler Benz reworked its financial statements and changed its governance provisions so as to be able to list its common shares on the New York Stock Ex-change. Pension funds, wherever situated, have much in common with other pension funds. As the quintessential long-term investors, they can be a worldwide force for governance reform.

Following the repudiation of socialism, the major industrialized coun-tries are struggling to articulate policies to guide their economic systems. The trend to privatization of formerly government-run or -sponsored en-tities in the United Kingdom, France, and Italy indicates a move from the traditional centralized "finance capitalism" and toward a more decen-tralized model. The worldwide pensions systems—public and private—with trustees appointed and elected by different constituencies provide the raw material with which a new diversified structure can be created.

Shareholder activism fits well with a variety of possible successful gov-ernance systems. It both can become an indispensable part of a system like that in the United States, which relies on extensive transparency of financial data and hostile takeovers as a final—if drastic—market re-sponse to poor management and can also play an important role in other countries, such as Japan or Germany, where the law, tradition, and cul-ture are very different.

An Action Program for Pension Plans

[The pension funds] are not owners because they want to be owners but be-cause they have no choice. They cannot sell. They also cannot become owner-managers. But they are owners nonetheless. As such, they have more than mere power. They have the responsibility to ensure performance and results in America's largest and most important companies. (Drucker 1991)

Much of the financial history of the 1980s could be written as the rapid but unacknowledged (even by themselves) acquisition of power by pension plans. Because the pension plans did not at first understand the power conferred by their vast ownership, a vacuum was created that was filled by "takeover entrepreneurs." If the pension plans fail to use their power responsibly in the future, a conferral of power on to others will again result. As the volatility of the takeover era showed, this is a significant risk. Pension funds, not only by virtue of their size but also by virtue of their long-term perspective and their fiduciary obligation to a broad section of society (as proxy for the 100 million participants in retirement schemes), are better suited for this role than many, including arbitrageurs, takeover entrepreneurs, and the government.

Only if the pension funds recognize their power and organize to become effective, however, can this work. CalPERS has been a leader since the early days, from establishing the Council of Institutional Investors, to both company-specific and broad-based initiatives, to the lengthy effort to reform the proxy rules. As noted above, the amendment of the proxy rules in 1992 was an enormous step forward, making communication among shareholders much easier. Significant obstacles remain, however. As Fisch (1993) noted, "The extent to which the federal proxy rules frustrate shareholder democracy has been chronicled extensively elsewhere. Many of these issues were brought to the attention of the SEC by the CalPERS letter, but the SEC chose not to address them. In spite of its continued re-examination of the regulatory system and its never-ending series of amendments, the SEC continues to limit shareholder participation in corporate governance both through sins of commission and omission in connection with its proxy rule. Accordingly, the rules remain an unauthorized and misbegotten regulatory endeavor." A beginning agenda of what remains to be done in other federally regulated areas was set forth by Conard (1988:1198–99). The Council of Institutional Investors has been very effective in pressing for pension plan legislative and administrative reforms.

One of the most pressing is prompt and unequivocal definition of the "exclusive purpose" rule of ERISA (and comparable rules applicable to public pension funds under the laws of most states). The language itself is clear: the pension plan must be administered "solely . . . and for the exclusive benefit of the plan participants." What is unclear is what that means in real-life application. The Department of Labor has been firm in stating that it does not mean the plans should be administered for the employees' benefit as employees or as members of the community, but for their benefit as pension plan beneficiaries. The only goal is the long-term health and growth of the pension assets.

Among the inevitable compromises in drafting and administering ER-ISA was the creation of what has been called "the fundamental contradiction of ERISA" (Fischel and Langbein 1988). Plan sponsors were given the right to appoint and control plan trustees. Despite the fact that the legislative history makes it clear that the statute is intended to incorporate the strictest fiduciary standards of the common law, and then add additional strictures to them, from the outset, the position of trustee has been equivocal. Nominally an independent fiduciary, in practice trustees serve the person from whom they are supposed to be independent. We have earlier considered Peter Drucker's twenty-year-old perspective that pension fund management is too important to be a secondary activity of a financial institution. Drucker notes, "But setting up pension fund management as an autonomous institution would only be the first step. It is equally important that pension funds be organized for legitimacy and accountability" (1976:88).

There is no need for the pension funds to wait for governmental action. The pension fund industry generates sufficient fee revenue to support an industry of special-purpose money managers. Pension fund trustees can make a difference by simply insisting on retaining money managers that limit themselves to pension funds as clients. Existing fiduciary banks can rationally elect either to continue their multifaceted relationships or to limit themselves to serving as employee benefit plan fiduciaries—there is a large enough market under either alternative to support their operations. Further, there would be opportunity for new "special purpose" pension-fund-only trust institutions.

Who will start this effort? Once again, the public plans are most likely to lead the way, as they do not run the risk of commercial reprisal in redirecting business. When the public plans have enabled the building of a "pension fiduciary industry" the private plans will find themselves at a competitive disadvantage and may be forced to follow suit. Beneficiary pressures may abet the development of an independent fiduciary system.

Further steps along the lines prescribed by PWBA chief Olena Berg in July 1994 may be necessary. As the Department of Labor notes, it "believes that active monitoring and communication with corporate management is consistent with a fiduciary's obligations under ERISA where the responsible fiduciary concludes that there is a reasonable expectation that such activities by the plan alone, or together with other shareholders, are likely to enhance the value of the plan's investment, after taking into account the costs involved" (USDOL 1994). While PWBA here plainly authorizes the expenditure of funds on appropriate shareholder initiatives, there will need to be precedent, publicity and, ultimately, judicial authority before risk-averse trustees become comfortable risking their beneficiaries' money. In the public plan arena, the problem is politics; state legislatures will not like their pension systems incurring all manner of expenses that have not been legitimated through the appropriations processes. Moreover, the targets of these initiatives are sure to have substantial political clout.

Large fiduciaries are bureaucratic institutions with the same inherent weaknesses as large companies. How can we protect ourselves against simply substituting one bureaucracy for another, increasing costs, and having little or even negative impact on efficiency? Fiduciaries have experience in engaging the services of professional advisors on a competitive basis. To the extent that shareholder activism becomes perceived as simply another potentially value-adding service, providers can be competitively selected and evaluated. The marketplace will be the ultimate judge.

Conclusion

The ancient Greeks believed that, in order for democracy to succeed, citizens had to devote their full time to participation. We now have a shareholder—the pension fund manager—who does devote full time to ownership, the shareholder's equivalent of citizenship. Size makes possible, and fiduciary obligation makes enforceable, the exercise of this citizenship on behalf of those real citizens, the pension beneficiaries. They are the citizens whose interest in the future makes them ideal stewards of America's corporations.

Appendix 1: Letter to Exxon Shareholders

April 3, 1992
Dear Exxon Shareholder:
    You have by now received Exxon's proxy statement for the 1992 annual meeting. I wish to call to your attention a shareholder proposal I am making for the establishment of a committee of shareholder representatives. This is the sixth item of business at the meeting and appears at pages 16 to 17 of the proxy statement.
    Let me explain what this proposal is all about. I believe a company does better for its shareholders if shareholders get actively involved in seeing that the company is managed well. Companies are managed by their boards of directors, so that positive shareholder involvement means intelligently evaluating what the directors do and interacting constructively with the board. This calls for an active, informed shareholder representative.
    In the case of large publicly held companies like Exxon, there usually is not a large shareholder who can fill this role. The largest shareholders of most large

United States companies are institutional investors—mutual funds, insurance companies, public or private employee benefit plans—that hold significant equity stakes in many hundreds of companies. These institutions don't have the resources to play an active, informed shareholder role in their various portfolio companies.

My proposal would establish a three-person committee to take on the role of active, informed shareholder representatives. The three persons would be selected by shareholders, and the cost would be borne by the company—hence proportionately by all shareholders.

How would this work? At each annual meeting shareholders would elect three persons to be members of the committee. Candidates would be nominated by shareholders. Large long-term shareholders, *i.e.*, shareholders (or groups of shareholders) who beneficially own, and have owned continuously for three years, at least US $10 million in market value of common stock, would have the right to have their nominees included in the company's proxy statement. (Other shareholders could nominate candidates, but I would expect those candidates that are included in the company's proxy statement would have the best chance of being elected.)

Committee members would be paid by the company in an amount equal to half the average amount a nonemployed Exxon director is paid and would be entitled to a reimbursement of expenses and the same indemnification rights as an Exxon director.* I believe this is necessary in order to attract capable and responsible individuals as committee members.

Sometimes the active, informed shareholder role requires expert assistance— for example, investment banking advice on whether shareholder interests would be served by some type of recapitalization or reorganization. No one shareholder can be expected to spend its own money exploring such issues in depth. The committee would be authorized to engage such expert assistance at the company's expense. I would not expect such expenses normally to be significant in amount. In any event, such expenses in any year would be limited to 1 cent per share outstanding (approximately US $12.4 million).

The committee's functions would be (1) to review the management of the business and affairs of the company by the board of directors, (2) to advise the board of its views and the views of shareholders which are expressed to the committee, and (3) to report to shareholders (in a report of not more than 2,500 words in the company's proxy statement) its evaluation of the management of the company by the directors and its recommendations on any matters proposed for action by shareholders. I would expect the committee to fulfill these functions by informing itself (hopefully, with the help of company management) on the fundamental strategic issues facing the company, obtaining independent expert assistance (if necessary) in evaluating these issues, and seeking and receiving input from shareholders on these matters.

I do not believe having such a committee need be "cumbersome and expensive." I do not believe such a committee "is likely to interfere with and reduce the efficiency" of the management of Exxon by its board of directors. Nor do I believe such a committee "would duplicate the shareholder communication efforts of the Investor Relations Department" of Exxon.

---

*The compensation of nonemployee Exxon directors is set forth on page two of the proxy statement.

I fully understand why a board of directors would be reluctant to endorse a proposal to establish a committee to review and evaluate the board's performance. I believe, however, that shareholders, as owners, would be better off—and shareholder values would be enhanced—if they got actively involved in seeing that their company is managed well. This is a responsibility of share ownership. I believe my proposal to establish a shareholders' committee to take on the role of active, informed shareholder representatives is a positive first step in this process. I urge you to support it.

Sincerely,
Robert A. G. Monks

Robert A. G. Monks is the president and sole shareholder of Institutional Shareholder Partners, Inc. (ISP), a consulting firm for institutional shareholders, whose office is located at 3333 Water Street, N.W., Suite 220, Washington, DC 20007. Mr. Monks owns 1,325 shares of Exxon common stock. Mr. Monks and ISP are soliciting the execution of Exxon proxies in favor of Mr. Monks' proposal for a committee of shareholder representatives but are not furnishing their own form of proxy for use at the annual meeting of Exxon shareholders. Their interest in the matters set forth herein is solely in connection with their business activities of providing services to institutional shareholders. Mr. Monks will bear the entire cost of the solicitation. Under rules of the Securities and Exchange Commission, this letter may constitute proxy soliciting material, and all the information in the Exxon proxy statement dated March 6, 1992 is incorporated herein by this reference. Mr. Monks and ISP, through its officers, employees and agents, may contact shareholders and others personally, by telephone or in writing, and intend to respond to inquiries, orally or in writing, regarding the matters set forth herein.

Appendix 2: Exxon Shareholder Proposal

RESOLVED: To adopt the following new by-law:
Article IIIA
COMMITTEE OF SHAREHOLDER REPRESENTATIVES

1. The corporation shall have a committee of shareholder representatives consisting of three members. The committee shall review the management of the business and affairs of the corporation by the board of directors and shall advise the board of its views and the views of shareholders which are expressed to the committee. The committee may, at the expense of the corporation, engage expert assistance and incur other expenses in a reasonable amount not to exceed in any fiscal year US $.01 multiplied by the number of common shares outstanding at the beginning of the year. The committee shall be given the opportunity to have included in the corporation's proxy statement used in its annual election of directors a report of not more than 2,500 words on the committee's activities during the year, its evaluation of the management of the corporation by the directors, and its recommendations on any matters proposed for action by shareholders.

2. The members of the committee shall be elected by the shareholders by plurality vote at their annual meeting. Elections of members shall be conducted in the same manner as elections of directors. Each member shall be paid a fee equal to half the average fee paid to nonemployee directors, shall be reimbursed for reasonable travel and other out-of-pocket expenses incurred in serving as a mem-

ber, and shall be entitled to indemnification and advancement of expenses as would a director.

3. The corporation shall include in its proxy materials used in the election of directors nominations of and nominating statements for members of the committee submitted by any shareholder or group of shareholders (other than a fiduciary appointed by or under authority of the directors) which has owned beneficially, within the meaning of section 13(d) of the Securities Exchange Act of 1934, at least US $10 million in market value of common stock of the corporation continuously for the three-year period prior to the nomination. Nominations must be received by the corporation not less than ninety nor more than 180 days before the annual meeting of shareholders. The corporation's proxy materials shall include biographical and other information regarding the nominee required to be included for nominees for director and shall also include a nominating statement of not more than 500 words submitted at the time of nomination by the nominating shareholder or group of shareholders.

4. Nothing herein shall restrict the power of the directors to manage the business and affairs of the corporation.

5. This Article IIIA shall not be altered or repealed without approval of shareholders.

ACCOMPANYING STATEMENT

The proposed by-law would establish a three-member committee of shareholder representatives which would review and oversee the actions of the board of directors in managing the business and affairs of Exxon. We believe such a committee could be an effective mechanism for shareholders to communicate their views to the board and would serve a useful advisory function at relatively little cost.

Notes

1. This is money held and managed by intermediaries—pension funds, insurance companies, mutual funds, endowments, etc.—for the benefit of individuals (investors, pension plan participants, etc.) or non-profit organizations (charities, universities, etc.). All statistical material is provided from Brancato (1995), unless a different edition is indicated.

2. During the first quarter of 1995, the Public Employee Retirement System of California indicated an increase in its targeted percentage of equity investment to 63 percent.

3. In the 1986 Federal Employee Retirement System Act, Congress provided that federal employees may elect to invest in an equity index but not in individual companies.

4. "Soft dollars" are a sort of frequent flyer miles for stock transactions and are an off-budget resource that can be used to pay for research (rather broadly defined).

5. We have found a very significant difference at those companies that give their shareholders the protection of confidential voting. At companies that insist on knowing how their shareholders voted (and that often use this knowledge to push anyone voting against management to change their votes), it is far more difficult to get a strong showing of support for shareholder initiatives than at companies that guarantee that all votes are confidential.

References

Brancato, Carol. *The Brancato Report on Institutional Investment*. vol. 2, January 1993 and 1995.

Conrad, Alfred E. "Beyond Managerialism Investor Capitalism?" *Michigan Journal of Law Reform* 22 (1988): 117 ff.

Drucker, Peter F. *The Unseen Revolution: How Pension Fund Socialism Came to America*. New York: Harper and Row, 1976.

———. "Can Pension Funds Lead the Ownership Revolution?" *Harvard Business Review* (May–June 1991): 169 ff.

———. "Reckoning with the Pension Fund Revolution." *Harvard Business Review* 69, 2 (1991): 106–14.

Ellis, Charles D. *Investment Policy*. Homewood, IL: Dow Jones-Irwin, 1989.

Fisch, Jill E. "From Legitimacy to Logic: Reconstructing Proxy Regulation." *Vanderbilt Law Review* 46 (1993): 1129, 1198.

Fischel, Daniel and John H. Langbein. "ERISA's Fundamental Contradiction: The Exclusive Benefit Rule." *University of Chicago Law Review* 55, 4 (1988): 1105–60.

Gillan, Stuart L. and Laura T. Starks. Relationship Investing and Shareholder Activism by Institutional Investors. University of Texas working paper, February 1995.

Nesbitt, Stephen L. "Rewards from Corporate Governance." Santa Monica, CA, Wilshire Associates, February 1992.

———. "Long Term Rewards from Corporate Governance." Santa Monica, CA, Wilshire Associates, January 1994.

Romano, Roberta. "Public Pension Fund Activism in Corporate Governance Reconsidered." *Columbia Law Review* 93, 4 (1993): 795–853.

———. "Politics and Public Pension Funds." The Manhattan Institute, 1994, New York.

Stein, Benjamin J. "A Saga of Shareholder Neglect." *Barron's* (May 4, 1987): 8–75.

U.S. Department of Labor. *Interpretive Bulletin 94-2, Title 29—Labor*. Part 2509. Pension Welfare Benefits Administration, Washington DC: USGPO, 1994.

Wahal, Sunil. "Public Pension Fund Activism and Firm Performance." University of North Carolina working paper, November 1994.

Chapter 9
Using Pension Funding Bonds in Defined Benefit Pension Portfolios

Robert M. Lang

Nearly 300 state and local governments in the United States maintain 451 retirement plans with collective assets of approximately US $1 trillion. These plans cover more than 13,000,000 municipal employees nationwide, in occupations ranging from state troopers and prison wardens to city clerks and school teachers (Zorn and Eitelberg 1994). When a state government's actuaries determine that the present value of plan benefits exceeds the present value of plan assets, the state is said to have an unfunded actuarially accrued liability (UAAL), meaning that it owes money to its retirement plan. Approximately 200 state and local retirement plans are collectively underfunded by more than US $162 billion (Zorn and Eitelberg 1994).

This chapter initially seeks to examine the current funding and investment practices of state and local government retirement plans in a manner designed to provide an introductory discussion for government decisionmakers, taxpayer groups, and municipal employees. In this context the concept of pension funding bonds (PFBs) is introduced as a mechanism for meeting public plans' unfunded liabilities.

When a municipal government owes money to its retirement plan, it typically funds the deficiency, the UAAL, by making amortization payments to its plan each year. In addition to amortizing the principal amount of the UAAL, the municipality must pay interest to its public retirement plan on the outstanding balance of the UAAL at an interest rate set by the plan's actuary. The "actuarially assumed interest rate" attempts to compensate the plan for the opportunity cost of not having money (the UAAL) available to invest in stocks and bonds. In recent years, this rate has typically been set at 8.09 percent (Zorn and Eitelberg 1994).

As an alternative to repaying the UAAL over time at the actuarially assumed interest rate, several municipalities, particularly those in California, have issued pension funding bonds. PFBs are publicly issued securities sold to bond investors in the well-established United States municipal securities marketplace; the proceeds are deposited to the municipal retirement plan to fund the UAAL. Under certain market conditions, bond investors in the municipal securities marketplace will lend funds to the government employer at an interest rate that is lower than the actuarially assumed interest rate, providing substantial savings.

Pension funding bonds are typically backed by the same security as other state and local debt instruments, requiring the governments either to appropriate money annually from generally available funds to pay debt service or to back the bonds directly with dedicated revenue sources, such as property taxes. The funds raised by the PFBs are irrevocably deposited to the state or local government retirement plan and invested by the plan to meet the future retirement needs of its municipal employees.

For example, the City of Fresno, California issued US $245 million of PFBs in March 1994. Fresno borrowed the funds at a 7.5 percent interest rate, deposited the proceeds with the City's retirement system, and hoped that the system would earn a long-term rate of return of at least 7.5 percent over the next twenty years. There were no guarantees that the system would be able to achieve this objective, but the system's actuaries had projected that the system would earn at least 8 percent per year, and the City was paying interest on the US $245 million UAAL at that 8 percent actuarially assumed interest rate. If the system is able to earn 8 percent each year on the invested assets, Fresno will earn US $18 million more over the next twenty years than it would earn as a result of an annual contributions approach. In fact, in the 12 months following the deposit of the additional US $245 million, Fresno's retirement system realized a total return in excess of 20 percent—or a gain of US $50 million on the funds provided by the PFBs. While Fresno benefited from uniquely fortuitous timing and generated savings in excess of its expectations, any public employer that earns a rate of return equal to or greater than its PFB borrowing cost would realize cost savings by funding its retirement plan with PFBs.

However, the potential cost savings, which come with attendant reinvestment risk, need not be the primary motivation for issuing PFBs. Perhaps the strongest argument in favor of PFB issuance is that a municipality's irrevocable obligation to make bond debt service payments may be a more predictable and less discretionary method of funding unfunded liabilities than a voluntary annual contribution. While the municipal employer, which is by definition governed by a political body, may choose to postpone or reduce an annual retirement fund contribution, it is unlikely that it would consider defaulting on an annual principal or interest payment due on publicly issued debt. Therefore, PFBs can introduce a higher level of discipline into the plan funding process.

These potential benefits also carry attendant drawbacks. First, if the public plan should fail to earn a long-term rate of return equal to the borrowing cost, such as 7.5 percent, the plan may be worse off than if the employer had continued to make annual contributions to decrease the unfunded liability. It should be noted, however, that even in the absence of PFBs a plan that earns less than its assumed rate of return will become underfunded.

Second, the financial discipline introduced by PFBs also comes at a price—decreased flexibility. While some state constitutions forbid employers from withholding annual contributions or lowering future retirement benefits, other state constitutions do permit such actions. Once PFBs are issued and the proceeds are deposited into the plan, federal law prohibits municipalities from withdrawing funds. Furthermore, bond holders must receive their annual payments or the municipality would be in default.

Furthermore, while it is certainly legal in most states to obligate future legislatures' actions (long-term highway, school, and hospital bonds are issued regularly), the decision to issue long-term debt should be given due consideration as a matter of public policy. One mechanism that somewhat mitigates the decrease in financial flexibility relating to unfunded liability payments is that the municipality may retain the ability to suspend or decrease its future annual contributions even though it would be obligated to pay the debt service on the PFBs.

Finally, taxpayers and elected officials should be aware that all PFBs are not created equal. PFBs need not be structured with level annual debt service payments like a home mortgage. Particularly for large debt issues, principal amortization can be heavily weighted toward the latter maturities, including the use of zero-coupon bonds, or can contain sophisticated embedded derivatives. While these types of bond structures may achieve desired payment patterns, PFB issuers would be well advised to evaluate both the financial risks and intergenerational equity implications of a given PFB amortization pattern.

This chapter focuses exclusively on state and local government employers and public retirement plans in the United States, but the fundamentals of the discussion relating to the creation of unfunded liabilities, the investment of plan assets, and funding plan liabilities by issuing debt securities will hopefully inform discussions in other countries.

Background

Before discussing current funding and investment practices and subsequently examining of PFBs, it will be helpful to make four general observations about public sector plans.

First, each of the fifty states has its own authorizing legislation governing retirement plans. This legislation often specifies contribution practices, actuarial and accounting assumptions, and investment practices. State and local government plans are exempt from nearly all federal legislation relating to retirement plans, including ERISA. Therefore, states are bound only by self-imposed rules relating to funding levels and contributions practices. Readers familiar with United States private-sector pension plans, or retirement plans in other countries, are forewarned to abandon attempts to understand these public plans through the lens of another paradigm.

Second, public sector plans are overwhelmingly defined benefit, necessitating additional employer payments if previous contributions and investment returns are not sufficient to pay benefits. More than 90 percent of public plans are defined benefit, whereas less than 4 percent are strictly defined contribution, and the remaining 6 percent are combinations of the two approaches (Zorn and Eitelberg 1994).

Third, more than 85 percent of the assets of the median municipal plan is invested in publicly traded domestic equities and domestic bonds (Zorn and Eitelberg 1994).

Finally, it is assumed that all state and local governments are experienced issuers of bonds in the capital markets. In fact, more than US $160 billion of municipal debt instruments are issued each year to fund the construction of schools, roads, hospitals, and other public projects.

Current Practices for Determining Public Plan Benefits and Contributions

To understand how PFBs can be used to change contribution mechanisms, it is helpful first to examine the status quo methods for estimating future benefit levels and determining the amount of annual contributions necessary to fund plan liabilities.

Policymakers face three challenges in addressing projected funding shortfalls. First, future benefit levels, which are the liabilities of the retirement plan, are difficult to predict. Second, even if liabilities can be determined with certainty, different funding methods have different consequences for how liabilities are shared between current and future taxpayers. Third, because benefits are practically irrevocable once granted, employers cannot pursue reductions in plan benefits as a means for matching assets and liabilities.

Plan Liabilities

Defined benefit plans expose municipal employers to significant financial uncertainty due to the possibility that the actual level of benefits paid to retired members may significantly diverge from projections.

Estimated Funding Levels

Paul Zorn and Cathie G. Eitelberg have compiled an excellent database of information about public pension plans for the Public Pension Coordinating Council (PPCC) from the responses of 300 public pension systems (some with multiple retirement plans) that account for more than 75 percent of all public plan membership in the United States (Zorn and Eitelberg 1994). Approximately 200 of the 451 state and local government plans in the PPCC survey are collectively underfunded by more than US $162 billion (Zorn and Eitelberg 1994).

It is helpful to put these liabilities in perspective. The average funding ratio of public plans has increased from 79.8 percent in 1991 to 82.1 percent in 1992 (Zorn and Eitelberg 1994). Only 16 percent of public plans are less than 70 percent funded, while 47 percent are more than 90 percent funded (Zorn and Eitelberg 1994). However, further exploration into the arcane world of actuarial projections reveals that projected plan liabilities are relatively uncertain, and plan valuations change when different actuarial methods and assumptions are used.

Different Actuarial Methods Indicate Different Funding Levels

There are many accepted actuarial methods for forecasting a system's future assets and liabilities, just as an equity can be valued using the cost, market value, or discounted cash flow methods. Describing the differences between actuarial methods, such as the "entry age normal" method and the "projected unit credit" method, is beyond the scope of this chapter. It is sufficient to note that different actuarial methods produce vastly different indications of a plan's funding ratio (the present value of plan assets over the present value of plan liabilities).

The decision to change a plan's actuarial accounting method can have important political implications, as a low funding ratio could require a state to make additional contributions to its retirement plan while a high funding ratio may provide employers with bargaining power to avoid further increases in employee benefits. It is not uncommon to find jurisdictions with similar local retirement plans (such as adjoining water districts in the same metropolitan area) using different actuarial methods.

Changes in Actuarial Assumptions Affect Funding Levels

Even among plans with the same actuarial method, underlying assumptions can vary widely. One plan may forecast inflation at a 3 percent annual rate of increase, while another may assume a 5 percent annual increase—producing vastly different outcomes. Because federal laws such as ERISA do not apply to public plans, actuarial assumptions can be changed under state or local law, either for sound financial reasons or to obtain politically desirable funding projections and annual contribution levels.

Political Motivations for Changes in Funding Methodologies and Assumptions

Some state and local lawmakers have become proficient at manipulating actuarial assumptions and methods to provide additional retirement benefits without increasing the level of annual contributions during their term of office.

Public employees are a powerful constituency—they are numerous, unionized, have a strong motivation to participate in the democratic process, and perform functions essential to the jurisdiction's well-being. For these reasons, publicly elected officials take employee requests for additional compensation quite seriously. Should the lawmakers agree to increase employee compensation, they may choose to increase either current wages or future pension payments (or a combination of the two.)

State and local governments are required to maintain balanced annual budgets. Therefore, current wage increases would necessitate either cuts in funding for other programs or higher taxes. However, lawmakers may instead choose to grant unfunded retirement benefits, pleasing both public employees and beneficiaries of other programs (whose funding would otherwise be cut). Increased benefits without additional contributions create, or augment, an unfunded liability, thereby shifting the cost of the wage increases from current taxpayers to future taxpayers. For state and local governments, the ability to create unfunded off-balance sheet obligations, such as unfunded pension liabilities, is almost as powerful as the ability to print money.

To address this problem, some states require by law that benefits cannot be increased if the action will create or increase the state's unfunded pension liability. To overcome this obstacle some lawmakers have creatively recognized that even small changes in actuarial assumptions, such as an increase in projected investment returns, can create a plan surplus large enough to absorb additional benefits. Alternatively, a state legislature may choose to change or make an exception to its own law and grant state employees additional benefits despite the creation of unfunded liabilities.

These observations do not suggest that the majority of changes to actuarial methods and assumptions are politically motivated. However, a discussion of funding levels and annual contributions practices for public plans would be incomplete without addressing the political implications of different approaches.

Actual Results Vary from Assumptions

Even plans with stable actuarial methods and assumptions find that actual plan experience differs from projections. For example, a municipality's actual payroll growth rate will be determined by both inflation and raises for merit and seniority. Similarly, the amount of benefits that a plan must pay will be influenced by the plan's actual mortality and disability experience. Plans that have few members, are concentrated in a small geographic area, or are segregated by occupation, for example, may experience large gaps between statistically predicted outcomes and actual results.

Benefits Reductions Legally Prohibited

Once benefits are granted to state and local government employees, strong legal protections as well as political pressures largely preclude cuts in pension benefits. This rules out benefit cuts as a financial tool for matching assets and liabilities.

Analysis of the Government Finance Officers' Association (GFOA) database reveals that benefit levels for 96 of the 286 plans with unfunded liabilities (33.5 percent) cannot be reduced, as mandated by state constitution, city charter, or a court order (Zorn and Eitelberg 1994; author's computation).

These protected plans account for US $53.7 billion of unfunded liabilities, or one-third of municipal employers' collective unfunded liability of US $162 billion. This protection is fairly strong, as changes to a state's constitution or a city's charter require difficult procedural maneuvers and must additionally be directly approved by a vote of the people.

A further 181 plans, or 40 percent of the total, have benefit levels protected by state statute (Zorn and Eitelberg 1994; author's computation).

While this statutory protection is somewhat weaker, benefit decreases still require the approval of both houses of a state legislature as well as the signature of the state's governor.

Plan Contribution Practices

Annual contributions to public plans include both "normal contributions" to meet the future liabilities of current employees and "UAAL amortization payments" to pay off the municipality's unfunded pension liability. Total annual contributions exceed US $37 billion per year, with US $24.6 billion provided by employers and the remaining US $12.9 billion provided by employees (Zorn and Eitelberg 1994).

However, municipalities are becoming increasingly aware of the budgetary benefits of creating money by "deferring" pension plan contributions. In 1995 New York City was scheduled to contribute US $106 million per month to its plans but, according to a spokesperson, "New York City was forced by a cash shortage to defer US $212 million in [two] monthly payments to its pension funds" (Adler and Sacco 1995). Thus New York City chose to spend its revenues on higher priorities, including bond debt service, increasing its future obligations to its pension plans.

Even though plans are generally healthy now, the continued adequate funding of public plans is an important matter of public policy. Particularly in small states or political subdivisions, plans that become severely underfunded could either impose severe burdens on future taxpayers or force public retirees to accept lower benefits than they had been previously promised.

Practices for Repaying Unfunded Pension Liabilities: Level Percentage of Payroll Versus Level Annual Payments

Many municipalities with unfunded liabilities choose to fund the UAAL through a standard actuarial method, the contribution of a "level percentage of payroll" each year. For example, a city's normal contribution may be 12 percent of its payroll, and its UAAL amortization payment may be an additional 8 percent of payroll each year. While the "level percentage of payroll" repayment method is widely practiced and is consistent with actuarially accepted standards, it causes the UAAL to increase dramatically for many years despite its claim to be an amortization method. The repayment of a UAAL in this manner requires steeply increasing annual payments. Alternatively, plans may choose to amortize unfunded liabilities using a "level annual payment" method, but this practice requires much higher annual payments in the short run.

In comparing the two approaches, it is useful to consider a conventional fixed-rate mortgage for a home or business loan. Lenders generally require equal monthly payments, divided between principal and interest. In certain situations, if the amount of the loan is very large relative to the borrower's income, the lender may permit a short period of time in which interest is paid but no principal is amortized. However, it is very unusual for the lender to allow the borrower to incur additional indebtedness in order to pay the interest due on the original loan, an ignominious practice known as negative amortization.

Level Percentage of Payroll and Negative Amortization

When a municipality amortizes its unfunded liabilities through the "level percentage of payroll" method, the employer frequently fails to make large enough annual contributions even to cover the interest due on the UAAL.

For example, the State of Louisiana has a total unfunded liability of more than US $7.2 billion. The average actuarially assumed interest rate for the State of Louisiana's various plans is 8.25 percent and therefore, just to make interest payments on its UAAL each year, the state should pay US $600 million per year to its plans (Office of Legislative Auditor State of Louisiana 1993; author's computations).

In fact, in accordance with standard actuarial practice, state forecasts call for only US $400 million in annual contributions over the next few years, adding another US $200 million per year to its UAAL. Due to this logic, the state's unfunded liability is projected to grow for the next twenty years until it reaches a maximum of US $10.5 billion. At that point, it is projected that the state will rapidly amortize its UAAL with US $1.5 billion per year of amortization payments (these payments will be in addition to the normal contributions due). The state's total payments to meet interest and principal on the US $7.2 billion UAAL over the next 32 years are projected to exceed US $27 billion (Office of Legislative Auditor State of Louisiana 1993; author's computations).

Louisiana has very strong state constitutional protections precluding decreases in public employee benefits (Office of Legislative Auditor State of Louisiana 1993). Therefore, the only choice available to the taxpayers and their elected officials is between significantly increasing current UAAL payments at least to meet the current interest cost or to continue to incur negative amortization by deferring the payments into the future at an even greater cost.

Louisiana should not be uniquely criticized for these practices. Its experience is typical, as over 200 public plans have UAALs (Zorn and Eitelberg 1994), and the level percentage of payroll method is a commonly accepted practice for the amortization of unfunded liabilities.

Proponents of the level percentage of payroll method argue that if future payrolls are not as large as projected, future benefits requirements will not be as large either, and thus plans are not exposed to significant funding risks. However, use of this amortization method raises important public policy questions. Many of these implications are beyond the scope of this chapter, but one consequence—the difficulty that this practice causes when attempting to refinance the UAAL—will be addressed below in the discussion of pension funding bonds.

To summarize the liability outlook, plans are generally healthy, but defined benefit plan liabilities are difficult to predict, reductions in benefits are often legally prohibited, and some actuarially recommended funding methods allow the UAAL to increase for decades before meaningful principal repayments are contributed. Despite the overall strength of most public plans, the dollar amount of public plan unfunded liabilities should convince state and local governments to explore mechanisms to fund their retirement plans more efficiently.

This discussion of liabilities provides important background information necessary to understand how PFBs can be used to alter current contributions practices. It is also helpful to understand how public plans invest the contributions that are made by public employers.

Public Plan Investments

In sum, public plans primarily invest in marketable securities, such as publicly traded equities and investment grade bonds. Investments may also include assets as commodities, real estate, non-investment grade bonds, but these types of investments typically account for only a small portion of a plan's asset allocation. Most public plans operate in perpetuity and attempt to meet all current obligations with current contributions and income from invested assets. Therefore, the corpus of a public plan's assets are generally invested to provide protection of principal, and a balance between capital appreciation and current income.

Investment Policy and Asset Allocation

The investment policy and asset allocation of a public pension plan is either defined by statute or determined by the retirement plan's board members. This policy may prohibit the plan from owning certain types of assets, such as foreign real estate or derivatives. As noted above, a typical public plan allocates 85 percent of assets among domestic equities and bonds. Typically, less than 10 percent of plan assets are held in so-called "risk-free" investments such as short-term United States government securities (Zorn and Eitelberg 1994). Because ERISA standards do not apply to state and local government plans, public retirement boards retain the discretion to take a great deal of financial risk or no risk at all (except to the extent that investment policies are directed by state and/or local laws).

Public plans do change their asset allocations over time, based on both fluctuating expectations about the relative returns of different asset classes and the forecasted cash-flow needs of the individual plan. To the extent that a public plan reallocates its assets among different asset classes based on a particular forecast of equity returns or interest rates, the plan engages in market timing. While plan contributions do come in over time, such as US $25 million per month, and therefore provide plans with the opportunity to realize returns similar to "dollar cost averaging" techniques, in reality when a plan shifts its asset allocation it moves a tremendous amount of funds from one sector to another. These reallocations more than offset the long-term averaging effect that could result from consistently investing a fixed amount of money in a fixed-asset allocation. The practice of market timing is not necessarily harmful (in fact, as discussed below, public plan returns in recent years have been above expectations); however, it is important to recognize that public plans actively make decisions about movements in interest rates or equity prices and take meaningful financial risks every day with a significant amounts of funds.

Investment Return Objectives

The typical (median) public plan assumes that it will earn an 8.09 percent long-term rate of return on its investments. Public plans responding to the PPCC survey cited above realized an average investment return of 10.62 percent per year from 1988 through 1992 (Zorn and Eitelberg 1994).

Why Do Public Plans Invest in Equities and Corporate Bonds Instead of Treasury Bills?

State and local governments take financial risks, including both market risk and credit risk, by purchasing equities and corporate bonds. Plan investments also typically include long-term government bonds, such as federal agency securities, which protect the plan from credit risk but still carry interest-rate risk. Taxpayers can benefit from this investment approach because these asset classes have historically provided a greater long-term rate of return than Treasury bills, requiring less taxpayer contributions to the public plan.

It is important to recognize, however, that the vast majority of public plan assets are invested in securities whose values fluctuate over time. Public retirement plans actively make investment decisions, involving billions of dollars each year, to choose which securities to sell, hold, or buy based on a plan's view of the relative performance of different market sectors. For example, a plan may previously have given 5 percent of its portfolio to a particular money manager focusing on overseas equities; after reevaluating its investment alternatives, the plan may choose to shift the funds to a domestic money manager focusing on "small-cap" domestic equities.

The reallocation of assets among asset classes is a well-established and widespread practice for public funds; in fact, if public funds were subject to ERISA, a diversification among asset classes and particular holdings would be required by federal law. While this practice of investing in marketable securities and making sector decisions among asset classes may appear relatively straightforward to seasoned pension money managers, public plan investment practices may be relatively unknown among the general public. In fact, as will be discussed below, one of the primary concerns raised by opponents of PFBs is that a public employer may erroneously decide that interest rates are unusually low, issue PFBs, and provide the bond proceeds to its public employee retirement plan, which then purchases investments that perform poorly.

It is helpful to put the general discussion of PFBs into context by recognizing that public retirement plans make multi-billion dollar judgment calls (more eloquently described as "investment decisions" or "asset allocations") about future interest rates and equity prices every day through their actions in purchasing securities, selling securities, or even by simply holding existing positions. There is nothing inherently wrong with public plans making judgment calls; in fact, each public plan is required by its own investment policy guidelines to make such decisions. Despite what may be conventional wisdom, public plans (and to some extent their contributing employers, who often participate in retirement board meetings) are not inexperienced in considering sophisticated issues relating to market timing and the relative performance of different asset classes.

Legal Status of Public Plan Investment Ownership Is Risky

One feature of public plans that not only raises concerns about whether PFB proceeds should be contributed to public plans, but more generally concerns both retirees and taxpayers, is that public plan assets remain under the ownership of the contributing employer in the event of a municipal bankruptcy.

The credit quality of the employer is important not only because the employer is the source of future contributions but also because the employer often holds all assets purchased with past contributions. "[P]articipants in 457 (state and local) plans are particularly nervous following the Orange County, California bankruptcy. Because 457 plans . . . are the property of the employer, the assets are subject to the claims of general creditors if the employers go bankrupt. In contrast, corporate retirement plans . . . are required by ERISA to hold employee contributions in separate trusts" (Adler and Sacco 1995).

The use of plan assets is one of the few instances in which federal regulations govern state and local retirement plans. Prior to the Tax Reform Act of 1986, municipal employers would borrow money by issuing low-interest rate *tax-exempt* PFBs and invest the PFB proceeds into its public retirement fund, which invested in higher-yielding taxable securities (but was not required to pay tax on the investment returns). This approach created arbitrage gains, at the expense of the federal government, by exploiting the power Congress gave municipalities to issue tax-exempt bonds. As a result of the 1986 federal tax reform act, municipalities may not issue tax-exempt bonds to fund retirement contributions, and all contributions made to public plans are irrevocable. (Ironically, this prevented Orange County, California from using retirement fund investments to avoid bankruptcy while simultaneously jeopardizing public employee retirement funds once the County was in bankruptcy by subjecting the employee funds to the claims of general creditors.)

As a result, public employees face meaningful credit exposure to the future financial condition of their employer, both for job security and retirement security. In some jurisdictions, such as a city or a state, the government may be able to make up for poor investment returns in its retirement plan by using surplus funds, making cuts to government programs, or raising taxes to increase contributions. If a public employer declares bankruptcy, or has no taxing authority and only limited ability to increase revenues (e.g., a turnpike authority), employees may ultimately be forced to accept decreased pension benefits despite state constitutional and statutory protections. Public retirees who are citizens of the jurisdiction would be particularly impacted, as they may otherwise benefit from government programs that would be cut, would pay a share of the resulting tax increases, and would receive diminished retirement benefits. Federal government pension plan insurance does not extend to state and local government retirement plans, which are exempt from nearly all federal regulation and do not pay insurance premiums to the federal government.

In sum, state and local government plan assets are invested in securities that carry inherent credit and investment risk, state and local government plan assets are not protected from employer bankruptcy by legal structures, and public retirees' future retirement benefits are not protected by federal pension insurance.

Public Policy Implications of Current Public Sector Approach

The continuing performance of public sector funds will fundamentally impact the financial position of state and local governments. Meaningful adjustments to the current approach to public pension plans may be desirable. However, based on the legal hurdles to implementing changes, such as state constitution and city charter requirements, and the author's interviews with public plan decisionmakers, fundamental changes (such as adopting a defined contribution plan) are more likely to be discussed than implemented by the nation's largest public employers. Furthermore, federal law changes, such as alterations in the legal ownership of 457 plans or the integration of state and local government plans into the federal private-employer pension plan guaranty system, appear even more remote. Therefore, in the absence of major changes, the only course of action available to state and local government employers is to make the best of the pension system they have inherited, specifically by maximizing investment returns and minimizing funding costs at acceptable levels of risk.

Tremendous attention is given to maximizing public plans' investment returns, and performance results are carefully scrutinized each quarter to assure that plan returns match or outperform relevant benchmarks such as the S&P 500 index. Because public plans choose to maintain more than 85 percent of their assets in publicly traded securities, it is reasonable to conclude that public plans are well-served by the capital markets.

Comparatively less attention has been given to the idea of using the capital markets to fund US $162 billion in unfunded liabilities more efficiently. The following sections describe pension funding bonds and the impact that the approach can have on a municipality's ongoing financial operations.

Capital Markets Approach to Funding Liabilities: Pension Funding Bonds (PFBs)

Funding a defined benefit pension system with invested assets is a complex and dynamic process. Issuing bonds to provide contributions in a lump sum is only one of many changes that can be made to alter the status quo approach. Other approaches to funding an unfunded liability could include investing unexpected annual operating gains into the system or increasing annual contributions each year above the amount required by the system's actuary.

A decisionmaker contemplating a PFB issue should ask at least three important questions. What is a PFB and how did the technique gain widespread use? How does a municipality create the mechanisms necessary to issue PFBs? What impact will a PFB have on a municipality's finances, particularly with respect to funding cost, investment risk, financial flexibility, and long-term funding progress?

Definition of a Pension Funding Bond

A PFB is an obligation issued by a state or local government employer for the specific purpose of depositing the proceeds of the bond issue into the employer's public employee retirement fund. PFBs are typically long-term bond issues, with 20- to 30-year final maturities, and may have principal amortization in each year. Most PFBs have been issued as current-coupon, fixed rate bonds, but both zero coupon fixed rate bonds and variable rate current coupon PFBs have been issued. There is no single definition of a PFB, and each state has the right to issue any type of bond for which it can find an investor. The only characteristic common to all types of PFBs is that the interest earned by investors is subject to federal income tax, unlike most municipal bond issues, for which the interest earned by investors is tax exempt.

There are two fundamental reasons that a state or local government employer might issue a PFB. First, PFBs can introduce discipline into the UAAL amortization process. The municipal employer may feel that it does not have the discipline to make consistent annual UAAL amortization payments to its retirement plan (or, just as important, that future lawmakers may not have the discipline), but that the employer would always honor its obligation to pay principal and interest on publicly issued debt. Second, a municipal employer may believe that it can issue long-term bonds at a lower interest cost than its retirement plan will earn on the borrowed funds.

Evolution of PFBs

Municipal employers have issued debt to fund retirement obligations for at least two decades. The practice gained national attention in the mid-1980s when the County of Los Angeles, California and other municipalities issued more than US $500 million in bonds to invest in their public plans. Interest on these bonds was exempt from both federal and state personal income taxes (thus, carrying a below-market interest cost), and the investments purchased by the plans accrued tax-free until paid out as benefits. The Tax Reform Act of 1986 prohibited further issuance of federally tax-exempt bonds to fund public retirement plans, which eliminated the municipalities' risk-free tax arbitrage (although individual states may continue to exempt interest on PFBs from state taxes). After 1986, municipalities could only issue pension bonds at interest rates comparable to corporate bond interest rates, which were generally higher than the plans' projected rates of return. Therefore, given the changes in tax laws and proportionately high interest rates relative to plans' expected rates of return, PFBs faded into obscurity.

In 1993, however, long-term bond interest rates declined to their lowest levels in more than twenty years. Municipalities believed that it was cost-effective to issue PFBs to repay their UAAL in full, as the PFB borrowing cost declined below the plans' expected rates of return. By the end of 1994, California cities and counties had issued more than US $4 billion of PFBs. These California municipalities were able to access the markets quickly because the legal authority to issue PFBs, which derives from the powers provided to a municipality by each state's constitution, legislation, and court rulings, was already in place in California.

Prerequisites for Implementing PFBs

Pension funding bonds share many common characteristics with other types of publicly issued municipal securities. Investors demand that any municipal security, including PFBs, must be legally authorized by the municipality, debt service must be supported by a sufficient stream of municipal revenues, and bondholders must be entitled to reasonable protections.

Legal Authority

A municipality can derive the legal authority to issue PFBs in two ways. First, it may determine that existing state law permits the issuance and repayment of PFBs. To make this determination, the municipality may rely on the advice of a prominent law firm familiar with state law. However, to be confident that this new approach is unquestionably authorized under existing law, several PFB issuers have taken the additional step of validating the legal theory by challenging themselves in court. Specifically, California municipalities, including the city of Fresno and the counties of Alameda, Los Angeles, and Sonoma, have obtained rulings from the California Superior Court that pension bonds are legal, valid, and binding obligations of these jurisdictions, consistent with state laws and rulings dating from 1937 to the present. Second, legislation can be enacted, typically by the state legislature, that specifically authorizes the state and/or its political subdivisions to issue PFBs, proscribes the manner and method for issuing such bonds, and delineates the various sources of government revenues that can be pledged to the repayment of the principal and interest due to bondholders.

Regardless whether PFBs are authorized by either existing or newly enacted legislation, many state and local jurisdictions have legal requirements that a majority of voters must directly approve any new debt obligation. However, these legal requirements typically exempt the refinancing of an existing obligation from reauthorization. The California cities and counties mentioned above have successfully validated in California Superior Court that municipalities are legally bound to pay unfunded pension obligations. Therefore, because pension bonds refinance existing obligations, in some states PFBs do not need to be reauthorized by direct vote. This line of reasoning is commonly employed by municipalities to refinance an existing bond issue, to raise funds to comply with a court ruling such as school integration, or to satisfy a monetary judgment levied against the municipality.

In addition to obtaining the authority to issue debt and to use governmental revenues to repay the bonds, the municipality must specifically choose the revenue source it will pledge to bondholders to repay the principal and interest due on the PFBs.

Sources of Repayment

Municipal governments can issue different types of securities that carry different debt ratings, just as corporations can issue different classes of senior and subordinated debt. Four types of repayment mechanisms will be discussed here. First, the "general obligation pledge," which carries the full faith and credit of the municipality, is the strongest type of security. This pledge would require the government to increase taxes until sufficient revenues are generated to repay the full amount of debt service due each year on the bonds.

Alternatively, the municipality may provide a "general fund pledge" by agreeing that it will budget and appropriate funds each year to repay the bonds, but only to the extent that money is available to pay debt service. This general fund pledge carries a slightly weaker credit rating than a general obligation pledge and therefore carries a slightly higher interest cost, but is still widely accepted by investors as a creditworthy security. A general fund pledge to only pay debt service if revenue is available in a given year closely parallels the current arrangement for repaying the UAAL, providing credibility to the argument that the PFBs are merely a refinancing of an existing obligation. Most California PFBs carry a general fund pledge.

Third, the PFB issuer may pledge a specific source of revenue to the repayment of the bonds, such as funds generated by a gasoline tax or a sales tax. This type of security can either be stronger or weaker than a general fund pledge, depending on economic conditions affecting the volume of sales being taxed. This type of pledge often requires voter approval.

Finally, to the extent that state law permits, cities and other political subdivisions may provide bondholders with a "state aid intercept mechanism" whereby the jurisdiction assigns its rights to receive state aid (such as a share of state motor vehicle licensing fees) to the PFB investors through a bond trustee. The bond trustee will directly receive the municipality's share of state funds, which are used to pay bond debt service, and only the remaining funds are passed through to the municipality that issued the PFBs. The municipality may also make additional payments if the state intercept money is not sufficient to repay the bonds fully.

A municipality may combine several of the above revenue sources to provide a particularly strong security, or it may create an entirely different type of security. These four security structures are only a few permutations of "pension funding bonds." In practice, nearly any debt incurred when pension fund contributions are modified can be construed as PFBs.

Debt Ratings

Consistent with the judicial rulings discussed above, Moody's Investor Service and Standard & Poor's Corporation have taken the view that pension bonds simply refinance a municipality's existing obligation to repay its UAAL. A recent Standard & Poor's rating analysis observed that the PFB being reviewed "shifts a portion of an off-balance sheet UAAL to on-balance sheet" (S&P 1995:30).

To the extent that pension bonds are used only to fund unfunded liabilities, this analysis may be reasonable. However, because there is no standard accepted definition of a PFB, it is possible to issue pension bonds not only to refinance a UAAL amortization schedule but also to borrow funds to make the current fiscal year's normal contribution. Depending on the municipality's overall debt burden and alternative borrowing costs, this approach may be prudent, but it may also serve as a mechanism for generating one-time budgetary relief that is similar to a decision to skip an annual normal contribution. Any irresponsible use of debt could cause a municipality's debt ratings to be lowered, not only for the PFB bond issue but for all other outstanding debt issues. The strength of a municipality's credit ratings will strongly influence its ability to earn a positive net rate of return by issuing PFBs. The interest rate for a pension bond issue will be determined by investor perception of the municipality's credit risk relative to other bonds available in the market.

Municipalities with weak credit ratings may prefer to continue to amortize the UAAL at the actuarially assumed interest rate. Under the current arrangement, a poorly rated government's employees take material credit risk by maintaining a UAAL as a plan asset. Bondholders will not welcome the opportunity to step into the plan's shoes as creditors of a poorly rated municipality, and PFB interest rates may be higher than the plan's projected rate of return. On the other hand, municipalities that enjoy strong credit ratings, consistently make retirement plan contributions, and maintain sound actuarial and accounting practices may find it cost-effective to issue PFBs.

Under the assumption that the PFBs are well structured, the investment of the proceeds by the public plan is also an important ratings factor. The rating agencies are not troubled by public plan investments that are consistent with commonly accepted investment practice. Equities and bonds are acceptable, but exotic derivatives raise questions. For example, Moody's determined that "the asset allocation plan" of Alameda County, California "is viewed as prudent, with investments distributed 40 percent in equities, 37 percent in fixed-income, 12 percent in real estate, 10 percent in international, and 1 percent in cash" (Schaffer et al. 1995). Whether the rating agencies should be more concerned about the market and credit risk of these investments is subject to further debate.

Impacts of PFB Approach on Public Employers and Public Plan Beneficiaries

A PFB issue alters the municipal employer's UAAL amortization payments to its retirement plans, changing the status quo funding cost, investment risk, financial flexibility, and long-term funding progress of the municipality and its employee retirement plan.

To the extent that municipalities maintain a defined benefit plan and invest capital in risky assets to fund such plans, municipalities perform the role of an investment company. The basic purposes of an investment company are first, to borrow at the lowest possible cost and second, to invest the borrowed funds at the highest rates of return that can be obtained at acceptable levels of risk. In concept, PFBs allow municipalities borrow funds against their excellent ratings at a low cost, enabling public retirement plans to invest in capital markets assets such as equities and corporate bonds. It is helpful to note that, in the absence of a PFB issue, the municipal employer would continue to make annual UAAL amortization payments into its plan, and the plan would invest these funds in equities and corporate bonds.

Funding Cost

Municipalities with high-quality debt ratings (at least "A" from Moody's and/or Standard & Poor's) have been able to access the credit markets at interest rates ranging from 25 basis points more than Treasury securities in the shorter maturity ranges to interest rates of approximately 90 basis points more than Treasury securities for longer-term (such as thirty-year) maturities. These relationships fluctuate constantly under changing market conditions.

By issuing serial bonds that have principal maturing each year rather than a single long-term maturity, PFB issuers are able to benefit from the slope of the yield curve, or the difference between short-term and long-term interest rates. The County of Sonoma, California and the City of Fresno, California issued PFBs at an overall interest cost of approximately 6.75 percent and 7.50 percent, respectively. To date, both the Sonoma and Fresno plans have earned double-digit rates of return on the PFB proceeds, and both plans continue to project long-term rates of return in excess of their employers' respective borrowing costs.

The most significant risk in locking in the funding cost is that the plans' actual returns will fluctuate over time. If the long-term return on plan investments is equal to the employer's borrowing cost, the employer will break even relative to its borrowing cost. If the average return exceeds projections, the municipality will realize increased savings from the PFB issue (although the employer is forbidden by federal law from removing excess funds from the plan, the employer may choose to eliminate normal contributions temporarily when the plan is projected to be overfunded). If the average return declines below the PFB borrowing cost, the municipality's borrowing rate will exceed its investment return, causing a net loss and necessitating additional unfunded liability payments from the employer.

Two other potential risks that must be considered are the additional investment risk that may be created by a lump-sum deposit of bond proceeds, and the excessive optimism required in a public plan's rate of return forecast if it believes that it can earn a higher long-term return than the employer's PFB borrowing cost.

Investment Risk

First, a plan receiving a lump-sum payment may invest the funds at a particularly poor time in the market cycle. For example, a municipality with a US $2 billion UAAL might issue US $two billion of PFBs, as the County of Los Angeles did in 1994. This lump sum was deposited to the public plan all at once, as opposed to a series of relatively smaller contributions over many years.

One issue is whether the lump sum would be invested in the same types of securities that would have been purchased with annual amortization payments. Because all funds deposited, whether from normal contributions, UAAL amortization payments, or PFB proceeds, are invested in equities and bonds, it is unlikely that a lump-sum deposit would be invested any differently than annual payments, particularly if the public fund passively indexes its investments. PFBs do not appear to increase the types of risks assumed by public plans. A second consideration is whether a large investment by any one public plan will materially affect market prices. Assuming that the plan maintains a fairly typical asset allocation or indexes its investments within each asset class, market prices for equities and bonds purchased by the plan should remain relatively unaffected.

Therefore, if PFB proceeds do not change the types of assets purchased, and the size of the purchase does not independently increase the cost of the assets purchased, the remaining question is whether the plan assumes a large incremental risk by investing the PFB proceeds at any one point in time. Under the status quo, the employer typically makes bimonthly UAAL amortization payments to the plan, thus providing the plan with a fairly consistent stream of revenue to invest each month. Therefore, investing the present value of the future UAAL payments at one point in time could cause the plan to experience higher or lower returns over the long run than if the funds were invested over time. It is difficult to evaluate whether a plan would be better off or worse off by changing its investment of the UAAL amortization payments. Theoretically, there is no way to predict which method will yield better future returns.

What may be helpful is to compare the PFB lump-sum investment activity in the context of the plan's other investment activities. Public plans regularly reallocate funds among asset classes, based either on judgments about future market conditions or to match investment income more closely with their projected cash-flow needs. Therefore, a plan's ongoing investing activities emulate lump-sum investments. For example, a public plan may have US $100 billion of plan assets, of which it may choose to increase its asset allocation in equities by 5 percent and decrease its asset allocation in bonds by 5 percent. Even such a modest reallocation will involve the sale of US $5 billion of bonds and the purchase of US $5 billion of equities, presumably over as relatively short a time horizon as a three-month period. Unless the PFB proceeds provide a substantially large increase in plan assets, the risk associated with the lump-sum investment of the PFB deposit will closely resemble the risks that the plan regularly takes when reallocating its assets.

Therefore, the incremental risk introduced by the lump-sum investment of the PFB proceeds may be material and should not be underestimated, but any determination of the acceptability of this risk must be placed within the context of a plan's ongoing risk-taking activities.

Projected Rates of Return

When a retirement plan believes it can reinvest bond proceeds at a higher rate of return than the employer's borrowing cost, it is logical to ask whether the plan's projected rate of return (also referred to as actuarially assumed interest rate) is realistic.

There are three factors that may help a plan may to consider why its rate of return is projected to be higher than the PFB borrowing cost. First, the general level of market interest rates may have declined rapidly over a recent period of time, and the plan's forecasts do not adequately reflect changing market rates of return. A decline in interest rates would enable the employer to issue relatively low-cost PFBs, for example, at an interest rate of 6.75 percent, while a plan's projected long-term rate of return may remain unchanged at 8.09 percent. If the plan's return on future investments is closely correlated to the future level of interest rates, declines in market interest rates may be a signal that the plan's projected long-term rate of return should be lowered.

However, a plan may believe that interest rates have declined only temporarily and, while the employer will benefit from borrowing at low rates, the plan will invest its assets gradually over a 12-month period to capture increases in interest rates. Acting on the belief that interest rates are only temporarily lower may appear to be a bold market call, particularly for a public plan, but as discussed above a US $100 billion public plan with 40 percent of its assets in bonds is already taking a meaningful position on the future level of interest rates.

Another possible reason that the plan may not need to reduce its expected rate of return after a sharp decline in interest rates is that retirement plans' actual returns of 10.62 percent between 1988 and 1992 have exceeded the plans' projected rates of return of 8.09 percent (Zorn and Eitelberg 1994). Thus, plans may already believe there is a sufficient margin for error embedded in their projected returns.

When comparing a plan's projected investment returns with a public employer's borrowing cost, a second factor to consider is the difference in credit quality between the public employer's bond issuer rating and the average rating of securities in which the plan is invested. If the employer carries a "AA+" rating from Standard & Poor's, for example, and the plan invests in securities with an average credit rating of "A," then the employer's borrowing cost should be lower than the plan's returns.

Some may argue that a public employer may be leveraging its excellent credit rating to fund the plan, but recall that the employer is already obligated to make the annual UAAL amortization payments if it does not issue the PFB, and the rating agency's assessment of the employer has already included the projected UAAL amortization payments. Furthermore, the plan is already investing in securities of a certain credit quality, independent of the employer's decision to issue PFBs, and under either the status quo or PFB alternatives, the employer remains obligated to pay any unfunded liability of the plan.

Beyond considerations of whether a plan's currently projected rate of return has an adequate margin for error, or whether net returns are generated by differences in credit ratings, a third factor to consider is whether a plan's overall investment returns can remain high even when bond yields decline. Assuming that a recent drop in bond yields is permanent and not a temporary opportunity to borrow at unusually low interest rates, a plan's asset allocation may still enable it to generate higher rates of return than the employer's borrowing cost.

For example, if the plan invests 60 percent of its assets in equities and 40 percent in corporate bonds, the plan could earn a high total rate of return on its equity investments, such as 9 percent, even though it may only break even on the corporate bond portion of its portfolio, which could yield a return equivalent to the employer's borrowing cost, such as 7.5 percent. Even for the bond portion of its portfolio, the municipal employer still enjoys the benefit of a small tax arbitrage because interest on the municipality's bonds are exempt from state taxes and therefore carry yields slightly below comparably rated corporate bonds.

A municipal employer considering the issuance of PFBs should very carefully consider these issues relating to its retirement plan's projected rates of return. If the plan should fail to earn a rate of return equal to its projected rate of return, the plan will have an additional unfunded liability and the employer will be obligated to make additional future UAAL payments to the plan.

Financial Impact: Precludes Ability to Skip Payments

Employers that have unfunded liabilities enjoy certain repayment provisions unavailable to other debtors, such as the ability to skip a payment at will or to extend the final maturity of the obligation each year. However, when plan returns exceed borrowing costs, this flexibility comes at a price.

Some municipalities may not value the flexibility to skip UAAL amortization payments, being satisfied that the ability to skip a future normal contribution preserves sufficient financial flexibility. Other municipalities may want to retain the ability to skip both normal and UAAL amortization contributions. In the latter case, taxpayers or public employees may benefit from the discipline imposed by the externalization of the debt (if they believe that the employer would not default on its debt service obligations to PFB investors).

If legislation is necessary to implement the PFB, policymakers may choose to mandate that no additional unfunded liabilities may be intentionally created. This may be helpful not only to ensure that the municipality does not skip future normal contribution payments but also that public employees—seeing that the plan is fully funded—do not create pressure to create new unfunded liabilities by increasing benefits.

Financial Impact: Additional Unfunded Liabilities Still Possible

Additional unfunded liabilities may still arise unintentionally. Due to the defined benefit nature of the employer's obligation, it is difficult to predict a plan's actual liabilities. It is possible that in a given year a municipality would have to pay both PFB debt service and the amortization of a newly created UAAL. A political risk created by PFBs is that voters may be unwilling to begin amortizing a new UAAL within a few years after bonds were issued fully to extinguish the formerly projected UAAL.

Financial Impact: Possible to Overfund Plan

Actuaries have raised the concern that under some circumstances a PFB issue could result in the "terminal overfunding" of a plan. This would occur if a plan reached a high enough surplus that its investments were projected to generate enough income each year to pay all plan benefits, even without any annual normal contributions from the employer. (Once PFB proceeds are deposited to the plan, the funds cannot be withdrawn by the employer.)

For open (ongoing) public plans, employment will typically increase over time and benefits will continue to be increased, both of which would decrease the plan's surplus if additional normal contributions were not made. Despite the permanence implied in the diagnosis, "terminal overfunding" for open plans is only a temporary condition, and one that would be welcomed by most public plans.

The terminal overfunding concern is relevant, however, for closed plans, which do not accept new members. A closed fund facing terminal overfunding could invest a substantial proportion of its assets in Treasury bills, lowering the expected surplus (due to a lower rate of return on Treasury bills than the projected return of a diversified portfolio) but protecting the plan from any investment performance risks. Furthermore, plan benefits could be increased to draw down the plan's assets faster than original projections. Employers funding a closed plan's UAAL with PFBs should be particularly cautious, as there are far fewer mechanisms available to adjust the plan's ongoing cash flows over time.

Financial Impact: PFBs Do Not Allow Negative Amortization

If plans are currently making actual funding progress, contributing funds each year to pay the full amount of interest due on the UAAL plus a portion of the principal amount of the UAAL, it is possible under certain market conditions to structure pension funding bonds that will provide a financial gain to the employer. However, as discussed above, some municipalities have severe negative amortization, and even a PFB issued as a single, long-term maturity would require the municipality to make interest payments which may exceed the current UAAL amortization payments. Investors are accustomed to receiving interest and principal payments each year, and converting a level percentage of payroll payment to a flat-level dollar payment may require cash flow changes.

Gary Finley, the Executive Director of the Missouri State Employees Retirement System and a skeptic of PFB issuance, has analyzed the mismatch between amortization patterns, concluding that special structuring techniques are often needed to avoid this dilemma (Finley 1994). One structuring alternative available is the issuance of discount (zero-coupon) PFBs that do not pay interest until maturity. However, PFB investors have not widely accepted such a structure at a cost-effective interest rate. Municipalities with severe negative UAAL amortization patterns have the most to gain over the long term by increasing their annual payments to amortize the UAAL, as interest on interest is avoided in the later years—potentially saving billions of dollars for some state governments.

Leaving aside a retirement plan's potential to earn a higher rate of return than the employer's borrowing cost, a primary benefit of issuing PFBs is that the employer may not have the discipline to make the annual UAAL amortization payments, which is how the negative amortization pattern may have been established. Similarly, a current state legislature that has begun to make progress on the UAAL amortization may not feel confident that a future legislature will continue these efforts. In either circumstance, a PFB issue can impose much-needed discipline into the funding process. An employer that has adequate financial discipline, and does not believe that it would benefit from the potential difference between its borrowing cost and its retirement plan's investment returns, would be well-advised simply to increase its own annual UAAL amortization payments without issuing a PFB. The self-disciplined approach would enable the employer to save the administrative costs associated with PFB issuance.

To summarize the financial impact of pension funding bonds, it may be possible for public employee retirement plans to earn long-term rates of return that exceed employers' PFB borrowing costs, but it is also possible that projected rate of return may be overestimated. Government employers that need the added financial discipline imposed by annual debt service payments, or are concerned about the discipline of future elected officials, may welcome PFBs as a mechanism for increasing UAAL amortization payments. However, this may prove difficult for municipal employers with severe negative amortization patterns, who would have to increase their annual payments to refinance their UAAL with pension funding bonds. Furthermore, employers that have the self-discipline to increase their contributions without the added obligation imposed by the capital markets can save administrative costs by increasing their contributions of their own volition.

Gary Finley summarizes three of the most important financial concerns relating to pension funding bonds. First, public officials may misunderstand that funding the UAAL does not extinguish the employer's ongoing obligation to meet all defined benefits. Second, employees may view the municipality's cost savings as an opportunity to increase benefits. Third, employers must consider whether an internal restructuring of contributions to the plan could accomplish similar results (Finley 1994).

Conclusion

Public plans maintain over US $1 trillion in assets and are responsible for the well-being of more than 13,000,000 public servants. Municipalities would be well served to investigate the nature of the risks that taxpayers assume as the providers of a defined benefit plan with uncertain liabilities and as the effective guarantors of public plans' inherently risky debt and equity investments.

Given the assumption that the defined benefit nature of plan liabilities will remain unchanged and that public plans will continue to invest in equities and bonds, this chapter has explored pension funding bonds as a technique for efficiently funding employer liabilities.

PCBs offer the potential to fund liabilities at a lower interest cost than the public retirement plans' projected investment return. Furthermore, the funding discipline introduced by the obligation to pay an external debt may benefit both taxpayers and employees. However, this discipline is imposed through a reduction in financial flexibility.

It is important to recognize that the repayment of a currently projected unfunded liability does not prevent future unfunded liabilities from being created, either due to increased benefits or due to unexpected changes in assets and liabilities. Municipalities with severely unfunded liabilities, particularly those that presently incur negative amortization, have the most to gain from the discipline imposed by PFBs but also would experience difficult short-term financial adjustments. Municipalities with high-quality ratings (at least "A" by Moody's and Standard & Poor's) are most likely to issue PFBs and can successfully use the technique under certain market conditions to provide increased retirement security to public employees at a lower cost to taxpayers.

Pension bonds attempt to reconfigure complex flows of funds, taking into consideration dynamic effects that occur over time. The complexity of the predicted interactions among benefits due and plan assets are compounded for multiemployer retirement plans, such as statewide teachers' retirement systems.

This chapter has attempted to provide an introductory discussion of issues relating to the concept of pension funding bonds issued by state and local government employers, and the potential costs and benefits of the approach. A maxim familiar to students of American government is that "all politics is local." Similarly, the determination of whether pension funding bonds are suitable for a particular municipal employer and its public employee retirement plan is best evaluated on a case-by-case basis.

References

Adler, Lynn K. and Tracy Sacco. "Cash-Strapped Municipalities Defer Pension Funds as a Short-Term Solution." *Wall Street Journal* (May 1, 1995): B13C, cols. 5–6.

Finley, Gary. *To Bond or Not To Bond?* St. Louis: Gabriel, Roeder, Smith & Company, 1994.

Galant, Debbie. "How Safe Are Stocks?" *Institutional Investor* 24, 4 (1995): 133.

Leibowitz, Martin L., Lawrence N. Bader, Stanley Kogelman, and Ajay R Dravid. *Pension Fund Risk Capacity: Surplus and Time Horizon Effects on Asset Allocation.* New York: Salomon Brothers, September 1994.

Office of the Legislative Auditor, State of Louisiana. Daniel G. Kyle, Auditor. *1992 Comprehensive Actuarial Report on the Louisiana Public Retirement Systems.* Baton Rouge: State of Louisiana, 1993.

Rohrer, Julie. "IBM Rethinks Pensions." *Institutional Investor* 24, 4 (1995): 141–42.

Schaffer, Susan, Steven G. Zimmerman, Chris Irwin, and G. Kris Rao. "Alameda County, California." *Standard & Poor's Creditweek Municipal* 15, 3 (April): 27–31.

Schultz, Ellen E. "State Street Unit to Offer Public-Retiree-Plan CDs." *Wall Street Journal* (April 11, 1995): C1, cols. 5–6.

Standard and Poor's (S&P). *Standard & Poor's Creditweek Municipal* 15, 3 (April), 30.

Zorn, Paul and Cathie G. Eitelberg. *Survey of State and Local Government Employee Retirement Systems.* Chicago: Government Finance Officers Association (book and PENDAT computer database), 1994.

———. "Pension Agency Cuts Deficit on Single-Employer Plans." *Wall Street Journal* (May 1, 1995): A10, col. 1.

Chapter 10
Public Pension Plan Efficiency

Ping-Lung Hsin and Olivia S. Mitchell

Population aging and fiscal stress are exerting pressures on public retirement systems worldwide. Finding ways to reduce the high costs of public pensions without contributing to a serious reduction in the quality of retirement services is an issue of public concern in the United States, where aging patterns combined with early retirement trends are exerting pressure on state and local government pension plans. When viewed against the backdrop of probably limited opportunities for collecting new public revenue, public sector plan managers are increasingly focusing on ways to make their pension plans function more efficiently. The topic is also one of central concern to policymakers elsewhere in the developed world and increasingly a prime target for reform in developing countries (Reid and Mitchell 1995).

This chapter investigates the determinants of pension administrative costs in state and local pension plans in the United States, seeking to draw lessons which might improve the design and governance of public pensions both in developed and in developing countries. In particular, streamlining public employee pensions without contributing to serious reductions in the quality of retirement services is a topic of great current interest. For example, some policymakers argue that governments should contract-out pension services, following the path taken by Chile in 1981 when that country turned most of its retirement system over to private (albeit heavily regulated) pension managers. While in Chile the privatization approach appeared to be quite costly initially, plan costs have declined of late (Reid and Mitchell 1995). Administrative costs may also vary depending on how the pension plan is organized and managed. For instance, in the United States there is a great deal of variation across public plans in terms of how their fiduciary boards are constituted, who authorizes their administrative cost budgets, and what kinds of participants are included in the plans. These differences in structure may influence administrative efficiency of the plans and could afford insights into how changing the way plans are structured could help save taxpayer money. Each of these possibilities is examined in the analysis below.[1]

Prior Studies of Pension System Administrative Efficiency

Previous research on pension administration costs has been mainly limited to simple multivariate analysis of *private* pension plans. The hypothesis examined in the few available analyses is straightforward, namely, that administrative costs rise less than proportionately as the size of the pension plan grows because certain inputs such as computer, accounting, payroll, or money management systems are lumpy investments. As a result, one would expect that as a pension system expands, plan costs would rise less than proportionately. If it could be proved that there are substantial cost savings from larger pension plans, this would suggest in the public sector, at least, that efforts to merge and coalesce larger groups of participants and plan assets could save taxpayer money. Conversely, breaking up large pension pools would be likely to make retirement systems more, not less, cost effective.

The first empirical study in the US context to examine the scale economies hypothesis in pension plans was an early piece by Caswell (1976) who focused on a subset of private-sector plans in the construction industry. These were multi-employer plans, called this because they were jointly managed by employers and unions in a collectively bargained environment. That study used multivariate linear regression to relate pension administration costs to two separate outputs—the total number of pension participants, and the total value of pension assets. Only one set of results was reported, namely, with regard to costs as they changed with the number of participants; the elasticity of costs with respect to the number of participants proved to be significantly less than unity, equaling 0.80. The study also indicated that costs rose with the number of employers covered by the system, holding constant the number of pension participants. In other words, having more pension sponsors apparently complicates pension administration. A final interesting finding in Caswell's study was that the pension system's administrative expenditures were not significantly affected by using in-house administrative staff compared to externally contracted agencies.

Some years later a follow-up study on multiemployer plans was carried out by Mitchell and Andrews (1981), who drew on Form 5500 pension plan reports filed in 1975 with the Department of Labor. Those authors estimated a Cobb-Douglas cost function, and found evidence for scale economies in that administrative expenses rose by only 0.80 if the size of the participant pool rose by 1 percent. Similar results were obtained by Cooper, Crabb, and Carlsen (1984) who also used a Cobb-Douglas cost function to estimate the determinants of pension system operating expenses. That analysis concluded that for each of three measures evaluated (participants, net pension assets, and employers' annual contributions) there appeared to be scale economies. Finally, Parsons (1992) recently reiterated the conclusion of scale economies for private pension plans, this time using aggregate rather than micro (plan-level) data.

The finding that there are substantial scale economies in *private*-sector pensions has not yet been extensively evaluated using *plan-level* information for *public* pension plans, nor has much multivariate analysis been undertaken. An *aggregate* data effort collected cross-national information on social security systems in a large number of developed and developing countries and found wide variation in administration costs across that set of nations. For example, Social Security administration costs averaged only 2 to 3 percent of benefit expenditures in the United States Social Security system and likewise across the large plans hosted by the OECD nations. In contrast, for the far smaller systems of Latin America and the Caribbean nations, social security administration costs averaged 28 percent of benefit expenditures (Mitchell et al. 1993, 1994). While little information is available with which to conduct multivariate analysis of scale economies internationally, two exploratory studies are supportive of the scale economies hypothesis (Reid and Mitchell 1995; James and Palacios 1995). Thus far, however, no careful multivariate state and local analysis has been carried out, a subject we turn to in the next section.

Measuring Administrative Efficiency of Public Employee Retirement Systems

Having found that the hypothesis of scale economies is confirmed for private pension plans and national social security programs, the question we turn to next is whether the hypothesis holds for US state and local pension plans as well. A related question we ask is whether the simpler cost studies of the past may have erred in assuming that pension plans are managed as efficiently as possible. Conventional cost studies assume that an institution operates on the feasible and economically efficient frontier with minimum possible expenditures, given the size of the pension plan as well as technological and environmental factors. This assumption may not hold in the public sector, since public retirement systems are generally not subject to direct market competition. If public pension plans operate far inside the administratively efficient frontier, we would be led to ask how substantial this inefficiency gap is and what factors might be associated with substantial inefficiencies. In the analysis below we test for this possibility directly.

The data set used for this study is known as the 1992 PENDAT data file, a cross-sectional survey of more than 300 public employee retirement systems (PERS) that together administer almost 500 state and local pension plans in the United States (Zorn 1993). Depending on the state, these plans cover public employees of all kinds, including judges and teachers, police and firefighters, among others. In 1992, these public retirement systems as a whole held assets of US $791 billion and covered 10.6 million active members.[2] To assess the relative importance of administrative expenditures within these public employee pension plans, it is useful to note that such costs averaged 12 percent of public *employers'* annual pension contributions, or 9 percent of *total* pension contributions (including employees' payments) in 1992.

The Model

In this study, public pension plan administrative efficiency is evaluated by measuring the gap between *frontier* and *actual* administrative costs. The term "frontier costs" refers to the minimum possible cost for a given amount of output and given input prices, and is denoted as C_0. If a pension plan's actual administrative costs were C_1, where C_1 exceeded C_0, then that PERS would be judged not to be on the efficiency frontier. Efficiency comparisons across different PERS can be effected by comparing the ratio of their frontier to their actual costs, known as a "Farrell-type" efficiency measure, C_0/C_1 (Farrell 1957). By contrast, if a public pension system's Farrell measure C_0/C_1 is higher than average, this would imply that that system was administered more efficiently. A public pension system on the frontier will have C_0/C_1 equal to unity.

Reported costs C_1 are reported in the PENDAT file, but the frontier measure C_0 is unobservable and must be estimated. This can be derived using a "stochastic frontier cost function" approach for estimation purposes, a technique which has been applied to measure the efficiency of other public services in recent years but not for public pensions.[3] This approach begins by specifying a general multiproduct cost function:

$$C_{1i} = f(Y, W; \alpha) + \epsilon_i,$$

where C_{1i} represents the actual administrative costs of a public retirement system i, Y is a vector of system outputs, W is a vector of input prices faced by each system, α is a vector of parameters, and ϵ_i is the error term.

For estimation purposes the model assumes that ϵ_i is made up of two independent components:

$$\epsilon_i = v_i + u_i, \qquad \text{where } u_i \geq 0.$$

The key to this approach is contained in the specification of the composite error term ϵ_i. The first component of the disturbance, v_i, captures random error and is posited to reflect exogenous independent changes in pension administration costs. The second error term, u_i, captures systematic technical factors that may lead to administrative costs exceeding the minimum frontier. If $u_i = 0$, then the retirement system i is said to be on the efficiency frontier.

To estimate the model, it is necessary to specify the exact functional form of $f(Y, W; \alpha)$, and the distribution of ϵ_i. Administrative expenditures of a PERS are incurred in producing two types of services: investment management and participant services. Of course in each case, it is somewhat difficult to define the PERS ultimate output. Nevertheless, following prior analysts, we identify two intermediate measures of output that are properly related to administrative expenditures: the value of assets held by the system (ASSETS), and the number of participants (PARTI), including both currently employed and retired members (Mitchell and Andrews 1981). Expenditures for investment management increase with the value of assets, but when scale economies exist, a system with more assets will be observed to incur lower administrative expenses per dollar invested. Similarly, expenditures rise with the number of participants, but economies of scale will be said to exist if an increase in the number of participants produces less than a proportionate increase in administrative expenses.

In addition to these two variables, public pension administrative expenditures are also likely to be influenced by the composition of participants and the complexity and quality of pension services provided. Thus serving retired participants may be more expensive than serving active participants (Caswell 1976; Mitchell and Andrews 1981). Extra expenses are also incurred for serving disabled retirees because of the necessary medical examinations. We also posit that administrative expenditures increase with the complexity of pension services, represented here by the number of pension plans administered by a PERS (NUMPLAN).[4] Typically, different state and local pension plans administered by the same PERS are from different localities or are negotiated with different unions (Zorn 1993). Required age and service years for receiving retirement benefits are also different among these pension plans.[5] Therefore, the more pension plans a PERS administers, the more complicated its pension services are likely to be. Finally, we seek to measure the quality of pension services by the annualized rate of return on pension assets over the previous five years (Y5ROR).[6] Other things being equal, administrative expenditures may increase with pension service quality, because more and better inputs are used.

As in most cross-section cost function studies, input prices are not explicitly included in the analysis. Their omission from the PENDAT file is probably not serious because the most important wage costs for public pension systems cover the services of actuaries, lawyers, accountants, and financial advisors. Salaries for these professionals are nationally competitive and hence are not expected to vary systematically across systems (Mitchell and Andrews 1981).

To summarize, the empirical formula employed in examining public pension plans' administrative costs is expressed as a log-linear cost function:[7]

$$\ln(C_{1i}) = \alpha_0 + \alpha_1\ln(\text{PARTI}_i) + \alpha_2\ln(\text{ASSETS}_i) + \alpha_3\text{SERRATE}_i$$
$$+ \alpha_4\text{DISRATE}_i + \alpha_5\text{NUMPLAN}_i + \alpha_3\text{Y5ROR}_i + \epsilon_i \tag{1A}$$

where

C_{1i} is the actual administrative expenditure of the retirement system I; and SERRATE and DISRATE represent the fractions of normal retirees and disabled retirees in the total pension participant pool.

ASSETS and PARTI are highly correlated, causing problems of collinearity when both are included in the model. Hence we multiply assets per participant, ASTPER by PARTI, and rearrange equation (1.A) as follows:[8]

$$\ln(C_{1i}) = \alpha_0 + \alpha_1\ln(\text{PARTI}_i) + \alpha_2\ln(\text{PARTI}_i{*}\text{ASTPER}_i) + \alpha_3\text{SERRATE}_i$$
$$+ \alpha_4\text{DISRATE}_i + \alpha_5\text{NUMPLAN}_i + \alpha_3\text{Y5ROR}_i + \epsilon_i$$
$$= \alpha_0 + \alpha_1{'}\ln(\text{PARTI}_i) + \alpha_2\ln(\text{ASTPER}_i) + \alpha_3\text{SERRATE}_i$$
$$+ \alpha_4\text{DISRATE}_i + \alpha_5\text{NUMPLAN}_i + \alpha_3\text{Y5ROR}_i + \epsilon_i \tag{1.B}$$

where $\alpha_1{'} = \alpha_1 + \alpha_2$.

It will be readily seen that this equation is a Cobb-Douglas type cost function; thus, coefficients on output measures, α_1 and α_2, represent output cost elasticity. The incremental proportion of administrative expenditures caused by a 1 percent increase in the number of participants is represented by $\alpha_1{'}$. These incremental expenditures include expenses for non-investment services to the added participants and the expenses of managing the assets maintained for these participants. The incremental proportion of administrative expenditures caused by a 1 percent increase in the value of assets is α_2. The difference between $\alpha_1{'}$ and α_2 is the cost elasticity with respect to non-investment services provided to participants. Economies of scale in public pension administration would be said to exist if α_1' is less than one.

The administrative cost frontier of retirement system i is derived by setting the error term u_i, which is part of ϵ_i, to zero in equation (1.B). Since the determination of the cost frontier still involves the noise error term, v_i, the cost frontier specified in this setting is called "stochastic."[9] Following Aigner, Lovell, and Schmidt (1977), we assume that u is drawn from a half-normal and v is from a normal distribution. In this event the model can be estimated by maximizing likelihood approach, and the Farrell-type efficiency indicator of retirement system i, C_{0i}/C_{1i}, is equal to $\exp(-u_i)$. Although u_i is unobservable, the expectation of u_i, conditioned on ϵ_i can also be estimated.[10]

Results

Table 1 reports descriptive statistics on all variables of interest for the PENDAT state and local pension plan sample. In these data, the measure

TABLE 1 Multivariate Analysis of Administrative Expenditures of Public Employee Retirement Systems

	Mean (S.D.)	Frontier Function Estimate
Dependent variable		
COST (US $K)	6.95	
ln (administrative expenditures)	(1.88)	
Independent variables		
PARTI	8.94	0.74**
ln (N. active & ret. participants)	(2.34)	(0.03)
ASSETS (US $M)	−2.92	0.49**
ln (mkt assets per participant)	(0.72)	(0.08)
SERRATE (%)	24.35	−0.004
Normal retirees to total participants	(11.41)	(0.006)
DISRATE (%)	2.72	0.02
Disabled retirees to total participants	(3.61)	(0.02)
NUMPLAN	1.38	0.03
N. pension plans per PERS	(1.00)	(0.10)
Y5ROR (%)	10.83	0.02
Annualized rate of return—5 year av	(1.69)	(0.03)
Constant		1.03**
		(0.63)
Log-likelihood ratio		−230.93
No. of pension systems		197

Source: 1992 PENDAT file; see text.
**Indicates significance at 0.05 level.

of pension plan participants per system is computed as the sum of participants across all individual plans in each retirement system. This measure includes active and retired members, but not vested terminated members, due to the way the survey asked the question; nevertheless, since job turnover is uncommon in the public sector, excluding vested terminated members is not a matter of concern. Pension system assets are measured as the reported market value of each pension system's holdings. Administrative expenditures of public employee retirement systems are taken from annual administrative budgets reported by each pension system.

After excluding systems with missing values for these key variables, the sample for analysis consists of 197 state and local pension systems, covering a total of 272 separate retirement plans.[11] The first column of Table 1 presents means and standard deviations of key variables. Per-plan administrative expenditures for a state/local retirement system averaged about US $130 per participant per year, a cost that compares favorably to median administrative expenditures per participant in large private defined benefit pension plans of about US $110 (in 1992 dollars).[12]

Maximum likelihood estimates of the coefficients from the efficiency model (the α's) appear in the second column of Table 1.[13] Of most interest is the estimated coefficient on (the log of the number of) participants, which is about 0.74. The fact that it is substantially less than 1 implies that scale economies are powerful in the public pension arena. Specifically, a 1 percentage point increase in plan participants would be predicted to increase public plan administrative expenditures by 0.74 of a percentage point, holding assets per participant constant. This number is remarkably close to the 0.80 figure reported in the private pension arena by Caswell (1976), Mitchell and Andrews (1981), and Cooper, Crabb and Carlsen (1984).

Even greater economies are revealed in the estimated coefficient on (the log of) the market value of assets per participant. The term is equal to 0.49, suggesting that a plan with 1 percentage point additional assets would be expected to have costs rise by less than half a percent. This is not quite twice the same elasticity found for private plans (0.27; see Mitchell and Andrews 1981). Using the derivation above, we compute that administrative expenditures also rise less than one-for-one with respect to non-investment services, where the elasticity is equal to 0.25 (calculated as the difference between 0.74 and 0.49). This cost elasticity is about half that estimated for private pension plans (0.56; see Mitchell and Andrews 1981). While the overall pattern of results between the private and public plans seems similar, there is clear evidence of some differences between the way public and private pension agencies allocate money management expenditures.[14] In general these results confirm

that there are significant economies of scale in public pension administration for both investment and non-investment services.

Another conclusion from Table 1 is that there is evidence of substantial inefficiency in the data. Estimated $\exp(-u)$ has an average value of
65 percent; the farther is this coefficient from 1.0, the less efficient is the
pension plan. In other words, as much as one-third of pension administrative expenditures are attributable to inefficiency using this methodology. Whether this number is larger or smaller than other similar
institutions is not known, but public plan efficiency in administration
appears somewhat less than that of other publicly managed institutions
in the United States. For example, in local police departments, about a
quarter of local administrative costs have been attributed to inefficiency
(Davis and Hayes 1993), and almost one-fifth in city government offices
(Hayes and Chang 1990). Research on heavily regulated United States
reports that inefficiency measured in the same manner seems to be
roughly 15 percent of costs (Zuckerman, Hadley, and Iezzoni 1994; Newhouse 1994). The extent of inefficiency in public pension plans appears
comparable to, or even a bit lower than, levels reported by researchers
studying the heavily regulated property liability insurers, where up to
45 percent of costs are due to inefficiency (Berger, Cummins, and Weiss
1995).

Turning to other results in Table 1, the findings offer no support for
the hypothesis that public plan administrative expenditures differ depending on the type of workers covered. This is different from results in
the private sector reported by Mitchell and Andrews (1981), who found
that services provided to retirees were more expensive. Table 1 also
shows that administrative performance in the public pension environment is not sensitive to the number of pension plans administered, a
finding which differs from Caswell's (1976) analysis of the construction
industry. Finally, the investment performance of public pension assets
has no statistically significant influence on administrative expenditures,
although the coefficient of $Y5ROR$ is positive.

Determinants of Pension Administrative Efficiency

In this section we move from documenting the extent of pension administrative inefficiency to a closer examination of particular institutional
features that seem to be associated with inefficient outcomes in the pension plan arena. One observation is that public retirement systems differ
according to who is scheduled to pay for administrative expenditures
incurred in running the plans. In nearly two-thirds of the PENDAT systems, these expenses must be paid out of plan investment earnings or
from pension contributions, while in the remaining one-third of the sys-

tems such expenditures are paid out of general revenues by the sponsoring employer. We hypothesize that pension boards may spend more per unit of output if they are permitted to authorize their own budgets, an effect which could be enhanced if the board need not cover its costs out of its own budget.

A second aspect we investigate is public plan governance, namely, who is responsible for the authorization of pension benefit levels, contribution, and funding decisions in a given plan. In about half the retirement systems under study, public pension administrative budgets are authorized by the governing boards of the pension systems themselves. In the other half of the cases, regulations require the state legislature or a specific outside council to authorize administrative budgets. Whether this oversight structure has a potent effect on administrative efficiency is explored below empirically.

A different dimension along which pension board governance varies pertains to the makeup of the board itself. PERS trustees are either elected by pension participants, appointed by governor, or serve ex officio, and board composition varies a great deal across systems. On average, one-third of board trustees are elected by pension participants, while the other two-thirds are appointed or serve ex officio. In earlier analysis we found that pension funding and investment performance was somewhat lower when participants served on their pension system's board (Mitchell and Hsin 1994). It may be that having participant-elected members on pension boards also reduces measured pension administrative efficiency. On the other hand, participant-elected trustees may have fewer incentives to expand administrative budgets because they may be less concerned with their own power, prestige, or patronage and more concerned with the welfare of their constituents. Therefore, the net effect of the fraction of participant-elected trustees on pension administrative efficiency is an empirical matter.

Pension administrative efficiency may also differ between state and local governments, as argued by analysts who contend that state pension plan staffers are better trained than are staff members of local plans (Bleakney 1972). Whether this is true can be examined directly by investigating whether state pension plans prove to be administered more efficiently than local plans: in the PENDAT data file, about one-fifth of public employee retirement systems are administered by state governmental units whereas local governmental units provide day-to-day administration of the remaining systems. The type of employees may also be important along the same lines; more educated participants, such as teachers, might be in a better position to monitor plan expenses as compared to a broader mix of covered workers. Similarly, it may be that public sector unions exert a watchdog function over costs, in which case it would be expected that plans covering unionized employees would experience measured efficiency (Mitchell and Smith 1994).

A final aspect of interest is the possible influence of contracting-out on public pension plan administrative efficiency. One form this takes among US public pension systems is that boards frequently hire professional money managers to invest fund assets. Many PERS have in-house investment staff, of course, but it is common for a public system to use at least one external private investment manager or performance measurement service (Mitchell and Hsin 1994), and, in some instances, all of the investment decisions are handled exclusively by external agents. Advocates of privatization suggest that contracting out may improve efficiency in providing public services because of different incentives driving private versus public sector managers.[15] Thus it is worthwhile investigating whether contracting out pension investment services to private agents improves public pension plans' administrative efficiency.

An examination of the influence of these several administrative features on pension administrative efficiency is facilitated using the following multivariate linear regression model:

$$
\begin{aligned}
\exp(-u_i) = &\ \beta_0 + \beta_1 \text{EXTPURE}_i + \beta_2 \text{BUDPAYOK}_i + \beta_3 \text{BUDOK}_i \\
&+ \beta_4 \text{PAYOK}_i + \beta_5 \text{BDELMEM}_i + \beta_6 \text{STADMIN}_i \\
&+ \beta_7 \text{TCHRPLAN}_i + \beta_8 \text{POFIPLAN}_i + \beta_9 \text{UNIONRT}_i + \kappa_i
\end{aligned}
\tag{2}
$$

where $\exp(-u_i)$ is the efficiency indicator derived in the previous section; EXTPURE is set to 1 when the public plan's investment management function is handled exclusively by external private contractors (else 0); BUDPAYOK is set to 1 if the plan's board both sets the administrative budget and must pay for it via pension investment earnings or contributions (else 0); BUDOK is equal to 1 if the plan's board authorizes administrative budgets but is not required to pay for it out of plan revenues (else 0); PAYOK is equal to 1 if the plan's board must pay for the administrative budgets are but cannot authorize administrative expenses (else 0); BDELMEM is the fraction of participant-elected trustees on the pension board; STADMIN is equal to 1 if the retirement system is administered by a state governmental unit (else 0); TCHRPLAN is equal to 1 if the major participants of the system are teachers or school employees (else 0); POFIPLAN is equal to 1 if the plan covers mainly police or firefighters (else 0); UNIONRT is the fraction of active members of the system represented by unions; and κ is assumed to be a normally distributed error term.

This multivariate model is estimated using ordinary least squares, and descriptive statistics of all variables used are given in Table 2. Here we note that, across the systems under study, about two-thirds used external

TABLE 2 Multivariate Analysis of Administrative Efficiency of Public Employee Retirement System

	Mean (S.D.)	OLS Estimate
Dependent Variable:		
exp($-u$)	65.01	
Efficiency ratio	(8.73)	
Independent Variables:		
EXTPURE	0.64	2.48*
External money managers only	(0.48)	(1.38)
BUDPAYOK	0.42	−4.01†
Admin. budget authorized & paid by pension board	(0.49)	(1.84)
BUDOK	0.18	−4.81†
Admin. budget authorized by board but paid by employer	(0.39)	(2.10)
PAYOK	0.23	0.68
Admin. budget authorized by employer but paid by pension board	(0.42)	(2.02)
BDELMEM	35.27	0.014
% of pension board elected by participants	(25.74)	(0.03)
TCHRPLAN	0.14	1.33
Teacher/school employee retirement system	(0.35)	(1.88)
POFIPLAN	0.16	−1.10
Police/fire fighter retirement system	(0.37)	(1.78)
STADMIN	0.20	−1.87
Retirement system admin. by state government	(0.40)	(1.75)
UNIONRT	73.95	0.012
% of actives rep. by union	(43.35)	(0.015)
Constant		64.82†
		(2.14)
R-squared		0.10
N. pension systems		197

Source: 1992 PENDAT file; see text.
*t-value ≥ 1.65
†t-value ≥ 1.96

money managers to handle exclusively their investment decisions. Pension boards both authorized and paid administrative budgets through pension investment earnings or contributions in 42 percent of the retirement systems; in another 23 percent of the cases boards paid administrative expenses but did not authorize the budgets, and in 18 percent of the cases the boards only authorized expenditures. In the remaining systems, the administrative budgets were neither authorized nor paid for by pension boards. The averages also show that about one-third of public pension board trustees are elected by pension participants, with most of the remaining trustees appointed or serving ex officio. Most of the retirement systems were general public employee plans, and only 14 percent were teacher-only systems, with 16 percent police- or firefighter-only systems. Most plans included some members covered by unions, averaging a 74 percent coverage rate across these PENDAT pension plans (state-only systems were one-fifth of these plans).

Estimated parameters (β's) appear in the second column of Table 2.[16] The first estimated coefficient, which is positive and statistically significant, indicates that plans are more efficient if they contract out investment services to private money managers. This offers convincing evidence that public pension plan administrative efficiency is improved by using external investment managers, holding other factors constant. Above we hypothesized that efficiency will be lower when plan administrative cost budgets are authorized by pension boards; this hypothesis is upheld in the data as is evident from the two negative and statistically coefficients on these variables. Specifically, we find that granting pension boards authority over their administrative budgets decreases systems' administrative efficiency. This effect persists, and is indeed somewhat stronger, when administrative budgets can be charged to a sponsoring employer, as opposed to having the system cover its own costs directly.

Turning to other estimation results, there appears to be no systematic linkage between a public pension plan's degree of administrative efficiency and board makeup, as indicated by the coefficient on participant-elected board members. There were also no significant differences in pension administrative efficiency discerned between state versus local retirement systems, or more or less unionized plans, or between plans covering different types of employees. In general, the relatively low R-squared shows that the overall variance in plan relative efficiency is only partly associated with hypothesized explanatory variables.

Implications

To explore further the magnitudes of these estimation results, we simulate how public pension administrative costs would be posited to change if plans could be structured more efficiently. To do this we use statistically significant coefficients in Table 2 combined with estimated inefficiency magnitudes from Table 1. The exercise to arrive at the cost savings per plan that would result from greater administrative efficiency is as follows: assume that on average 35 percent of all plans' administrative costs are inefficient based on the frontier function model; then multiply this fraction by the average dollar figure devoted to pension system administration by public plans in the PENDAT sample. As Table 3 points out, an average plan would be expected to save approximately US $370,000 per

TABLE 3 Simulation Analysis of Public Pension Plan Administrative
        Expenditures

Public Pension Management Technique	Yields Change in Annual Plan Administrative Expenditures
1. If all state and local plans were administered on the efficiency frontier.	Pension administration costs would fall by US $365 K per plan / US $876 M PERS-wide.
2. If all state and local plans contracted out their entire investment activity to private money managers.	Pension administration costs would fall by US $25 K per plan / US $6 M PERS-wide.
3. If all state and local plans' administrative budgets were authorized and paid for by pension boards.	Pension administration costs would rise by US $41 K per plan / US $100 M PERS-wide.
4. If all state and local administrative budgets were authorized by pension boards, but paid for by the public employer.	Pension administration costs would rise by US $50 K per plan / US $120 M PERS-wide.

Source: Derived from coefficient estimates in Table 2 and median per-plan administrative
expenditures of US $1 M per plan.

year (in 1992 dollars) by operating on the efficiency frontier. This translates into estimated cost savings for the approximately 2,400 public pension plans in the country of about US $876 million in administrative
expenses.[17]

What if existing plans switched investment practices and utilized external money managers exclusively? Based on the figures given above, the
average public pension system would save about US $25,000 per year in
administrative expenditures by contracting out all investment services
to private money managers as efficient as those used by plans in the
PENDAT sample. Taking this figure to the PERS universe, it is estimated
that about US $6 million per year could be saved from such a strategy.

Alternatively, what might be the result of changing pension board authority so as to permit all PERS boards to authorize, and pay for, their
own administrative budgets? The results in Table 3 indicate, that for
the average public plan, this move would increase administrative costs
US $41,000 per year. Averaging this figure across all PERS, administrative
expenditures would be predicted to rise by about US $100 million per
year. If, instead, PERS boards' powers were restricted to authorizing administrative budgets, but administrative costs were charged to and paid
for by the sponsoring employer, administrative expenditures would be
predicted to rise by US $120 million per year.

Conclusions

Reducing the high costs of public pensions without cutting the quality of the retirement services provided by these plans is an important issue of public concern everywhere. This chapter has examined a new data set on state and local pension plans in the United States in order to investigate the determinants of pension administrative costs. Our goal has been to draw lessons which might improve the design and governance of public pensions both in developed and in developing countries.

This analysis of a large number of US state and local pension plans reveals that, on average, administrative expenditures per participant are high but not apparently higher than in private pension plans. In both cases, to take advantage of scale economies, pension plans could benefit from merging and coalescing into larger pension pools.

We have also offered evidence that pension administrative costs could be substantially reduced if the systems were operated more efficiently. A multivariate frontier function approach was used to show that, on average, the public pension systems examined here operated at about 65 percent efficiency, suggesting that substantial cost savings might be derived from better management.

In examining patterns of public pension inefficiency, we found evidence that efficiency is higher when administrative budgets are authorized by a group other than the pension board. We also find that contracting out pension investment services to private money managers improves administrative efficiency. Finally, the extent of public plan administrative efficiency varies widely among PERS. While our model revealed only some of the variation, there remain many other factors influencing public plans' administrative efficiency. To investigate these factors, more comprehensive data must be gathered, including additional information on administrative structure and control. That it is critical to do so is obvious, given the increasing authority that the federal government is devolving to states and eventually to locally run public-sector institutions.

Opinions are those of the authors and not the institutions with whom they are affiliated.

Notes

1. We recognize that reducing administrative costs will not save insolvent and chronically underfunded pension systems; see Reid and Mitchell (1995) and Hsin and Mitchell (1994) for further discussion of this issue.

2. The public employee retirement systems included in the PENDAT data file represent the vast majority of state and local pension participants, covering 86 percent of total state and local pension plan assets and 83 percent of active pension plan members. Nevertheless the fact that the survey does not include all plans must be kept in mind when interpreting results; these plans are among the largest in the nation and perhaps are better managed than some smaller systems. Previous research on public pension funding outcomes using this data set (Hsin and Mitchell 1994) suggested no potent effect of selectivity bias, however.

3. The stochastic frontier cost approach has been applied in assessing the efficiency of several public-sector activities including municipal government (Hayes and Chang 1990; Deller and Rudnick 1992) and police departments (Davis and Hayes 1993). An early survey of the frontier function approach appears in Forsund, Lovel, and Schmidt (1980); recent developments in this approach appear in Bauer (1990).

4. This follows Caswell's specification for measuring private pension plan complexity.

5. The actuarial assumptions and the benefit accrual rates are usually the same for state and local pension plans administered by the same PERS.

6. We recognize that the service quality provided by a PERS cannot be represented solely by the rate of return on pension assets. For instance, some might argue that covered participants' satisfaction level might be a good measure of system performance. However in the PENDAT survey, the plan's rate of return is the only performance measure available in this data set.

7. We also investigated a translog cost function. However, the hypothesis that all the coefficients of the quadratic terms are equal to 0 cannot be rejected at the 1 percent significance level.

8. A different way to handle the collinearity problem is to include PARTI and ASSETS separately in two different models (e.g., Caswell 1976; Cooper et al. 1984). The cost elasticity for investment and non-investment services, however, cannot be distinguished using this approach.

9. A different type of cost frontier excludes the error term and is called "deterministic" (Greene 1980). The advantage of the stochastic specification is that estimation of the cost frontier is less likely to be influenced by data outliers. For a comparison between the two cost frontier approaches see Forsund, Lovell, and Schmidt (1980).

10. For estimation of $E(u_i | \epsilon_i)$ see Jondrew et al. (1982).

11. The PENDAT sample is diminished by almost two-fifths due to item non-response. However, omitted plans were very small as a rule; systems analyzed still held US $691 billion in assets, only 12 percent less than the initial group of systems surveyed. As a consequence, results reported here probably represent upper-bound estimates of public plan efficiency.

12. Expenditures per participant in private *multiemployer* pension plans averaged about US $50/year (1992$); see Caswell (1976), Mitchell and Andrews (1981), Turner and Beller (1989), and Reid and Mitchell (1995). The gap in administrative expenditures between public and private pension plans may be larger than described above, however, once different accounting systems in public versus private sectors are taken into consideration. Private pension systems are likely to report most administrative expenditures, including operating expenses and such expenses as building and capital depreciation, but these may not be properly accounted for by public pension plan administrations. Public plans might also understate their costs if they share equipment or offices with other

government branches. Hence administrative expenditures reported by public pension agencies almost certainly understate the full cost of resources devoted to providing pension services, a point that should be kept in mind when comparing the administrative efficiency of public and private pension systems; c.f. Reid and Mitchell (1995). The US $130 median figure (= exp(6.95)/exp(8.94)) in the text is higher than the average of US $260 derived by dividing costs by participant by plan. Because outliers thus strongly influence the simple averages, we use medians in the discussion below.

13. Some may question whether the regression results are biased since some portion of the administrative costs are not fully reported in plans that have been partially or fully contracted out. However Paul Zorn (personal communication) suggests this is a modest problem, and we conclude that the regression results might be biased, but the bias is not serious.

14. These differences could also be the result of differences in model specification; for instance, collinearity between output levels of investment and non-investment services was not addressed by Mitchell and Andrews (1981).

15. The World Bank (1994) summarizes the case for privatizing or contracting out public pension plans. For a general discussion of public/private differences in the production process and their effects on incentive structures and monitoring see Hirsch (1991), who notes that owners of a private-sector production process have incentives to monitor quality because they can transfer their ownership and reap the residual profits. In the public sector, however, voters (owners of the public production processes) cannot generally transfer their ownership, which discourages profit seeking and hence monitoring. Although they can reap the residual profits in paying lower taxes, these profits must be shared with all the residents in a jurisdiction, regardless of whether they pay the costs of monitoring. As a consequence, the costs of producing goods may be higher in public than in private production. For a discussion of the impact of bureaucrats' behavior on efficiency see Niskanen (1971).

16. In alternate analyses (results not presented here) we estimated models which included fewer variables in the first-stage and more in the second-stage equation. However, results for included variables did not differ from those presented in Tables 1 and 2.

17. This computation uses median (unlogged) administrative costs per PERS of US $1 million in 1994 (exp 6.95). Outliers make average administrative costs higher, at about US $4 million but the text uses the more representative amount.

References

Aigner, Dennis, C.A. Knox Lovell, and Peter Schmidt. "Formulation and Estimation of Stochastic Frontier Production Function Models." *Journal of Econometrics* (1977) 6: 21–37.

Bauer, Paul W. "Recent Developments in the Econometric Estimation of Frontiers." *Journal of Econometrics* 46, 1–2 (1990): 39–56.

Berger, Allen N., J. David Cummins, and Mary A. Weiss. The Coexistence of Alternative Distribution Systems for the Same Financial Services: The Case of Property-Liability Insurance. Mimeo, Philadelphia: Wharton Financial Institutions Center, 1994.

Bleakney, Thomas P. *Retirement Systems for Public Employees.* Homewood, IL: Pension Research Council and Richard D. Irwin, 1972.

Caswell, Jerry W. "Economic Efficiency in Pension Plan Administration: A Study of the Construction Industry." *Journal of Risk and Insurance* 43 (1976): 257–73.

Cooper, Robert D., Connie Ann Crabb, and Melody A. Carlsen. *Pension Fund Operations and Expenses—The Technical Report*. Milwaukee, WI: International Foundation of Employee Benefit Plans, 1984.

Davis, Michael L. and Kathy Hayes. "The Demand for Good Government." *Review of Economics and Statistics* (1993): 148–52.

Deller, Steven C. and Edward Rudnicki. "Managerial Efficiency in Local Government: Implications on Jurisdictional Consolidation." *Public Choice* 74 (1992): 221–31.

Farrell, M. J. "The Measurement of Productivity Efficiency." *Journal of the Royal Statistical Society* General Series A, 120, 3 (1957): 251–83.

Forsund, F. R., Christopher A. K. Lovell, and Peter Schmidt. "A Survey of Frontier Production Functions and of Their Relationship to Efficiency Measurement." *Journal of Econometrics* 13, 1 (1980): 5–25.

Greene, William H. "Maximum Likelihood Estimation of Econometric Frontier Functions." *Journal of Econometrics* 13, 1 (1980): 27–56.

Hayes, Kathy and Semoon Chang. "The Relative Efficiency of City Manager and Mayor-Council Forms of Government." *Southern Economic Journal* 57, 1 (1990): 167–77.

Hirsch, Werner Z. *Privatizing Government Services: An Economic Analysis of Contracting Out by Local Governments*. Los Angeles: Institute of Industrial Relations, University of California, 1991.

Hsin, Ping-Lung and Olivia S. Mitchell. "The Political Economy of Public Pensions: Pension Funding, Governance, and Fiscal Stress." In Patricio Arrau and Klaus Schmidt-Hebbel, eds., *Revista de Analisis Economico: Special Issue on Pension Systems and Reform* 9, 1 (June 1994): 151–68.

James, Estelle and Robert Palacios. "Costs of Administering Public Pension Plans." *Finance and Development* (June 1995): 12–15.

Jondrew, James, C.A. Knox Lovell, Ivan S. Materov, and Peter Schmidt. "On the Estimation of the Technical Inefficiency in the Stochastic Frontier Production Models." *Journal of Econometrics* 19 (1982): 233–38.

Mitchell, Olivia S. "Retirement Systems in the Developed and Developing World: Institutional Structure, Economic Effects, and Lessons for Economies in Transition". In A. Van Adams, E. King, and Zafinis Tzannatos, eds., *Labor Market Policies for Managing the Social Cost of Economic Adjustment*. Washington, DC: World Bank, forthcoming.

Mitchell, Olivia S. and Emily S. Andrews. "Scale Economies in Private Multi-Employer Pension Systems." *Industrial and Labor Relations Review* 34, 4 (1981): 522–30.

Mitchell, Olivia S. and Ping-Lung Hsin. "Managing Public Sector Pensions". In John B. Shoven and Sylvester Schieber, eds., *Public Policy Toward Pensions*. New York: Twentieth Century Fund, fothcoming.

Mitchell, Olivia S and Ping-Lung Hsin. Public Pension Governance and Performance. NBER working paper, 1994.

Mitchell, Olivia S. and Robert Smith. "Public Sector Pension Funding." *Review of Economics and Statistics* (May 1994).

Mitchell, Olivia S., Annika Sunden, and Ping-Lung Hsin, "An International Comparison of Social Security Administration Costs" *International Compensation and Benefits* (1994).

Mitchell, Olivia S., Annika Sunden, Ping-Lung Hsin, and Gary Reid. An International Appraisal of Social Security Administration Costs. Mimeo, Washington, DC: World Bank, 1993.

Newhouse, Joseph. "Frontier Estimation: How Useful a Tool for Health Economics?" *Journal of Health Economics* 13 (1994): 317–22.

Niskanen, William A., Jr. *Bureaucracy and Representative Government.* Chicago: Aldine-Atherton, 1971.

Parsons, Donald O. "Recent Trends in Private Pension Coverage." Ohio State University, mimeo, 1992.

Reid, Gary and Olivia S. Mitchell. Social Security Administration in Latin America and the Caribbean. Paper prepared for Public Sector Modernization and Private Sector Development Unit, The World Bank, March 1995.

Skinner, Jonathan. "What Do Stochastic Frontier Cost Functions Tell Us About Inefficiency?" *Journal of Health Economics* 13 (1994): 323–28.

Turner, John A. and Daniel J. Beller, eds. *Trends in Pensions 1989.* US Department of Labor. Washington, DC: USGPO, 1989.

World Bank. *Averting The Old Age Crisis: Policies to Protect the Old and Promote Growth.* New York: Oxford University Press, 1994.

Zorn, Paul. *Survey of State and Local Government Employee Retirement Systems: Data Base User's Guide.* Public Pension Coordinating Council, 1993.

Zuckerman, Stephen, Jack Hadley, and Lisa Iezzoni. "Measuring Hospital Efficiency with Frontier Cost Functions." *Journal of Health Economics* 13 (1994): 255–80.

Part III
Cross Currents in National Retirement Income Policy

Chapter 11
Analytical Framework for Retirement Policy Decisions

Constance F. Citro and Eric A. Hanushek

It is commonly recognized that the process of policy development and implementation is not closely linked to research and analytical efforts. This situation became very clear during recent policy debates on health care. As task forces, executive branch agencies, and Congress strove to define new organizational and regulatory policies to improve provision of health services, they repeatedly found that knowledge about key underlying relationships was missing. The dearth of relevant information was most apparent when analysts attempted to price out reforms and arrived at conclusions that differed by integer multiples. In some key ways, however, the situation with respect to health care policy is better than the situation with respect to retirement income policy. The heterogeneity of circumstances and the long delays between policy and effects place special analytical requirements on modeling retirement income policy. Moreover, the analytical infrastructure for many policies actively being considered today is noticeably weak.

In recognition of this situation, the Pension and Welfare Benefits Administration of the U.S. Department of Labor requested that the National Research Council form a Panel on Retirement Income Modeling.[1] This panel of experts was charged with recommending how the government could be better positioned to make decisions concerning various elements of retirement policy,[2] and here we describe the issues taken up by the Panel. The Appendix lists some of the specific recommendations issued by the Panel.

Background Perspective

This effort is not aimed at designing public policies. Instead, its objective is to ensure that appropriate analytical tools are available when policies are being designed. The development of appropriate tools, however, is complicated by the difficulty of the problem.

Retirement income for any individual results from a series of lifetime decisions and an array of current and past governmental policies. Some of these decisions appear quite remote from anything to do with retirement, even though they have strong implications for ultimate retirement income and well-being of the individual. For example, the private pension income of an individual is directly linked to occupational and firm employment choices made throughout the lifetime, even though the immediate circumstances of income and job satisfaction may loom much larger in these career choices. Government tax regulations may similarly affect the path of savings accumulation of individuals, having significant effects on the security provided by private savings.

The lengthy time periods involved in savings and retirement and decisions present special modeling challenges. Actions taken today will not have their full effects for many years to come; similarly, the need for various policies may not be apparent today because the problem will not be felt until some time in the future. Understanding savings and retirement decisions that unfold over the work life of individuals necessitates either extensive longitudinal data sets that follow individuals across careers and/or strong assumptions about how today's outcomes might relate to those in the future.

In many areas of research, we attempt to infer what will develop over time for one group by comparing this group today to an older group today. For example, if we are interested in life-cycle earnings of people with different amounts of education, we frequently take data from a cross-section of individuals and implicitly assume that todays 25-year-old twenty years from now will look like today's 45-year-old. Recently, however, data have become available both for repeated cross sections (e.g., the Current Population Survey) and for true panels that follow a set of individuals over time (e.g., the Panel Study on Income Dynamics or the National Longitudinal Surveys). Analyses of these suggest that observations and inferences about the future earnings of 25-year-olds differ significantly from those that would result from simple cross-sectional projections. At the very least, the economic environment and the relative demands for individuals with varying amounts of schooling have changed dramatically over the past two decades, and, while there are still debates about the correct interpretation of how earnings patterns have changed, there is no disagreement that the simple cross-sectional analysis is prone to very distorted pictures. The availability of rich longitudinal data has taken us along the road of being able to separate the natural life-cycle changes from effects of different time periods and from being in different age cohorts (even though analytical difficulties still remain).

With savings and retirement decisions, the same basic analytical difficulties are present and are, if anything, stronger. Analysis of individual decisions in these areas must sort out life-cycle changes from other effects that occur over time. But layered on top is the much more central role of governmental policies that are in place at any point in time and that might be expected to change over time. A similar statement holds for the policies of firms and organizations providing private pensions. Thus, the active and continuing decisions of individuals are conditioned by expectations about firm and governmental decisions, making the evolution of decisions much more complicated. Moreover, because of the undeniable importance of the evolving policy environment, the data and modeling requirements become much more central—or, put the other way, assumptions required to convert simple cross-sectional analyses into statements about future outcomes are much more tenuous.

A related issue is the interaction of individual and institutional decisions. If we take the traditional view that retirement income results from a combination of Social Security support, individual pension incomes, and private savings, it is immediately apparent that interactions among the various components are likely to be very important. Decisions that materially affect the expected pattern of Social Security payments almost certainly will have an impact on how individuals prepare for retirement through their own savings behavior. They may also influence the patterns of firm-provided pension plans. Thus, even though individual components of the retirement income package might usefully be separated for some purposes, understanding the full implications for retirement income security of policy initiatives is unlikely to be possible without careful consideration of the interactions across areas.

Many of the most important implications for the consideration of retirement income policy flow from distributional considerations. Specifically, the heterogeneity of circumstances—related to past employment decisions, individual savings behavior, health considerations, and luck—implies that retirement situations vary widely. Moreover, some of the worst off in terms of retirement incomes are just those who are least self-sufficient or least able to deal with unfortunate circumstances. Because these people typically are a focal point of public policy concerns, it is important to understand the distribution of possible retirement outcomes and how public policies will affect this distribution. Obtaining information about distributional outcomes adds yet a further complexity to modeling efforts. Many approaches to understanding behavioral outcomes are better suited to describing average behavior than to identifying the distributional impacts. This, again, is further complicated by the presence of important programmatic and behavioral interactions across areas.

The difficulties of modeling and projecting the impacts of various policies itself introduces another element. The complexity suggests that there will remain considerable uncertainty about the ramifications of any given policy. Read backwards, the development of sound policies would be aided by an understanding of the magnitude of any uncertainty in the analysis. Importantly, because projections and uncertainty may vary significantly across different policies proposals, estimation of the underlying uncertainty involved would allow proposals to be compared in natural ways.

The provision of information about uncertainty is, however, seldom done in any policy setting. There are natural reasons for this. First, many models used to assess possible effects of policy are very complex, making conventional calculation of uncertainty, confidence intervals, and the like very difficult. Second, projections of the impacts of policies can seldom be compared with what actually happened, because the policies that are simulated are seldom actually put into place. In other words, in developing a set of policies, a wide range of alternatives is frequently discussed and evaluated, but the ultimate policy might not even be among those that were evaluated. Third, as discussed previously, the projections of outcomes far into the future makes assessment of accuracy difficult or impractical if it is necessary to wait for the full evolution of outcomes. Fourth, there has never been very strong desire by policymakers to have information about uncertainty in policy analyses. Indeed, they frequently make known their explicit preferences for point estimates of any outcomes. Nonetheless, a sensitivity to uncertainty in analyses would seem valuable if not essential, but providing such information requires different approaches than commonly available now.

Some Immediate Conclusions

Within this background and following the preliminary analysis of the Panel on Retirement Income Modeling, some conclusions begin to emerge. While details on how to design a research and modeling program to prepare best for future policy decisions are unclear at this time, some basic foundations emerge.

Current Lack of Integrated Models

Current retirement modeling is marked by special-purpose models which focus on very specific factors or issues. Perhaps the broadest model in regular use is the Social Security model(s) that provide projections of the status of the Social Security system. This cell-based approach to understanding the evolution of Social Security income is the primary tool for evaluating proposed changes in the Social Security system, such as those flowing from the current imbalances in the trust fund. While powerful from the narrow viewpoint of the Social Security system, this model does not provide for consideration of other components of retirement income and their interactions, does not provide distributional information about retirement incomes, and does not assess the underlying analytical uncertainty involved. (Additionally, as discussed below, the model itself is not available for use or assessment by outside researchers and users.)

While there have been past attempts to integrate the various components of retirement income in microsimulation efforts, these proprietary models have not been maintained or evaluated in recent years. The most significant of these (DYNASIM2 and PRISM) do not provide a current basis for analyzing policy issues and would require considerable modification and updating to be useful. Some other scattered efforts to model retirement incomes are available, but few would believe that these are ready to be used in active policy debates.

Almost any effort to provide policy analysis and advice will require some way to integrate the effects of policies across different components of retirement income (and across the underlying behavioral decisions). This is not to say that all modeling efforts will have to be the "grand model" that considers all facets, but it is to say that there must be mechanisms for understanding the feedbacks within and across areas of policy changes.

Data Shortcomings

Matched data that combines administrative information with other descriptions of individuals have been particularly important in modeling retirement incomes and behavior. During the 1970s, important efforts were made to obtain exact matches of individual Social Security histories with Current Population Survey data. These databases, remarkably, provide the most up-to-date historical information that is publicly available. (A subsequent exact match by Social Security has not been available for public use.) Such matches of administrative records and of basic survey data provide an extraordinarily important source of information upon which to build models of retirement income.

Concerns about confidentiality of data frequently enter these discussions, as they rightfully should. On the other hand, a variety of statistical, legal, and organizational approaches are available to protect the confidentiality of individuals. None of the concerns, if dealt with in an appropriate manner, appears sufficient to overcome the importance and usefulness of creating new matched data sets that incorporate the wealth of historical data available from administrative records.

Panel data on individuals over time have also proved to be an essential element of modeling efforts for behavior that evolves over the life cycle. In recent years, researchers and analysts have discovered the power of panel data for distinguishing the effects of individual differences from more fundamental behavioral responses. Further, the insights gained from observing how individuals respond to different stimuli and circumstances are often clearer and less complicated than efforts not based on actual data about specific individuals. Panel data are considerably more expensive because the same people must be followed and coaxed into repeated responses, but there is a growing appreciation for the fact that panel data are sufficiently superior to more extensive data available only as a single cross section to warrant such spending.

The importance of obtaining panel data is built into recent efforts such as the Health and Retirement Study (HRS). The HRS effort is designed as an ongoing panel with data collections already fielded in 1992 and 1994. Nonetheless, because of the expense of panels and because many budgetary decisions are made myopically, there is constant pressure to let large panel data efforts lapse. Doing so in the area of retirement decisions would be very shortsighted.

Finally, because an important component of retirement income comes from firm-based pension plans, any general modeling effort must consider the interaction of individuals and firms. Yet few data that match individuals with firms are currently available. Such data as exist generally are very limited in information about firms (if based on household surveys) or on individuals (if based on firm surveys). The need for better data matching individuals and firms has been long recognized, but concerns about expense and about confidentiality have prevented such developments. For understanding the full character of retirement plans and prospects, more attention to such data seems essential. Further, in line with the previous point, panel data offer exceptional analytical promise, even though such data are almost never available for firms.

Organizational Issues

A series of organizational issues also seems important to questions of developing adequate policy models. At the top of the list comes a concern about the fractionated nature of policy concerns and policy modeling. Within the federal government many different organizations and agencies, each with its own mission, enter into policy decisions. The Social Security Administration is perhaps largest and most noticeable, but the Department of Labor, the Department of Health and Human Services, and the Department of the Treasury have important programs and policies that influence the income and security of retired persons. From initial investigation, it would appear that each of the separate agencies involved in retirement income policies tends to stick quite closely to its mission and not to allow its policy analysis and modeling to stray far off into other areas. This would be sensible if policies could be segregated and well-insulated from other institutions—a situation that does not appear to hold.

Fundamentally, it appears critical that any design of sensible retirement income policies comes from the joint efforts of the affected agencies. A corollary is that developing useful policy models should involve the active interaction (and support) of the various agencies. As with many collective action problems, achieving good results will almost certainly involve some organizational changes, such as cross-agency commissions or the more active involvement of the Office of Management and Budget. Without taking a position on the specific institutional structure, it is clear that some institutional structure is needed.

Another aspect of the organization of modeling efforts relates directly to the construction of integrated models. In the past, private contractors have developed some of the most complete models related to retirement incomes (DYNASIM2 and PRISM). These very large microsimulation models were a result of the available technology. They attempted to manipulate data and simulate complicated family behavior at the level of the individual household. As such, they were constructed to operate on mainframe computers. The pattern of funding and support also dictated that, while complicated, little documentation was available. As a result, they have always been black boxes that have not been subjected to close scrutiny and validation efforts by people other than their designers. A similar story holds for the models of individual government agencies. For example, the details of the one or more models supporting Social Security Administration projections are unknown to outside researchers and analysts.

Given the current changes in technology, which make most computational efforts a relatively small portion of total costs, it is natural to expect (and demand) that future developments proceed in much different ways. Specifically, modeling efforts, capitalizing on current computer technologies, should be much more transparent and portable. The idea behind this is quite simple: scrutiny by the scientific community is likely to improve the reliability and acceptance of policy models. Further, there is little argument for government creation of analytical monopolies in situations where the government is a primary funder of development and where the results of the modeling efforts could have important ramifications for the formulation of public policies.

The implementation of such an idea is complicated. It rests not only on how models are developed but also on issues of documentation, portability across computer platforms, ease of use, and the like. Nevertheless, the general principle is clear, even though not a central part of any past decisions.

A final organizational issue relates to the interaction between the research community and the policy community. The design of databases and of policy models is a complicated issue fraught with possibilities for serious mistakes. Because we do not currently have an existing structure to build on in developing integrated policy models of retirement income, the best way to proceed is uncertain. One implication, since both initial and continuing design decisions can have very long-term effects, is that regular mechanisms for getting both the broad policy community and the broad researcher community to evaluate plans and progress should be instituted. An ongoing and broadly based advisory panel is an obvious approach.

Conclusions

The conclusions are simple. First, we appear to be a long way from having an adequate base for making informed decisions about retirement income policy. Part of this is very explicable. The problems are particularly difficult, and solutions will demand the joint efforts of different agencies and researchers when an appropriate institutional structure is currently lacking. Nevertheless, almost any general consideration of future policy debates would place various aspects of retirement income high on the agenda. The issue is simply whether or not we make these decisions based on a good understanding of the likely ramifications of any policies. Second, much of any more complete policy modeling effort will require more extensive data than are currently available. Because there are long lead times in developing good databases, efforts should be directed at these issues immediately (and currently existing efforts such as the Health and Retirement Study (HRS) and the Study of the Assets and Health Dynamics of the Oldest Old (AHEAD) efforts should receive continued support). Third, the organization of the research and development effort will undoubtedly have a strong influence on the results. The current approach of highly compartmentalized efforts seems inefficient and possibly very limiting.

Appendix

The translation of the various considerations into operating principles for government agencies is easiest to see through the recommendations in the Panel's interim report (National Research Council, 1995).

Openness in Governmental Model Development

Much of prior policy modeling sponsored by the government and conducted by various agencies has not been widely available to outside users and analysts. While there are some circumstances which might justify closed modeling, in general it leads to inferior policy analysis. The models escape scrutiny of other analysts and cannot be subject to the same verification process.

Recommendation 1. Retirement-income-related policy models that are operated by government agencies or that are developed with government funds should be made publicly available to the policy and research communities in a timely manner.

Recommendation 2. Retirement-income-related policy models should be adequately documented so that analysts other than the model developers can readily use them.

Recommendation 3. Government agencies should take advantage of the dramatic changes in computing technology and the dramatic reductions in computing costs to develop (or support the development of) retirement-income-related policy models that are fully accessible to the research community

Ensuring Availability of High Quality Data

One lesson of many policy initiatives of the past has been that having relevant data at the time of discussion is extremely important. Analysis can seldom overcome the limitations of incomplete or erroneous data. At the same time, data collection efforts must begin well before any analytical uses are contemplated. There must also be a commitment to continuing the data collection efforts, particularly given the greatly enhanced value of having panel data.

Recommendation 4. Relevant agencies should continue to support existing retirement-income-related panel surveys of individuals. Such surveys, which permit analyzing behavioral responses to policy changes over time, are essential for retirement-income-related research that can inform the development of adequate policy models. They must be continued if they are to provide sufficient longitudinal information for analysis purposes.

Recommendation 5. Relevant agencies should develop and implement data collection systems that provide improved information on the nature and extent of employer retirement-income-related benefits and on employer and worker behavior relevant to retirement. The new data should include panel studies of employers and samples of their employees. Researchers and policy analysts who will use these data should be involved from the outset in the design of the data systems.

Recommendation 6. Relevant statistical and administrative agencies should create up-to-date matched files of survey responses and administrative records that, with suitable protections to maintain the confidentiality of individuals or employers, are available for retirement-income-related research and policy analysis use.

Organization of Modeling and Research

The difficulties of mounting a coherent research effort with decentralized agencies and without good mechanisms for agency/academic cooperation are especially noteworthy. While coordinating devices have the chance of introducing extra regulation and bureaucracy, some balance seems necessary.

Recommendation 7. Relevant agencies should explore ways to integrate retirement-income-related research, data collection, and policy modeling, so as to obtain the most cost-effective use of available resources. Such integration should represent a high priority goal in order to minimize duplication of effort, ensure that important issues are not overlooked, and ensure that priorities are set in light of the full range of policy concerns.

Recommendation 8. Relevant agencies should explore mechanisms for bringing academic researchers and government analysts together on a regular, routine basis to facilitate the development of high quality, relevant models and associated data for addressing retirement-income-related policy concerns.

Notes

1. Financial support for this panel was also provided by the National Institute on Aging and by TIAA-CREF. See National Academy of Sciences (1995).

2. The Panel members were Henry Aaron (Brookings Institution), Alan J. Auerbach (University of California, Berkeley), Christopher Bone (Actuarial Sciences Association), Peter Diamond (MIT), Eric A. Hanushek (University of Rochester), Michael Hurd (SUNY, Stony Brook), Olivia S. Mitchell (University

of Pennsylvania), Samuel H. Preston (University of Pennsylvania), John P. Rust (University of Wisconsin, Madison), Timothy M. Smeeding (Syracuse University), and James P. Smith (Rand Corporation).

References

National Research Council of the National Academy of Sciences. Toward Improved Modeling of Retirement Income Policies. Washington, DC: National Academy of Sciences interim report, 1995.

Chapter 12
Reforming Social Security?

Edward M. Gramlich

Like many other public pay-as-you-go (PAYG) systems, the United States Social Security system is running into long-run financial difficulties. Workers are now living long past their retirement age, fertility rates are below the zero-population-growth level, and long-term rates of real wage growth are at a historically low level. These difficulties are reflected in the recent Report of the Social Security Trustees (1996) that implied that significant austerity measures will be necessary to restore long-run balance in the system. Moreover, cohort rates of return on payroll contributions are declining to levels well below going real interest rates for young people. Polls indicate that increasing numbers of young people do not trust that Social Security benefits will be there for their own retirement (Friedland 1994).

As with other PAYG systems, Social Security and disability benefits are paid by trust funds that have time-related schedules (i.e., future benefit liabilities can be predicted from present tax payments). Every year the Trustees of the system (the Commissioner of Social Security, three cabinet members, and two outside members) report on the long-run actuarial soundness of the system, and every four years an outside Advisory Council (such as the one I chaired from 1994 to 96) is established to review the methods and assumptions of the Trustees as well as to suggest new policy departures. These bodies have developed the tradition of requiring the system to be in "close actuarial balance" over a 75-year period, though it would make perfect sense to go to an even longer planning horizon. In 1994 the Congress passed new legislation to make the Social Security Administration an independent agency, and one of the provisions of this legislation would create a permanent advisory body that will presumably develop its own long-term actuarial conventions.

In their 1996 report the Trustees confirmed again a proposition that is becoming increasingly familiar to Americans—rather than being in close actuarial balance for a 75-year period, the old age, survivors, and disability trusts funds are in close actuarial balance for only 35 years, under an intermediate set of assumptions regarding births, deaths, labor force participation, real interest rates, and real wage growth. Under these assumptions, the trust funds are accumulating assets now, that is, they are running a current account surplus, but the assets rapidly deplete and the net worth of the trust funds drops to zero by about year 2030. By this time fund outflows are expected to be running well ahead of inflows, so major changes would have to be made to bring the system back into close actuarial balance for a 75-year period. Even more significant changes would be necessary to bring the system into close actuarial balance in perpetuity. This chapter reviews briefly what some of these changes might be.

Incremental Change Options

Logically, any incremental change options must be either on the benefits side or the tax side. I first discuss some benefit and tax changes within the present system and then some more radical options for changing the system.

Raising the Retirement Age

The measure that first occurs to most people is to raise the normal retirement age. When Social Security first began in the 1930s, the normal male life expectancy at age 65 was 12 years. It is now 15 years and slated to rise to 18 years over the forecast horizon. Given this rise, and the fact that most workers are less likely to have had physically demanding work histories than in the 1930s, it might seem logical to raise the normal retirement age for payment of benefits above its present level of 65 years of age (and slated to rise gradually toward 67 beginning in year 2000 due to previous austerity reforms).

Although there are strong arguments for considering further rises in the retirement age, there are also some drawbacks. For one thing, not all workers now have easy jobs; some are still physically spent by age 65. For another, rises in the normal retirement age may have different effects on different racial groups, depending on their life expectancies. For a third, the fact that life expectancy at retirement has increased does not necessarily mean that retiree health has; the three added years on a retiree's life may be three years of relatively poor health for some individuals. But the biggest problem with raising the normal retirement age is that, because of the way benefits are computed, in the end this is nothing but an across-the-board cut in Social Security retirement benefits. Given the generally low level of these benefits already, and the fact that this low level already leaves many aged individuals in poverty status, there may be a better rationale for selective, not general, cuts in benefits.

Other Cuts in Benefits

There are many other ways of cutting benefits, as compared to present law. An across-the-board measure often suggested by legislators hoping for quick cuts in budget deficits is to delay or suspend the price indexing of benefits. One problem here is that the fact that a key value of Social Security lies in its protection against inflation. Suspension of price indexing, for any group of people or any time period, debases this value. Another problem, as already noted, is that for many people Social Security benefits are not very high, and even brief suspensions of indexing will throw many aged people into poverty status.

An approach suggested in the deficit-reduction plan of a group known as the Concord Coalition is to means-test current benefits (i.e., reduce benefits for high income retirees). While there eventually may be a need to scale back benefits for high income people, there are other ways of doing this that seem much more consistent with the underlying logic of Social Security than simple means-testing. One is to alter the benefit formula gradually over time so that high income replacement rates are lower. Another is to make benefits completely taxable within the general income tax, using either consumption or income tax principles.

There might also be a mixed strategy for scaling back benefits. One such package might consist of more complete taxation of all Social Security benefits, further increases in the retirement age, and further gradual reductions in high income replacement rates through the benefit formula.

Raising Payroll Taxes

The great unmentionable in American politics is the T word—should there be rises in taxes? Tax increases could be designed that would restore the close actuarial balance of the system, and they could be nicely delayed for ten or twenty years so as not to cause grief to present-day politicians. Should they be part of the actuarial balance rescue package?

One objection to the present payroll tax is that for high incomes the tax is regressive. It is assessed only on the first US $61,000 of annual wages, at the 87th percentile of the wage distribution. This regressivity could be partially corrected by simply removing the taxable ceiling, as has already been done for the health insurance component of the payroll tax. While this change would reduce the regressivity of the payroll tax, it would not eliminate all regressivity because much of the income of high income people does not come in wage form, a change that would bring in limited net revenue over the very long run unless the benefit schedule were flattened at the high end.

The other possibility is simply to raise the payroll tax rate. Adverse affects on economic competitiveness are probably modest due to the presumed inelasticity of overall labor supply and the fact that general payroll taxes are probably shifted back onto labor. But the real problem with this type of change, and also with all of the benefit reductions discussed above, involves an issue not yet raised that is likely to become increasingly important over time—rates of return.

By comparing payroll employer and employee taxes and subsequent benefits, it is possible to compute internal rates of return for different age cohorts from the Social Security system. For cohorts born in 1875, who paid in next to nothing and received benefits, annual real rates of return were on the order of 35 percent, better than almost any imaginable investment. For cohorts born in 1900, annual real rates of return were about 10 percent, and for cohorts born in 1925, about 5 percent, still well above the going real interest rate in the economy (approximately 3 percent). For cohorts born in 1950, roughly the beginning of the baby boom generation, rates of return are down to 2 percent, now below the going real interest rate, and they continue to drop slowly. These are real rates of return for the whole cohort. But as was pointed out above, because of the progressivity of the Social Security system, rich people of a cohort get a lower internal rate of return than the cohort as a whole (with constant life expectancies). For these relatively well-off young people, the internal rate of return is on the order of 1 percent or lower.

There are basically three reasons for this drop in rates of return. First, any PAYG system will experience rate of return drops as the system matures; those retired at the time the system starts get benefits without paying in and get infinite rates of return. Rates of return then drop asymptotically toward the rate of growth of real wages plus population growth, the equilibrium real rate of return in a PAYG system (Samuelson 1958). That suggests the other two reasons for the drop in rates of return. The second is that, because of the drop in national saving and other economic factors, overall productivity growth and the rate of growth of real wages has slowed in the United States. This rate of growth of real wages is projected to be only 1 percent per year, and even that low rate is above that experienced for the past two decades. The third reason is demographics. For the first time since the US Social Security system began, a cohort (the baby boom generation) was larger than the following cohort. But by now fertility rates are low enough that every cohort is predicted to be larger than its following cohort, at least apart from new immigration. Thus there are always likely to be relatively few workers paying the retirement costs of relatively more workers, or, in Samuelsonian terms, the equilibrium real rate of return on workers' Social Security contributions will be 1 percent or less.

Until now Social Security has been a uniquely popular public program. Poll after poll has recorded this popularity, and an important reason to maintain the generality of Social Security is to preserve its popularity. It is one public system that everybody is a part of, and the sheer accomplishment of paying out this much in benefits for this long a time should not be denigrated. But looked at in cold, calculating terms, any program that gives people 10 percent real rates of return should be pretty popular. What happens when the real rate of return drops to 1 percent or below, as it is bound to with further payroll tax increases or benefit cuts? Friedland (1994) already reports that young people seem to have much less interest in Social Security than their elders, commonly reporting that "there will be nothing there for me." There may be something there for young people, but if the internal rate of return is less than 1 percent, these same people can be excused for asking "just how much?"

This political popularity point, much more than economic distortions, seems to be the main argument against tax increases. They load costs even more on young people, who are already getting a low implicit rate of return on their tax payments. It is also a reason for going slow on reductions in benefits to high income individuals, which raise the same rate of return questions. But if tax increases and high income benefit cuts are ruled out for political reasons, how exactly does the nation restore actuarial balance in the system? There are not many obvious alternatives other than altering the way funds for retirement income are saved and invested.

Fundamental Changes

One possible answer to the question of how to make austerity cuts but still keep well-off young people feeling they have a stake in Social Security is to give these young people new pension saving opportunities, either collectively or individually. Macroeconomists generally agree that the United States economy is now undersaving. Were there added pension saving, it could be invested at the world real interest rate of about 3 percent. While one could not fight the fact that well-off young people received only 1 percent real return on their Social Security payroll taxes, these same young people could do much better on their whole retirement portfolio.

In addition to this macroeconomic rationale, there is also a micro-economic rationale for such a change. There are grounds for believing that the present US tax and retirement system unduly limits private pension saving. It is now possible to do some pension saving in the US tax code under consumption tax treatment, but there are tight limits on these possibilities. Recent income tax law changes have also discouraged pension saving in defined benefits plans (Committee for Economic Development 1995). Overall, it is estimated that the typical worker would need to save 18 percent of wages annually to provide for 50 percent replacement of income in retirement years (Schieber 1995; Cutler 1995). The typical worker in the United States now saves at rates well below 18 percent, even when including the 10.7 percent (12.4 percent including disability) of wages now paid in the form of Social Security retirement taxes.

There are two ways of capturing the gains from added national saving, one primarily a public or collective approach and one primarily a private or individual approach.

Higher Public Pension Saving

The most straightforward public way to raise national saving was proposed by Aaron, Bosworth, and Burtless (ABB 1989). They argue for pre-funding the rise in future benefit payments by raising payroll taxes now and investing the proceeds in government bonds, as the system now does. A more radical variant of this approach was recently suggested by one of the ABB team, Bosworth (1995). Under his new approach, payroll taxes would again be raised now, though by less than in the ABB proposal, but instead of investing the funds in government bonds, Bosworth would permit the Social Security trust fund to invest a portion of its assets in private equities, hence permitting the system to capture more of the benefits of the high rates of return on new saving. This approach would enable the Social Security system to take advantage of what economists call the "equity premium puzzle," the fact that over long periods of time equities pay substantially more than bonds, even with generous adjustments for portfolio risk (Congressional Budget Office 1994). Bosworth calculates that under realistic assumptions these changes alone would eliminate actuarial deficits for the foreseeable future, with only a 2 percentage point rise in payroll tax rates (from the present 12.4 percent to 14.4 percent).

Under either the ABB or the new Bosworth approach, it may be necessary to remove Social Security from the federal budget. As long as Social Security stays in the budget and deficit targets are imposed on the overall unified budget, it can almost be guaranteed that any added Social

Security saving will be offset by higher deficits elsewhere in the budget. This means that any added Social Security saving will not even raise federal government saving, let alone overall national saving, and that there will be no added national income to be used to solve the long-term difficulties of the Social Security system.

Under the new Bosworth approach it would also be important to regulate the investments of the new Social Security fund. One obvious reason is financial prudence; but there is another reason as well. Right now the Social Security fund is more than ten times as large as any other pension fund in the United States, and the disparity increases if Social Security payroll tax rates rise further. Given the size of this new pool of investment funds, and the possibility of it being used in a political way, it would be very important to neutralize the political impact of Social Security investment. There may be ways to do this, either by letting a number of competing fund managers do the investment or by having Social Security invest in broadly based index funds (Weaver 1994b), although this presents a formidable and perhaps unprecedented problem in financial politics.

Higher Private Pension Saving

The private approach features a variant of the dual pillar system that the World Bank, among others, has been advocating (World Bank 1994; Weaver 1994a). In a gradualist version of the dual pillar approach, future Social Security benefits for young, high income people might be scaled back, and then supplemented by mandatory defined contribution individual accounts layered on top of the Social Security system.

These individual accounts could be held inside or outside Social Security, with the individuals who own them given constrained choices about investing the accounts in index stock funds or index bond funds. Again overall pension saving is supplemented by new national saving, again invested at the going market rate of return for stocks or bonds. This time, since the investment is through the individual accounts, there would be no particular fear of government political control of large investment funds. Particular individuals or firms would choose their own funds managers, and these management decisions would be sufficiently diversified to eliminate most political control problems.

But there could be some other fears. One is the need to insure the safety of these individual accounts, both in terms of how the funds were invested and how the annuities were regulated. Another is the fear that, as high income people rely more and more on their individual accounts and less and less on Social Security proper, Social Security becomes more of a redistribution program and less of a communitarian program. This too could threaten the unique political popularity of the Social Security system.

It is also possible, however, to imagine an intermediate reform that still raises national saving, along the lines recently proposed by the Bipartisan Commission on Entitlement and Tax Reform (1995). Instead of simply raising payroll tax rates, it might be possible to designate some of these added contributions as made on behalf of the individual, and to fold these contributions into the normal Social Security indexed annuity that is now payable on retirement. The investment of these individual accounts could be done by constraining choices to broad investment options, as the federal thrift plan now does. This intermediate option raises national saving without raising taxes and solves the investment difficulties associated with direct-fund investment in equities. Whether it sets to rest fears that the individualized component will dominate the public component of Social Security over time is quite difficult to determine. A different form of intermediate measure is to make the individualized accounts voluntary, perhaps related to or constrained by the amount of benefit cuts certain individuals received.

However these issues play out, the underlying feature of all of these options is that there must be added national saving. This saving can be invested at attractive rates of return, and these returns can be used to raise overall national living standards and simultaneously to supplement pension income and ward off the looming financial difficulties amply documented in the Trustees' Report. This saving could be done collectively by the Social Security system, individually, or individually within the Social Security system. There are advantages and disadvantages of each approach, but the national saving does have to be added. Without this, society's living standards are no higher, and any greater returns from equity investment are only a form of higher Social Security tax on the rest of the economy (Congressional Budget Office 1994).

Implications

The US Social Security system has served remarkably well for a 60-year period in providing retirement income for hundreds of millions of people and in maintaining a high degree of political popularity. It should not be changed quickly or without careful planning. At the same time, some of the early assumptions on which the system was built are now changing: retirees are living longer, cohort sizes are stable or declining, and, most significantly, rates of national saving and productivity growth have dropped sharply. All of these changes are leading to drops in the internal rate of return on Social Security contributions to levels well below going real interest rates. The combination of these changes and other forces has led to a considerable reduction in the long-term actuarial health of the system, requiring some package of significant cuts in benefits and/ or payroll tax increases.

These cuts or increases may be difficult to accomplish in a way that preserves the historical popularity of the Social Security system. There might be several ways of breaking the impasse, from fine-tuning the present system to new approaches for saving and investing retirement funds. All approaches have their advantages and disadvantages, but it is generally true that the greater the level of new saving and the greater the ability of the system to invest safely in equities, the less are austerity cuts in benefits necessary and the higher are the overall rates of return on pension saving for younger people.

Opinions are the author's and should not be attributed either to the Advisory Panel or the Social Security Administration.

References

Aaron, Henry J., Barry P. Bosworth, and Gary Burtless. *Can America Afford to Grow Old: Paying for Social Security*. Washington, DC: The Brookings Institution, 1989.

Bipartisan Commission on Entitlement and Tax Reform. Final Report to the President. Washington, DC: USPGO, 1995.

Bosworth, Barry P. "Fund Accumulation: How Much? How Managed?" in Peter A. Diamond, David C. Lindeman, and Howard Young (eds.), *Social Security: What Role for the Future?* National Academy of Social Insurance, Washington, DC 1996.

Committee for Economic Development. Who Will Pay for Your Retirement? The Looming Crisis. Committee for Economic Development, New York, NY, 1995.

Congressional Budget Office. *Implications of Revising Social Security's Investment Policies*. Washington, DC: USGPO, 1994.

Cutler, David M. "Reexamining the Three-Legged Stool" in Peter A. Diamond, David C. Lindeman, and Howard Young (eds.), *Social Security: What Role for the Future?* National Academy of Social Insurance, Washington, DC 1996.

Friedland, Robert D. *When Support and Confidence Are at Odds: The Public's Understanding of the Social Security Program*. Washington, DC: National Academy of Social Insurance, 1994.

Samuelson, Paul A. "An Exact Consumption Loan Model of Interest with or without the Social Contrivance of Money." *Journal of Political Economy* (December 1958): 219–34.

Schieber, Sylvester J. Retirement Income Adequacy at Risk: Baby Boomers' Prospects in the New Millennium. Watson Wyatt Worldwide working paper. Washington, DC: The Wyatt Company, 1995.

Social Security and Medicare Boards of Trustees. *Status of the Social Security and Medicare Programs*. Washington, DC: USGPO, 1996.

Weaver, Carolyn L. The Current Status and Future Prospects of Social Security:
An Alternative View. The American Enterprise Institute mimeo, 1994a.
———. Social Security Investment Policy: What is it and How can it be Improved?
The American Enterprise Institute mimeo, 1994b.
World Bank. *Averting the Old Age Crisis: Policies to Protect the Old and Promote Growth.*
New York: Oxford University Press, 1994.

Chapter 13
Individual Social Security Retirement Accounts

John E. Porter

It is time to propose a change in the way we manage the Social Security Trust Fund reserve, and in this chapter I propose one viable method of approaching the system's financing problems. My plan, although not a complete solution to the larger, long-term financial ills of Social Security, would improve the long-term health of Social Security by converting the Trust Fund reserve from a pile of government IOUs into real savings controlled by individuals. Indeed, I have always been careful to note the specific focus of my plan—the management of the Trust Fund reserve. Clearly, Social Security's larger problems will have to be dealt with at some time through more comprehensive changes in order for the future of this vital and successful program to be guaranteed.

The purpose of the legislation, known as the Porter Plan, is twofold. First and foremost, it would take from the government the reserve Social Security payroll tax revenues, those not needed to pay current benefits and which are nominally being collected to help pay the baby boom generation's Social Security benefits. These are currently being spent to finance present-day deficits. Under the Porter Plan, the reserves would instead be refunded into mandatory, individually held accounts treated much like IRAs. This change in legislation would guarantee the availability of these funds for the baby boom generation's retirement, something I believe the current policy makes highly unlikely if not altogether impossible, as will be explained in greater detail below.

Second, by changing the management of the reserve so as to remove it from the federal government's hands, the government would be forced to raise more deficit capital in the private markets and the true size of the annual federal budget deficit would be revealed in sharp relief. I am hopeful that this change would put additional pressure on Congress and the President to cut spending further in order to stem the current, much-larger-than-understood river of red ink flowing from Washington.

The 1983 Social Security amendments increased Social Security payroll taxes in order to create a reserve within the Social Security Trust Fund intended to cover the shortfall between the Social Security system's tax and interest income and its benefit outgo which will occur when the baby boom generation retires and draws Social Security benefits. At that time, there will be approximately 25 million more retirees on the Social Security benefit rolls than there are today without a proportionate increase in taxpaying workers. The reserve is thus designed to protect future workers from sharp increases in payroll taxes which would occur if Social Security were operated under pay-as-you-go financing. While those tax increases could be mitigated through significant cuts in Social Security benefits, I doubt the likelihood of such cuts given the apprehension with which most Members of Congress approach the issue.

In light of the fiscal impact of the baby boomers and the need to protect future workers from higher taxes, the Trust Fund reserve is a wise and valuable management tool. Unfortunately, current law governing the investment and management of the reserve is fueling congressional profligacy and will eventually undermine the Social Security system.

Each year, the Social Security system receives various tax revenues. These funds are used first to pay the benefits of current beneficiaries. Surplus funds remaining after these payments (the annual reserves) are by law invested in special issue, interest-bearing Treasury bonds. Surpluses "invested" in these bonds are credited on government ledgers to the Social Security Trust Fund, and the United States Treasury receives the cash. The Trust Fund surplus, then, is simply a collection of government IOUs.

This transfer of reserve cash to the Treasury creates serious problems since this cash is, from the standpoint of the Treasury, indistinguishable from any other revenues paid to the federal government. Because current law does not require reserve moneys to be set aside or otherwise saved separately from other government funds, and because the federal government continues to run annual budget deficits, the reserve funds are used to finance present-day general operations of the government. In other words, the Social Security Trust Fund surplus finances part of today's deficit spending. The Congressional Budget Office (CBO) confirmed this analysis when it noted that "as long as the trust fund operates with an annual surplus, the policy of investing in special issues means that the government does not have to borrow as much from the public to finance the deficit in the rest of the government's accounts" (CBO 1994:1).

If left unchecked, current law governing the Trust Fund reserve will cause a serious fiscal crisis when the baby boomers retire. At that time, the Social Security system will begin redeeming its Treasury bonds in order to pay retirement benefits. When these transactions take place, the federal government will have to produce literally hundreds of billions of dollars in each of several years to pay back the bonds held by Social Security. Since the money obtained from issuing the bonds will have already been spent on today's deficits and will not be backed by any real assets, the government at that time will have to obtain it by either raising taxes or by sharply cutting spending on other federal programs. If these options are unpalatable, the government may instead choose to renege on its promise to the baby boomers and greatly reduce their Social Security benefits. Each of these options is likely, at the very least, to be economically disruptive and politically excruciating.

Because the excess money is simply making it easier for Congress to continue deficit spending, I have reintroduced legislation which would reduce Social Security payroll taxes by the amount not needed for current beneficiaries, namely, about 1 percent. Both employers and employees would now be required to contribute .50 percent into mandatory Individual Social Security Retirement Accounts, or ISSRAs. These IRA-like accounts would be held in private-sector entities and would accrue tax-free interest over the working lifetime of the individual. Individual recipients would own the accounts and would direct bonded ISSRA trustees—banks, insurance companies, brokers, or other money managers—in investing ISSRA moneys. While the Porter Plan contains no specific guidelines, I conceive of ISSRA account investments as being limited by law to safe, non-speculative investments such as time deposits, government obligations, AAA corporate binds, and certain mutual funds that would allow money to be saved and invested and grow as a nest egg for the future. The trustees would be required by law to abide by the investment guidelines and would only be able to pay the money to purchase an annuity when the owner reaches retirement age. The ISSRA system would be phased in gradually and would take roughly forty years to become fully vested. As mentioned above, my legislation affects only the management of the Trust Fund reserves. It does not change current law governing replacement rates, cost-of-living adjustments, or scheduled changes in the Social Security retirement age.

Under the Porter Plan, an individual's Social Security benefits would consist of two parts: an annuity purchased with the person's ISSRA funds and an adjusted payment from the Social Security Trust Fund itself. Payments from the Trust Fund would be adjusted to ensure that benefits would remain at the same level as they are today under current law, not increased by the amount of an individual's ISSRA payment. In a recent Social Security subcommittee hearing, the CBO criticized the Porter

Plan because it did not contain an offset mechanism which would ensure Social Security's progressive benefit structure. In the revised bill, I worked with the General Accounting Office of Congress (GAO) to implement a benefit adjustment that would maintain the progressivity under a mixed private/public Social Security system. GAO's analysis showed that an ISSRA system could actually increase benefits slightly given moderately good economic conditions. Interestingly, the analysis also showed that a 2 percent diversion into ISSRAs conducted during the period when Social Security was accumulating a reserve would increase benefits more than would a 1 percent diversion—even with an appropriate benefit adjustment (GAO 1990, 1994). CBO might wish to review GAO's work in this area, especially since CBO's hearing report largely discounts the notion that partial privatization would improve benefits.

Thus the Porter Plan would take from Congress the reserve funds it is supposed to save but which it instead spends on present-day deficit spending. This change would help protect baby boomers from cuts in Social Security benefits and protect future workers from huge tax increases. It would prevent the need for enormous future cuts in government programs to finance redemption of Social Security's special issue bonds. At the very least, establishment of an ISSRA system would give baby boomers the moneys they have in their ISSRAs to use for retirement. Under the current system, they may well end up receiving little if any money from Social Security given the demographic, fiscal, and Trust Fund management trends discussed above. Finally, it would force the federal government to borrow more from public markets to finance the deficit and thereby make the enormity of our fiscal problems far more readily apparent to the general public than it is today.

The Porter Plan has several other positive attributes. First, it would make every American worker an investor in our economy. Every worker in America who paid Social Security taxes would have an ISSRA and would thereby have a tangible stake in the success of our economy. Second, Americans who have not otherwise saved during their lifetimes would have savings that would be theirs, that they would manage, and which would grow and be available as part of their retirement. Third, it would give all workers an asset to pass on to their families. Today, if one dies prior to becoming eligible for Social Security old age benefits, those benefits are gone except for survivors' benefits in some cases. However, under my proposal, someone who dies prior to retirement age would pass on accumulated ISSRA funds as part of his or her estate. Fourth, my proposal would put US $3 trillion, in 1990 dollars, or at least a very substantial part of that, into private-sector investments. This infusion of capital, coupled with an expected drop in the deficit because Congress would not have the reserve to spend, should help drive down interest rates and speed future economic growth. Finally, my plan would create the basis of a completely portable private pension system. In other words, if I were a worker directing part of my Social Security into an ISSRA with every paycheck, I would go to my employer and say, "Forget the pension plan. I want my share paid into my ISSRA account." Years later when I am about to retire, I would not have to worry about whether the pension plan of the company had been mismanaged or stolen or gone broke. I would have the money in my own hands. I would have invested it and I would know that it is available for my retirement.

I realize that one criticism my colleagues might have of the ISSRA plan as described here is that the investment guidelines allow people to invest in Treasury bills, something I am trying on one level to prevent the government from doing. My answer is that allowing such investments leaves the choice up to the individual rather than having the government do so on autopilot, as under current law. I would note that a greater proportion of federal debt instruments would be held by American citizens, not foreign creditors.

I believe that most of us in Congress and, indeed, many members of the public understand the fact that the Trust Fund reserve is not real, that it has been spent, continues to be spent, and exists only on paper. Few if any of us really believe Social Security will have the money it needs to work as it should when the baby boomers retire and the system's "special issues" come due. We must soberly face this issue as an institution and change law accordingly. I offer the Porter Plan as a positive way to do so.

References

U.S. General Accounting Office (GAO). Social Security: Analysis of a Proposal to Privatize Trust Fund Reserves. GAO/HRD-91-22 (Dec. 12). Washington, DC: USGPO, 1990.

U.S. General Accounting Office. Social Security Retirement Accounts. GAO/HEHS-94-226R (Aug. 12). Washington, DC: USGPO, 1994.

Congressional Budget Office (CBO). 1994. "Implications of Revising Social Security's Investment Policies." CBO Working Paper (September). Washington, DC.

Contributors

Vickie Bajtelsmit is an Assistant Professor in the Department of Finance and Real Estate at Colorado State University. Her research focuses on corporate pension planning and institutional investment, and the relationship between pension plan generosity and labor productivity. She has a BA in linguistics and Russian language from the University of Virginia, a JD from Rutgers University School of Law, and a PhD in risk management and insurance from the University of Pennsylvania's Wharton School of Business.

Brad A. Blalock is a senior analyst with Mercer Investment Consulting, where he applies and develops tools for investment planning, for retirement program forecasts, and for solving client financial problems. His research also focuses on innovative methods of modeling defined contribution plan outcomes. He has a BS in actuarial science from the University of Illinois and a Master's degree in finance from Northwestern University.

Constance F. Citro is a senior staff member of the Committee on National Statistics at the National Academy of Sciences-National Research Council. She served as the study director for the Panel to Evaluate Microsimulation Models for Social Welfare Programs and the Panel to Evaluate the Survey of Income and Program Participation, and is currently study director for the Panel on Poverty and Family Assistance and the Panel on Retirement Income Modeling. She received her PhD in political science from Yale University and is a former vice president of Mathematics Policy Research, Inc.

Gordon P. Goodfellow is an associate of the Research and Information Center at Watson Wyatt Worldwide, where he has specialized in the analysis of social security policy and private defined contribution plans. Previously, he was with the Office of the Assistant Secretary for Planning and Evaluation as a senior policy analyst and project manager of the Panel Study of Income Dynamics.

Michael S. Gordon is a Washington, DC attorney specializing in pension law and the employee benefits field. He served as Minority Pension Council to the United States Senate Labor and Public Welfare Committee under Senator Jacob K. Javits (R. NY) and participated in the drafting of ERISA. Mr. Gordon was a Department of Labor legal advisor to President Kennedy's Cabinet Committee on Corporate Pension Funds and received a United States Department of Labor Distinguished Achievement Award for his contribution to private pension improvement. Since 1975 he has been Chairman of the Advisory Board to the Bureau of National Affairs (BNA) Pension Reporter, and served on the ERISA Advisory Council representing the public. He is also on the Board of Directors of the Pension Rights Center of Washington, DC and is a member of the Board of the Pension Research Council of The Wharton School.

Edward M. Gramlich is Dean of the School of Public Policy Studies at the University of Michigan, where he is also professor of economics and public policy. He chaired the Advisory Council on Social Security from 1994 to 1996. Dr. Gramlich served in the Congressional Budget Office, the Office of Economic Opportunity, the Brookings Institution, and in 1992 was the staff director for the Economic Study commission of major league baseball. He has written several books on benefit-cost analysis, macroeconomics, budget policy, income redistribution, fiscal federalism, social security, and the economics of professional sports. He received his MA and PhD from Yale University.

Eric A. Hanushek is professor of economics and of public policy and director of the W. Allen Wallis Institute of Political Economy at the University of Rochester, and was previously deputy director of the Congressional Budget Office. His research focuses on public finance and public policy with special emphasis on education, incomes and wages, housing policy, social experimentation, statistical methodology, and the economics of discrimination. He currently is Chairman of the Panel on Retirement Income Modeling for the National Academy of Sciences/National Research Council. He received his PhD from MIT.

Richard P. Hinz is the director of the Office of Research and Economic Analysis in the Pension and Welfare Benefits Administration at the United States Department of Labor. Mr. Hinz directs a program of research on policy issues related to the private employee benefits system within the jurisdiction of ERISA. His office provides comprehensive statistics on ERISA plans through a variety of regular publications, funds work on employment-based health care financing and labor market issues, and conducts research on private pension benefits. Since 1991, through a program administered by the United State Department of Labor's Bureau of International Labor Affairs, he has provided technical assistance in the reform of social insurance programs and the development of private pension systems to the governments of the Czech Republic, Slovakia, Romania, Bulgaria, Poland, and Hungary. He has a MPA from Columbia University and is a CFA.

Ping-Lung Hsin is an associate research fellow at Chung-Hua Institution for Economic Research, Taipei, Taiwan. His research areas are public pensions, informal labor markets, and the evaluation of labor market programs and legislation. He received his PhD in labor economics from Cornell University.

Robert M. Lang is a vice president in the Municipal Securities Group of BA Securities, Inc., BankAmerica Corporation's investment banking division, where he works with states, cities, airport authorities, and other public entities that issue municipal securities. Mr. Lang, as part of a team of public finance professionals, helped develop the tool of taxable pension obligation bonds (POBS), sold to investors by state and local governments. Mr. Lang received his undergraduate degree from the University of California at Berkeley, with majors in political economy and political science and a minor in city and regional planning. He was trained in quantitative public finance and earned a Master's Policy degree from the Kennedy School of Government at Harvard University.

Christopher A. Levell, ASA, is a consulting actuary and Associate at William M. Mercer, Inc. He focuses on applying and developing sophisticated tools for retirement program forecasts and for solving client financial problems. His research also focuses on innovative methods of presenting information to clients. He is an Associate of the Society of Actuaries and has a BS in actuarial science from the University of Illinois.

David D. McCarthy is an operations research analyst for the Office of Research and Economic Analysis, Pension and Welfare Benefits Administration at the United States Department of Labor. His research explores aspects of the private pension system, including benefit levels, rates of return, portfolio turnover, and ERISA enforcement. He also oversees research contracts, conducts regulatory analysis, and provides analytical support for litigation. Mr. McCarthy holds a MS in operations research from George Washington University and a BA in mathematics from Amherst College.

Olivia S. Mitchell is the International Foundation of Employee Benefit Plans Professor of Insurance and Risk Management, and Executive Director of the Pension Research Council, at The Wharton School of the University of Pennsylvania. Concurrently she is a research associate at the National Bureau of Economic Research. Dr. Mitchell is a senior fellow of the University of Pennsylvania's Leonard Davis Institute and research associate at the Population Studies Center, and serves on the Steering Committee for the Health and Retirement Survey at the University of Michigan. She previously taught labor economics at Cornell University for fifteen years and was a visiting scholar to Harvard University's Department of Economics. Dr. Mitchell received her MA and PhD in economics from the University of Wisconsin-Madison and her BA with honors in economics from Harvard University.

Robert A. G. Monks is a principal of LENS, Inc., which seeks to employ shareholder rights to make changes in poorly performing companies. Mr. Monks is also the founder of Institutional Shareholder Services, Inc., a leading corporate governance consulting firm advising shareholders. Past positions include service as a partner in a Boston law firm, vice president of the investment firm Gardner Associates, president and CEO of the New England-based energy company C. H. Spague & Son, member and later chairman of the board of directors for the bank holding company, Boston Company and its subsidiary, Boston Safe Deposit and Trust Co. In addition, Mr. Monks has been director of the United States Synthetic Fuels Corporation, member of Vice President Bush's Commission on Deregulation, administrator of the Office of Pension and Welfare Benefit Programs at the United States Department of Labor, and trustee of the Federal Employees Retirement System. Mr. Monks is a graduate of Harvard College, Cambridge University, and Harvard Law School.

John E Porter (R. 10th) of Illinois is serving his ninth term in the United States House of Representatives. Mr. Porter is a senior member of the House Appropriations Committee and is the Chairman of the Labor, Health and Human Services and Education Subcommittee. He also serves on the Foreign Operations Subcommittee, the Military Construction Subcommittee, and the Congressional Human Rights Caucus. He is a member of the Commission on Security and Cooperation in Europe, and co-founder of the Congressional Coalition on Population and Development. He received his undergraduate degree from Northwestern University and a law degree from the University of Michigan Law School. After admission to the Bar, he served as an Honor Law Graduate Attorney with the United States Department of Justice, practiced law in Evanston, Illinois, and served three terms in the Illinois House of Representatives.

Anna M. Rappaport, FSA, is a managing director of William M. Mercer, Inc. She is an actuary with many years of experience in consulting, research, and insurance company management, and consults with major clients on health care strategy, strategic benefit planning, retirement program management, and retiree health care. She is a member of the Board of the Pension Research Council, a member of the National Academy of Social Insurance, and a Board Member of the Society of Actuaries. She is fellow of the Society of Actuaries and has an MBA from the University of Chicago.

Sylvester J. Schieber is the director of the Research and Information Center in Washington, DC and sits on the board of directors of Watson Wyatt Worldwide. He specializes in the analysis of public and private retirement policy and health policy issues. He previously served as research director of the Employee Benefit Research Institute, was deputy director in the Office of Policy Analysis at the Social Security Administration, and was deputy research director at the Department of Health and Human Services. He is currently a member of the Social Security Advisory Council and of the Board of the Pension Research Council. He received a PhD in economics from the University of Notre Dame.

John A. Turner is deputy director of the Office of Research and Economic Analysis, Pension and Welfare Benefits Administration at the United States Department of Labor, and adjunct professor of economics at George Washington University. Dr. Turner formerly worked in the research office of the Social Security Administration. He received a Fulbright Senior Scholar award to do pension research at the Institut de Recherches Economiques et Sociales in Paris in 1994. He has written or edited eight books on pensions and employer-provided health benefits, one of which has been translated into Japanese, and he has published numerous articles on pension and social security policy. He has a PhD in economics from the University of Chicago.

Marc M. Twinney is a fellow of the Society of Actuaries and is currently serving on the Social Security Advisory Council. Until March 1995 Mr. Twinney was director of pensions at Ford Motor Company. He has been a member of many professional groups, including the Conference of Consulting Actuaries, the Washington Pension Report Group, the private-sector consultants to the United States Civil Service system, and the board of directors of American Academy of Actuaries. He is a member of the Board of the Pension Research Council. He holds a BA in mathematics from Yale University and an MBA from Harvard University.

Jack L. VanDerhei is an associate professor of risk management and insurance at Temple University and previously served on The Wharton School faculty. He is on the Board of the Pension Research Council, and is currently an EBRI Fellow for the Employee Benefit Research Institute and editor of *Benefits Quarterly*. He has served as a consultant to the International Foundation of Employee Benefit Plans, the Pension Benefit Guaranty Corporation, and the United States Department of Labor. He received his PhD in insurance from The Wharton School.

Mark J. Warshawsky is an economist at TIAA-CREF, and was formerly a senior economist and staff assistant to the assistant commissioner for Employee Plans and Exempt Organizations at the Internal Revenue Service. He also served as a senior economist at the Federal Reserve Board and was a visiting scholar at the American Enterprise Institute. He has published in the field of retiree health benefits, pensions, and life insurance.

Michael L. Young, FSA is a consulting actuary and Principal at William M. Mercer, Inc. He works with insurance company managers; consults with clients on retirement program issues, including plan financial management, plan design, investment of assets, and measurement of liabilities; and has developed unique tools for constructing a bond portfolio to model and document discount rates for FAS 87 and FAS 106. He is a fellow of the Society of Actuaries and has a Master's degree in business statistics from the University of Wisconsin.

Index

Aaron, Henry, 225
Account balance, 30
Accounting for pensions, 107–138
Accrual patterns in pensions, 30, 107–138
Activism. *See* Governance
Actuarial: assumptions, 135, 159; imbalance of Social Security, 220; methods, 163–166; pension liabilities, 25–26, 38–39, 42, 47, 107–138. *See also* Funding
Adler, Lynn, 166, 171
Administrative costs and pensions, 9–10, 187–205
Age: and investment decisions, 8–9, 67–90, 92; at retirement, 2, 8, 17–28, 191, 221–222; discrimination, 17
Aigner, Dennis, 193
Alameda County, 174, 177
Allis Chalmers Corporation, 117
American Express Company, 146, 150
Andrews, Emily, 188, 191–192, 194, 203
Annuities, 4, 5, 117–119, 232
Applebaum, Joseph, 129
Asset: allocation decisions in pensions, 7–8, 44–64, 67–90, 91–103, 159–186; and Health Dynamics of the Oldest Old Study (AHEAD), 216; management, 6–7, 139–158. *See also* Bonds; Equities; Governance; Housing; Pension investment; Portfolio; Saving
Automotive industry, 19

Baby Boom and retirement, 6, 29–30, 48, 48, 233
Bader, Lawrence, 127
Balanced fund, 53. *See also* Indexed fund
Bajtelsmit, Vickie, 8, 45, 92
Bank of America, 144

Bankruptcy, 113, 123, 172. *See also* Termination of pensions
Barsky, Robert, 92
Bauer, Paul, 202
Behavioral decision theorists, 54
Beller, Daniel, 202
Benefit: accrual in a pension plan, 30, 107–138; payments from a pension, 71, 165. *See also* Pension plans
Benefits manager, 7
Berger, Allen, 195
Bernasek, Nancy, 52, 56, 92
Berg, Olena, 153
Bernheim, B. Douglas, 48, 96
Bipartisan Commission on Entitlement and Tax Reform, 226
Blalock, Brad A., 29
Bleakney, Thomas, 196
Board of directors, 145, 168, 196. *See also* Governance; Trustees
Bodie, Zvi 6, 10, 27, 52, 97
Bonds, 52; in pension funds, 37, 51–59, 67–90, 91–103, 159–186. *See also* Investment
Borden Corporation, 150
Bosworth, Barry, 225
Brancato, Carol, 140, 157
Britain. *See* United Kingdom
Buffett, Warren, 149
Burtless, Gary, 225

California, 160–161, 173
California Public Employees' Retirement System (CalPERS), 144, 147–150, 152, 157
Canada, 150
Capital market risk, 4

The Pension Research Council

The Pension Research Council of the Wharton School at the University of Pennsylvania is an organization committed to generating debate on key policy issues affecting pensions and other employee benefits. The Council sponsors interdisciplinary research on the entire range of private and social retirement security and related benefit plans in the United States and around the world and seek to broaden understanding of the complex arrangements through basic research into their economic, social, legal, actuarial, and financial foundations. Members of the Advisory Board of Council, appointed by the Dean of the Wharton School, are leaders in the employee benefits field. While they recognize the essential role of Social Security and other public sector income maintenance programs, they share a strong desire to strengthen private sector approaches to economic security.

Executive Director

Olivia S. Mitchell, *International Foundation of Employee Benefit Plans Professor*, Department of Insurance and Risk Management, The Wharton School, University of Pennsylvania, Philadelphia

Institutional Members

Bankers Trust Company
Buck Consultants, Inc.
Ford Motor Company
General Electric Company
John Hancock Mutual Life Insurance Company
Hay/Huggins Company, Inc.
Instituto Cultural de Seguridade Social
Investment Company Institute
J.P. Morgan Investment Management Inc.

Richard B. Stanger, *National Director*, Employee Benefits Services, Price Waterhouse, Washington, DC

Marc M. Twinney, FSA, *Director*, Pension Department, Ford Motor Company, Dearborn, MI

Jack L. VanDerhei, *Associate Professor of Risk and Insurance*, Temple University, Philadelphia, PA

Paul H. Wenz, FSA, *Second Vice President and Actuary*, The Principal Financial Group, Des Moines, IA

Howard Young, FSA, *Adjunct Professor of Mathematics*, University of Michigan, Ann Arbor, MI

Pension Research Council Publications

Corporate Book Reserving for Postretirement Healthcare Benefits. Dwight K. Bartlett, III, ed. 1990.

An Economic Appraisal of Pension Tax Policy in the United States. Richard A. Ippolito. 1990.

Economics of Pension Insurance. Richard A. Ippolito. 1989.

Fundamentals of Private Pensions. Dan M. McGill and Donald S. Grubbs, Jr. Sixth edition. 1988.

Future of Pensions in the United States. Raymond Schmitt, ed. 1993.

Inflation and Pensions. Susan M. Wachter. 1987.

It's My Retirement Money, Take Good Care of It: The TIAA-CREF Story. William C. Greenough. 1990.

Joint Trust Pension Plans: Understanding and Administering Collectively Bargained Multiemployer Plans Under ERISA. Daniel F. McGinn. 1977.

Pension Mathematics with Numerical Illustrations. Howard E. Winklevoss. Second edition. 1993.

Pensions and the Economy: Sources, Uses, and Limitations of Data. Zvi Bodie and Alicia H. Munnell, eds. 1992.

Pensions, Economics and Public Policy. Richard A. Ippolito. 1985.

Positioning Pensions for the Twenty-First Century. Michael S. Gordon, Olivia S. Mitchell, and Marc M. Twinney, eds. 1997.

Providing Health Care Benefits in Retirement. Judith F. Mazo, Anna M. Rappaport, and Sylvester J. Schieber, eds. 1994.

Proxy Voting of Pension Plan Equity Securities. Dan M. McGill, ed. 1989.

Retirement Systems for Public Employees. Thomas P. Bleakney. 1972.

Retirement Systems in Japan. Robert L. Clark. 1990.

Search for a National Retirement Income Policy. Jack L. VanDerhei, ed. 1987.

Securing Employer-Based Pensions: An International Perspective. Zvi Bodie, Olivia S. Mitchell, and John A. Turner, eds. 1996.

Social Investing. Dan M. McGill, ed. 1984.

Social Security. Robert J. Myers. Fourth edition. 1993.